Longing for More

Longing for More

Man's Quest for Meaning and the Hope of Christ

Blake S. Hart

WIPF & STOCK · Eugene, Oregon

LONGING FOR MORE
Man's Quest for Meaning and the Hope of Christ

Copyright © 2025 Blake S. Hart. All rights reserved. Except for brief quotations in critical publications or reviews, no part of this book may be reproduced in any manner without prior written permission from the publisher. Write: Permissions, Wipf and Stock Publishers, 199 W. 8th Ave., Suite 3, Eugene, OR 97401.

Wipf & Stock
An Imprint of Wipf and Stock Publishers
199 W. 8th Ave., Suite 3
Eugene, OR 97401

www.wipfandstock.com

PAPERBACK ISBN: 979-8-3852-4500-0
HARDCOVER ISBN: 979-8-3852-4501-7
EBOOK ISBN: 979-8-3852-4502-4

VERSION NUMBER 05/19/25

All Scriptures in this book are derived from The ESV® Bible (The Holy Bible, English Standard Version®). ESV® Text Edition: 2016. Copyright © 2001 by Crossway, a publishing ministry of Good News Publishers. The ESV® text has been reproduced in cooperation with and by permission of Good News Publishers. Unauthorized reproduction of this publication is prohibited. All rights reserved.

To Every Pilgrim Searching for Answers...

Contents

Preface | ix

Part I: The Unraveling: Modernity and Its Discontents
1   Discovery and Disenchantment | 3
2   H. G. Wells: The Machine, the Man, and the Meaning | 19
3   Fyodor Dostoevsky: Faith, Freedom, and the Abyss | 32
4   T. S. Eliot: The Waste Land and the Collapse of Meaning | 45

Conclusion to Part I | 57

Part II: Deepening the Despair: Postmodernity, New Atheism, and the Growing Meaning Crisis
5   The Shattered Mirror: Postmodernity and Deconstructionism | 63
6   The Failed Horsemen: New Atheism and Its Attack on Faith | 80

Conclusion to Part II | 92

Part III: Voices of Restoration: Messengers of Meaning in the Modern Age
7   G. K. Chesterton: Wonder, Tradition, and the Sacredness of the Ordinary | 97
8   Gabriel Marcel: Mystery, Hope, and Relational Wholeness | 110
9   Reinhold Niebuhr: Christian Realism and Moral Responsibility | 120
10 Viktor Frankl: The Will to Meaning | 131
11 J. R. R. Tolkien: Myth, Beauty, and the Restoration of Hope | 143

12 C. S. Lewis: Faith, Imagination, and the Argument from Desire | 161

13 Jacques Ellul: Technology, Personhood, and Authentic Living | 178

14 Francis Schaeffer: Reclaiming the God Who Is There | 191

15 Dallas Willard: Spiritual Disciplines and the Renewal of the Soul | 204

Conclusion to Part III | 217

Part IV: Toward Wholeness: Reclaiming Meaning with a Restored Vision

16 The Fragmented Self: Moving Toward Integration | 223

17 The Resurgence of the Sacred: Longing for Transcendence | 232

18 Restoring Relationships: The Sacredness of Community | 241

19 Work, Calling, and the Kingdom of God | 251

20 The Sacred Balance: Embracing the Objective and the Subjective | 263

21 Towards a Christian Metanarrative: The Story That Won't Die | 273

Conclusion: Living as Restorers | 285

Bibliography | 297

Preface

ONE OF MY EARLIEST memories is lying in the damp grass of my childhood home in Florida, staring up at the brilliant stars scattered across the night sky. I was fascinated by their distant light and captivated by the vastness of the universe. In school, I learned that those stars were faraway suns, separated from us by incomprehensible distances. The Earth, I was told, was just a tiny speck in a sprawling galaxy that was itself, just one among billions. The sheer scale of it all filled me with awe. Yet, beneath that awe, a quiet but persistent question began to form: *What is my place in all of this?*

As a child, I was blessed with an unquenchable curiosity, a desire to understand the world and my place in it. This was nurtured by an extraordinary teacher, Cathy Hooper, who first opened my eyes to the wonders of science, history, literature, and philosophy. She had a way of making the past come alive, of showing how ideas shaped civilizations and how the quest for knowledge could transform not only our understanding of the world but also of ourselves. Under her guidance, my mind was set on fire with a love for exploration—not just of the physical world but of the deepest questions that have haunted humanity for centuries.

As my intellectual curiosity deepened, I found myself drawn not only to the world of science but even more intensely to the realms of philosophy, literature, and history. I was captivated by the profound questions that have preoccupied humanity for centuries—questions about existence, morality, the nature of reality, and the purpose of life itself. My school's library became my refuge, a place where I could dive into the works of great thinkers like Plato, Augustine, Nietzsche, and Kierkegaard. I pored over history books that traced the rise and fall of civilizations, searching for patterns that might reveal deeper truths about the human condition.

There was a thrill in exploring the great philosophical debates of history, understanding how ideas shaped entire eras, how revolutions in thought had the power to upend societies. I became fascinated by the way literature could capture the complexities of the human soul, how the epic poems of Homer, the existential musings of Dostoevsky, and the piercing wit of Shakespeare could speak to timeless struggles and hopes.

Yet, despite the breadth of human knowledge I encountered, there remained questions that none of these disciplines could fully answer. The philosophers could wrestle with concepts of meaning and morality, historians could recount the grand narrative arcs of empires, but they often fell silent when it came to the deepest cries of the human heart. As I sat alone with these books, lost in the thoughts of men and women who had grappled with the great mysteries of life, I could not shake the persistent questions that kept me awake at night: *Why are we here? What is the point of all this striving?*

Philosophy and history could explore the human experience in astonishing depth, but they often left me searching for more, unable to satisfy the yearning for something beyond mere human understanding. The study of ideas could illuminate how humanity had grappled with its existence, but it still left unanswered the most haunting question of all: *What is the purpose behind it all?* Philosophy, for all its insights, could not fill the void of meaning.

This longing for deeper answers began when I faced my first real brush with mortality. My mother passed away when I was 8 years old, a loss that left a gaping hole in my young life. Her death was a wound that refused to heal. I was thrust into a world where the comforting certainties of childhood were torn away. I found myself grappling with questions far beyond my years: Is there anything beyond this life? Is death the end? In the face of such loss, the neat explanations of science seemed cold and indifferent. They offered no solace for the pain that gnawed at my heart.

The comforting promises of religion seemed distant, while the materialist worldview that I was beginning to embrace offered little more than the bleak finality of death. I tried to tell myself that life was nothing more than a series of random chemical reactions, that consciousness was a mere byproduct of evolution. But no matter how hard I tried to embrace this view, something inside me rebelled. I found myself caught in a paradox: intellectually, I sought to deny the existence of God, but emotionally, I was angry at him. I raged against a God I claimed not to believe in, demanding to know why he had allowed such pain into my life.

For years, I wrestled with this inner turmoil. I tried to find answers in the realms of reason and logic, convinced that if I studied hard enough, I could explain away the mysteries of existence. But no matter how many books I read or how much knowledge I acquired, the existential void only seemed to deepen, and with it, a growing anger.

It was not until I was 17 that everything began to change. After years of grappling with my anger toward God and the emptiness I felt inside, I experienced a profound shift. I remember the night clearly. I was alone in my room, holding a letter my mom had written for me weeks before her death to read once I was older. In that letter, I read for the first time my mother's own thoughts for me, for God, and for the cancer that had taken her life. My mother was a woman of faith, but being so young when she passed, I never knew how deep it was. In her letter, she stated how she understood that I likely struggled with why God had chosen to take her this young, and in this way so did she at times; however, it was actually through this cancer that she had come to know the goodness of Christ in a way she never had before. She pleaded in her letter to me to trust Christ and that in him, I would know what true satisfaction meant, no matter what else life threw my way. That night, I truly opened my heart to the possibility of faith. In that moment, I found myself praying—truly praying—for the first time in my life. It was not a prayer of certainty but a cry for help: *God, if you are there, show me.*

That night marked the beginning of my conversion to Christianity, a turning point that would set the course for the rest of my life. The journey was not an easy one. It involved a lot of unlearning, a lot of surrendering the intellectual pride and anger that had kept me from faith for so long. But as I began to read the Bible and explore the teachings of Christianity, I discovered a depth of meaning, of hope, of life that I had never found in the pages of any other book.

After serving in the military, my growing faith eventually led me to get out and pursue service in the church as a pastor and then back to the military again, this time as a chaplain. As I stepped into these roles, I was brought face-to-face with the crisis of meaning that seemed to define the modern age. In my ministry, particularly among soldiers, I have found that the existential questions I had wrestled with were not unique to me. They were questions that haunted many of the men and women I encountered—especially young men.

In the military, I have witnessed a depth of suffering, loss, and moral injury that was impossible to ignore. I sat with soldiers who had seen the horrors of war, who had held dying friends in their arms, who had faced their own mortality in the starkest of terms. Many of them, despite being steeped in a culture of rationality and scientific precision, found themselves haunted by questions of purpose and meaning. They struggled with guilt, with the justifications for violence, with the tension between duty and conscience. In their darkest moments, they would come to me not just for comfort but for answers: *Why do we suffer? Is there any meaning to the sacrifices we make?*

It was in these moments that I began to see the crisis of meaning as not just a philosophical problem but a deeply personal one—a crisis that cuts to the heart of what it means to be human. My time as a chaplain has revealed to me that the crisis of meaning is not just an abstract concept discussed in academic circles. It is something that plays out in the lives of real people facing real pain. The questions that had haunted me as a child, as a teenager, and as a young man trying to make sense of the world, were the same questions that haunted my soldiers.

As I continued to study, preach, and counsel, my academic pursuits in intellectual history converged with the practical realities of ministry. I found that the crisis of meaning that so many people were facing today had deep roots in the presuppositions and ideas that lay at the core of the modern era. The rise of scientific materialism, the decline of religious faith, and the philosophical movements of the last two centuries all contributed to a worldview that was, at its core, devoid of transcendent meaning.

This book, *Longing for More*, is the culmination of my own journey, both personal and intellectual. It is an exploration of the crisis of meaning that has gripped our world and an attempt to understand how we got here. In the pages that follow, we will journey through the lives and ideas of thinkers like H. G. Wells, who placed his faith in scientific progress only to find himself disillusioned; Fyodor Dostoevsky and T.S. Eliot, who faced the spiritual desolation of modernity with raw honesty; and Viktor Frankl, who found meaning even in the darkest of circumstances. We will demonstrate the major ideas and movements that led to the unraveling of meaning and the growing despair produced by it.

We will also explore voices of hope, modern messengers of meaning—figures like G. K Chesterton, C. S. Lewis, J. R. R. Tolkien, Dallas Willard, and others—who offered a path toward restoration in a world that had lost its way. These thinkers, each in their own way, challenged their readers to see beyond the material to embrace a vision of life that is rich with wonder, purpose, and, ultimately, hope.

My hope is that this book will not only inform but inspire—that it will serve as an invitation for readers to embark on their own quest for meaning. In a world that often feels fragmented, where the search for purpose is dismissed as naïve, I believe that humanity's longing for more is not a weakness but a sign of something deeper. It is, I am convinced, the whisper of the divine calling us to a life that is fuller, richer, and far more meaningful than we can imagine.

May you find, as I did, that the journey toward meaning, toward beauty, toward goodness, toward truth is one worth taking. And I pray that it will lead you, ultimately, to the One who is, himself, the Source of all those things.

PART I

The Unraveling
Modernity and Its Discontents

1

Discovery and Disenchantment

God is dead. God remains dead. And we have killed him. How shall we comfort ourselves, the murderers of all murderers? What was holiest and mightiest of all that the world has yet owned has bled to death under our knives: who will wipe this blood off us?"

—Friedrich Nietzsche[1]

In a world that has mapped its stars and counted the sands of distant shores, what remains uncharted is the human soul, adrift in a sea of certainty yet filled with unanswered questions. The modern era emerged as a grand triumph of reason and discovery, a triumph where humanity harnessed knowledge with unprecedented power. With the advances of science and rational inquiry, the invisible world—the myths and beliefs once cherished as guiding stars—seemed to vanish, dismissed as mere relics of a less enlightened age. The dream of a universe governed by laws we could know, explain, and, most importantly, control had arrived, and with it, the confidence that we could live free from superstition, irrationality, and even the uncertainty of what comes after life.

---

1. Nietzche, *Gay Science*, 181.

Yet as the old gods fell silent, a new silence took their place—one that echoed not with meaning but with absence. The familiar world had grown disenchanted, stripped of its sacredness, and those who first glimpsed this new order began to feel its cold isolation. The story of modernity is a story of discovery, yet also of deep loss. As humanity lifted its eyes to the stars with the tools of science, it seemed to lose sight of the divine, the ineffable, and the source of meaning itself. Discovery had indeed come, but it brought with it an unanticipated companion: disenchantment.

This disenchantment is not merely a loss of faith or tradition. It is the slow unraveling of purpose, a hollowing-out of the very sense that there is something worth living and dying for. Figures like Friedrich Nietzsche warned that without a shared belief in something greater than ourselves, humanity risked falling into a chasm of despair and confusion. Sigmund Freud exposed the hidden and often disturbing layers of our psyche, revealing just how unknowable and fractured our "selves" truly are. Søren Kierkegaard, sensing the coming crisis, insisted that reason alone could not satisfy the human heart—that our deepest yearnings demanded a leap beyond the visible and measurable.

This chapter begins with a question: what happens when humanity believes it has uncovered the last mystery, only to find the world bleaker and colder in the revelation? How does a civilization, built on the promise of progress and certainty, handle the unraveling of its own meaning? The thinkers we will explore grappled with these questions, each in their own way uncovering the shadows cast by modernity's brightest lights.

Scientism and the Rise of the "Objective" Worldview

The modern era did not merely mark a time of unprecedented discovery; it ushered in a new worldview, one that saw the universe as a vast machine governed by knowable laws, awaiting our intellectual conquest. Enlightenment thinkers argued that reason and empirical investigation were the only trustworthy guides to truth, and with these tools, humanity would uncover answers that had evaded the world's greatest philosophers, mystics, and priests for centuries. The mysteries of nature, once seen as a testament to a divine creator, began to shrink in awe as science expanded. No longer was the world viewed as enchanted; it was now an object to be dissected, analyzed, and explained.

Yet this was not simply the age of science but of scientism: the belief that science alone, as a discipline, could answer the most fundamental questions about existence, purpose, and human nature. While science undoubtedly advanced human understanding, scientism took this respect for empirical study and stretched it into a creed of its own, reducing truth to what could be observed, quantified, and classified. This was science exalted to an almost religious stature, implying that anything beyond its scope was unknowable, or worse, irrelevant.

To many, this shift felt like liberation from superstition and dogma, a new dawn of intellectual independence. No longer shackled by the "dark ages" of religious explanation, humanity could explore the universe on its own terms. Newton's laws mapped the celestial bodies with mathematical precision, and Galileo's telescope brought the distant reaches of space into focus, heralding a brave new world of certainties. The heart of this revolution was clear: anything that could not be tested or proven by science was to be viewed with skepticism. It was a form of faith in reason itself, a belief that knowledge gained through human effort could illuminate every shadowed corner of the cosmos.

This "objective" worldview came with a price. While it revealed much, it dismissed the unseen, the unmeasurable—the things that stirred the soul, gave comfort in suffering, and framed life's most profound questions. With science as the arbiter of truth, religious and metaphysical beliefs were increasingly viewed as relics of a less enlightened time. The notion of a transcendent purpose, something beyond flesh and bone, was redefined as a psychological crutch, a comforting story but no longer to be taken seriously. A gulf opened between knowledge and meaning, and as scientism became the intellectual fashion, humanity began to see itself not as divinely fashioned but as a mere result of cosmic chance, caught between blind forces and indifferent processes.

Scientism, with its relentless drive for objectivity, left no room for the sacred, the mysterious, or the soul's longing for something greater. It rendered the cosmos as indifferent, a series of cold mechanisms governed by predictable laws. And while humanity might have been liberated from ignorance, it was also untethered from deeper beliefs that once provided meaning, comfort, and a sense of place in the world. This disenchanted view of reality was now set in stark contrast with the sense of wonder that earlier generations felt when looking at the night sky or pondering their purpose.

As the grip of scientism tightened, some saw a darker side to this relentless pursuit of "truth." If existence was merely a biological accident, if human beings were no more than highly evolved animals, then concepts like morality, purpose, and beauty had no grounding beyond our subjective preferences. The world may have become clearer, but the human soul had grown fogged, lost within a reality that spoke to the mind but left the heart desolate.

This was the dawn of the "objective" worldview, a perspective that taught humanity to see the world without awe, only analysis. It was a worldview that sought liberation from illusion yet, in doing so, invited a new form of bondage—a deep, existential loneliness in an indifferent universe. This chapter of human history was not just a story of enlightenment; it was the beginning of an unraveling, a retreat from meaning as humanity chose the light of knowledge and found itself cast into the shadow of disenchantment. In this age of science and objectivity, humanity had gained a new understanding but lost an ancient wisdom—the belief that some things, though unseen, are as real as the world we touch and see.

Nihilism and the "Death of God"

With scientism casting its cold light across the human landscape, a shadow loomed darker than any humanity had faced before. This was the shadow of nihilism, a profound existential crisis that questioned not only what we could know but also whether anything we did know truly mattered. The Enlightenment had liberated humanity from superstition, yet in discarding old beliefs, it left a void—one that rational explanations alone could not fill. As humanity turned to science and empirical certainty, it became clear that the things which gave life its deepest meaning—purpose, value, moral truth—had no secure footing in this new, "enlightened" world.

It was Friedrich Nietzsche who would step forward to name and confront this crisis. For Nietzsche, the relentless spread of secularism and the dismantling of religious belief marked a monumental shift in human history. As noted in the opening quote of this chapter, Nietzsche made one of his most striking declarations when he wrote in *The Gay Science* that "God is dead." With this statement, Nietzsche was not just challenging belief in a deity; he was proclaiming the end of a shared moral and existential framework that had supported Western civilization for centuries.

Humanity, he warned, was now adrift in a vast moral abyss, where every previously held value could be questioned, every purpose undermined.

This proclamation was not a celebration but a diagnosis, an alarming recognition that without the foundational belief in a divine order, civilization was at risk of losing its very sense of meaning. If God was indeed dead, then everything that followed from that belief—morality, purpose, objective truth—was now a "floating world" with no anchor. Nietzsche knew well the dangers that lay ahead, describing humanity's condition as one of "weightlessness," where individuals were free but left without direction, lost in the open sea of relativism and existential uncertainty.[2]

Nihilism, the consequence of this "death of God," is often misunderstood as simple despair or hopelessness. Nietzsche saw it as something far more pervasive: the conviction that life has no inherent meaning, that moral values are mere social constructs and that truth itself might be little more than a useful fiction. Where the medieval mind looked upward for purpose, and the Enlightenment mind looked outward to nature and reason, the modern mind looked inward—and found only a mirror, reflecting nothing but its own image back.

This vacuum of meaning did not go unnoticed by Nietzsche's contemporaries or successors. Søren Kierkegaard, writing decades earlier, had sensed this crisis long before Nietzsche named it. Kierkegaard spoke of what one might call an "existential dread" that arises when one confronts the limitations of human reason and the seeming absurdity of life without faith. For Kierkegaard, the solution was radical: only a leap of faith could restore meaning. This faith, however, could not be passive; it was an active choice to believe despite the apparent absurdity of existence. In a world where reason had failed to answer life's most pressing questions, faith alone, he argued, offered the means to transcend despair.

Nietzsche, however, took a different path, one fraught with inner conflict. He warned that if humanity did not find the strength to create its own values, it would fall victim to despair and, eventually, to an all-encompassing nihilism. With religious belief increasingly dismissed as fantasy, individuals and societies alike faced the temptation to construct new gods—values, ideologies, or leaders who might fill the void left by traditional faith. In Nietzsche's view, this was both dangerous and necessary. Humanity could either rise to the challenge of self-created purpose or sink into a cynical apathy that saw life itself as nothing more than a biological accident.

2. From Kaufmann's introductory notes to Nietzsche's *Gay Science*, 18.

The ideas that Nietzsche introduced would echo through the coming century as Western society struggled to reconcile the comforts of scientific progress with the void left by a loss of spiritual belief. As generations turned from the cathedral to the laboratory, existentialism emerged as the philosophy of the moment, an answer to the emptiness left by nihilism. Figures like Jean-Paul Sartre and Albert Camus took Nietzsche's premise and ran with it, famously claiming that without God, life itself has no meaning beyond what we ourselves impose upon it. Sartre argued that humans are "condemned to be free," burdened with the responsibility of creating their own meaning in a world without given values.[3]

Existentialism became both a challenge and a form of solace. If there were no inherent truths, then humanity was liberated to find or invent its own. Yet for all its optimism, this philosophy carried a heavy cost. The absence of absolute meaning placed an unbearable weight on the individual, whose choices became a matter of personal invention, untethered from the traditions and moral frameworks that once provided guidance. This was freedom, but it was also loneliness—the awareness that in the end, the individual stood alone in a vast, indifferent universe, armed only with personal resolve.

While existentialism offered a response, it could not fully dispel the specter of nihilism. Nietzsche's "death of God" was not merely a blow to belief; it was an opening to an age where all previous forms of certainty were questioned and the sacred was replaced by the secular, often to isolating effect. It was as if society had gained clarity but lost the very essence of what made life worth living. In this world, where faith was replaced with doubt, and purpose with personal preference, the soul found itself with nowhere to turn. The values that had once defined civilization now appeared as arbitrary as the social customs they emerged from, and humanity's heart grew heavy, craving something it could no longer find in the empirical and the "real."

Nihilism became the bitter fruit of a disenchanted world, a reminder that while humanity had shed the comforts of faith, it had also lost the meaning that came with it. In this age of reason, where even reason itself seemed powerless to satisfy, the question that haunted Nietzsche continues to echo: Without God, without purpose, without a guiding light, what becomes of us?

---

3. Sartre, *Being and Nothingness*, 129.

The Unconscious Mind and the Fragmented Self

As society struggled with the death of God and the encroaching shadow of nihilism, a new frontier of human understanding opened—not in the stars above but in the labyrinthine depths of the human psyche. If Nietzsche had shattered the foundations of moral certainty, Sigmund Freud would fracture the sense of self that humans had relied upon for centuries. Freud's discovery of the unconscious mind revealed an aspect of our inner lives that was not only unfamiliar but, in many ways, unknowable. What people once considered the self—rational, unified, capable of moral decision—now seemed to be but the surface layer of a deeper, chaotic inner world, marked by conflicts, desires, and forces that defied conscious control.

Freud's model of the mind was revolutionary. He proposed that much of human behavior was shaped not by our conscious decisions but by the unconscious, a repository of hidden urges and repressed memories. Beneath the apparent coherence of everyday life lay a constant struggle between the forces of instinct and the demands of society. Freud broke the mind down into three components: the id, the ego, and the superego, each competing for control. The id was raw and primal, driven by unbridled desires; the superego imposed societal expectations, acting as a moral censor; and the ego, caught between the two, sought to mediate this tension.[4] This model did not just complicate the view of human nature, it suggested that human beings were not entirely in control of their own actions, that they were strangers even to themselves.

Freud's ideas struck another disconcerting blow to a society already uneasy with the erosion of traditional beliefs. They revealed a humanity that was not only morally unanchored but psychologically fragmented. The unconscious mind was not a placid well of deep thoughts but a turbulent sea of conflicting urges and anxieties. Dreams, once considered random or even prophetic, were redefined as expressions of repressed desires, gateways into the unconscious that betrayed the raw, often disturbing forces at work beneath the surface. If the conscious mind was the rational captain of the self, Freud showed that it was steering a ship with a mutinous crew below deck.

Freud's theories raised a deeply unsettling question: If human beings are not wholly aware of or in control of their own minds, then what becomes of concepts like responsibility, autonomy, and even identity

---

4. See Freud, *Civilization and Its Discontents*.

itself? The unconscious challenged the very Enlightenment ideal of a rational, unified self, suggesting instead that our actions might often be the result of conflicts we cannot fully grasp or master. This was a profound departure from the view of humanity that had persisted since the Renaissance, where the self was seen as coherent and rational, able to pursue truth, virtue, and progress. Freud's work revealed the self as fragmented, at war within itself, and as complex as any social or cosmic system.

This fractured view of the mind found resonance in the cultural mood of the time. The Victorian world, which Freud both criticized and worked within, was one of repression and moral rigidity. Respectable society avoided open discussions of sexuality, violence, or mental illness, relegating them to the shadows of polite conversation. Freud tore open these veiled aspects of life, presenting sexuality as a fundamental driver of behavior and neurosis as a symptom of repressed desires and traumas. His patients, whose mental suffering he attributed to buried memories and hidden conflicts, became mirrors of a society that sought to deny its darker impulses, only to find them emerging in unexpected and often destructive ways.

As Freud's influence grew, the language of the unconscious began to shape the way people thought about themselves and each other. Terms like "repression," "projection," and "sublimation" became part of the cultural lexicon, reshaping the dialogue around human motivation and morality. No longer could individuals view themselves as masters of their own minds. Instead, they had to reckon with the reality that their choices, relationships, and even identities might be driven by unconscious forces beyond their control. This understanding eroded the last remnants of certainty about human nature, suggesting that our greatest mysteries were not only beyond the stars or buried in religious texts but lay within our own minds.

This fragmentation of the self contributed to the broader crisis of meaning, pushing humanity further down the path of modern disillusionment. Just as scientism had dispelled the sacred from the cosmos, Freudian psychology dispelled the notion of a sacred inner self. The mind, like the universe, became an object of analysis, a puzzle to be solved rather than a soul to be revered. And as people began to see themselves through Freud's lens, as products of drives, fears, and traumas, the possibility of true self-knowledge seemed to recede into the distance. To be human was now to be haunted by what lay beneath—to question whether one's motives, beliefs, and even loves were genuine or merely products of unseen psychological mechanics.

The ripple effects of Freud's discoveries extended far beyond the clinic or the consulting room. Art, literature, and philosophy began to reflect this darker, more fragmented vision of humanity. The modernist movement, with its disjointed narratives and experimental forms, mirrored the disintegrated self that Freud had revealed. Writers like Franz Kafka and Virginia Woolf drew on these themes, exploring characters whose lives were shaped by forces they could not understand. The unconscious mind, with all its ambiguity, became a central character in the story of modernity itself.

In revealing the unconscious, Freud forced humanity to confront its own complexity and contradiction, setting the stage for an era in which certainty and coherence were no longer possible. This was not merely an intellectual shift; it was an existential one. To be modern was to live in tension with oneself, to be both the seeker and the stranger within one's own mind. The age of reason had stripped the universe of meaning, but the age of psychology had done the same to the self. As humanity grappled with this internal dissonance, it began to ask: If we are not fully in control of our own thoughts, desires, or identities, then what can we truly know about ourselves?

Schopenhauer and the "Will" as Blind Force

As Freud cast light on the hidden depths of the mind, another voice spoke to a deeper, darker force driving not only the human psyche but all existence itself. For Arthur Schopenhauer, reality was not a rational, ordered system but a relentless force he called the "Will." This Will was not a deity nor a purposeful entity; it was a blind, insatiable drive, an endless hunger that both shaped and tormented life. Where Freud revealed internal conflicts within the self, Schopenhauer painted a picture of conflict as the very essence of the universe, embedded in every living thing. In Schopenhauer's vision, life itself was a manifestation of an unconscious Will, a force that pulls every creature into an endless cycle of desire, striving, and ultimately, suffering.

Schopenhauer's philosophy, bleak as it was, offered a mirror to a modern world that had grown suspicious of the comforting narratives it once told itself. As science unraveled the mystery of the heavens and psychology unraveled the mystery of the mind, Schopenhauer unraveled the mystery of existence, revealing it to be as devoid of benevolence as it was of meaning. The Will, he argued, is irrational, impersonal, and above all, indifferent. It is the impulse behind survival, the reason plants stretch toward the sun, animals hunt and reproduce, and humans labor and love. Yet all these acts, he claimed, are merely expressions of an unyielding force that cares nothing for the individual or for any notion of fulfillment. Life, in Schopenhauer's eyes, was an endless pursuit of desires that, even when met, gave birth to new ones, trapping every living being in a cycle that could never bring lasting satisfaction.

Schopenhauer's view of existence stood in stark contrast to the optimistic rationalism of his contemporaries, who saw science and human progress as the keys to a better world. Where they spoke of the Enlightenment as humanity's path out of ignorance and suffering, Schopenhauer described it as another layer of illusion, a veil over the brutal reality of life. His ideas echoed the sentiments of ancient Eastern philosophies, particularly Buddhism, which similarly sees desire as the root of suffering and liberation as an escape from this cycle. But while the East offered a path to freedom through detachment and enlightenment, Schopenhauer offered no such solace. For him, life was suffering, and the Will was the reason why.

The implications of Schopenhauer's philosophy were profound. In a world driven by the Will, morality, purpose, and even happiness become illusions. People could pursue these ideals but only as part of the larger, blind drive that would ultimately consume them. The Will was both the cause of all striving and the architect of its futility, creating a paradox in which every effort to achieve contentment inevitably led back to dissatisfaction. As Schopenhauer wrote, "All striving comes from lack, from a dissatisfaction with one's condition, and is therefore suffering so long as it is not satisfied. But no satisfaction is lasting; it is always merely the starting point of a new striving."[5] Here was a philosophy of existence that offered no comfort, only the brutal honesty that life's inherent nature was to struggle, endure, and seek in vain.

Schopenhauer's vision was more than a personal philosophy; it was a worldview that would deeply influence later thinkers, including Nietzsche and Freud. Nietzsche would take Schopenhauer's Will and reinterpret it as the "Will to Power," a creative force that could drive

---

5. Schopenhauer, *World as Will and Representation*, 309.

humanity to greatness even in the absence of transcendent meaning.[6] Freud, too, drew from Schopenhauer's ideas, seeing the id as a reflection of the primal, unconscious drives Schopenhauer had described. For both men, Schopenhauer's work opened the door to understanding life as a struggle—whether for dominance or for survival—and human nature as caught within forces beyond conscious control.

Yet Schopenhauer's pessimism went deeper, for he believed that even knowledge and art, the pursuits that many consider highest, were ultimately governed by the Will. While he acknowledged that art could provide temporary relief by lifting individuals beyond their immediate desires, he argued that this relief was fleeting. The artist, too, was driven by the Will, producing beauty not out of altruism or enlightenment but as a means of escaping his own dissatisfaction, if only for a moment. Even the philosopher, who might claim to be searching for truth, was, according to Schopenhauer, simply another expression of the Will, seeking to satisfy an inner need rather than to transcend life's inherent struggle.

For Schopenhauer, the only escape from this relentless cycle lay in renunciation, a turning away from desire itself. This idea, reminiscent of Buddhist teachings, presented asceticism as a path to quiet the Will, if not to defeat it. While he was skeptical of humanity's ability to overcome the Will entirely, he believed that a life of simplicity, humility, and detachment could at least alleviate some of the suffering inherent to existence. Yet even here, Schopenhauer was cautious, aware that the Will is insidious and that even the act of renunciation could become another expression of desire.

As we reflect on Schopenhauer's philosophy, we see an image of humanity that is stark, raw, and unadorned. In his eyes, we are creatures bound to an endless wheel, compelled by desires that are never satisfied and a Will that is indifferent to our suffering. This vision of life as an arena of ceaseless striving adds another layer to the existential crisis of modernity—a crisis already marked by the loss of faith, the disintegration of the self, and now, the revelation that even our deepest pursuits are the expressions of an indifferent, blind force. If scientism had disenchanted the cosmos and Freud had fragmented the mind, Schopenhauer had removed any pretense of cosmic purpose, leaving humanity to wrestle with the implications of existence as pure will. This bleak, uncompromising worldview provides a fitting backdrop to the journey of modernity's

---

6. Nietzsche, *Gay Science*, 292.

discontents. It calls into question every motive, every hope, every dream. In Schopenhauer's world, meaning does not lie in the heavens or the heart but in accepting that life is struggle, that suffering is inherent, and that peace may come not in conquering but in surrendering.

Agnosticism and the Limits of Knowledge

In the wake of Schopenhauer's bleak revelations about existence and the Will, modernity found itself increasingly wary of grand conclusions. With science dismantling the sacred, psychology questioning the coherence of the self, and philosophy exposing the blind forces beneath our striving, a deep uncertainty settled over Western thought. Humanity had grown suspicious, not only of ancient beliefs but also of the possibility of knowing ultimate truths. This suspicion took form in the work of T. H. Huxley, who championed a philosophy of restrained understanding: agnosticism. For Huxley, knowledge had limits, and humanity's ability to reach into the depths of reality would always be constrained by those boundaries. Rather than profess certainty about things beyond empirical observation, Huxley argued that true wisdom lay in acknowledging what could not be known.

Dubbed "Darwin's Bulldog" for his fervent defense of evolutionary theory, Huxley was a scientist at heart, one who believed in the power of inquiry but remained deeply aware of its limitations. He saw science as the best tool for understanding the natural world, yet he warned against confusing scientific inquiry with a means to answer life's ultimate questions. Agnosticism, for Huxley, was not a lack of curiosity but a disciplined humility. It was a refusal to assert belief in the face of unknowable mysteries. As he wrote in an 1889 essay:

> Agnosticism, in fact, is not a creed, but a method, the essence of which lies in the rigorous application of a single principle. That principle is of great antiquity; it is as old as Socrates; as old as the writer who said, "Try all things, hold fast by that which is good"; it is the foundation of the Reformation, which simply illustrated the axiom that every man should be able to give a reason for the faith that is in him; it is the great principle of Descartes; it is the fundamental axiom of modern science. Positively, the principle may be expressed: In matters of the intellect, follow your reason as far as it will take you, without regard to any other consideration. And negatively: In matters of the intellect do not pretend that

conclusions are certain which are not demonstrated or demonstrable. That I take to be the agnostic faith, which if a man keep whole and undefiled, he shall not be ashamed to look the universe in the face, whatever the future may have in store for him.[7]

Huxley's agnosticism was born out of an intellectual landscape brimming with both discovery and doubt. By the late nineteenth century, scientific advancements had transformed humanity's view of the cosmos and of life itself, presenting a vision of existence that seemed self-sustaining, indifferent, and often hostile to human significance. The Victorian public, fascinated yet unsettled, turned to science for answers that might once have been sought in religion. Yet Huxley, despite his enthusiasm for scientific progress, cautioned against this trend. He believed that science was a tool, not a creed, and that extending it into the realm of metaphysics would ultimately fail to satisfy humanity's deeper questions. For Huxley, the great mystery of life could be studied and explored but not solved in any final sense.

This concept of agnosticism, though seemingly straightforward, was revolutionary. It represented a deliberate shift away from certainty, an acknowledgment that the grandest questions—Why are we here? What is our purpose?—might forever elude definitive answers. In a society that had placed growing faith in the power of human understanding, Huxley's position was a stark reminder that knowledge had limits, that there were mysteries science might observe but could never fully explain. By coining the term "agnosticism," Huxley gave voice to a cautious form of intellectual honesty, one that held back from declaring absolute truths where evidence was lacking. This restraint was both a source of liberation and a burden, for in denying false certainties, agnosticism left humanity standing in a world stripped of clear purpose.

In a sense, Huxley's agnosticism was the natural response to a world that had lost its faith but had not yet found a new vision. If Nietzsche had warned of nihilism and Freud had fractured the self, Huxley urged a temperate path between belief and disbelief, a respect for the unknown. Yet his agnosticism also mirrored the modern spirit of skepticism, a growing reluctance to commit to ultimate claims about existence. Where previous generations had sought the transcendent, Huxley's approach was firmly grounded, focused on what could be known and what could not. It was a stance that valued intellectual humility over dogmatic belief, a recognition that humanity's reach would always exceed its grasp.

7. Huxley, "Agnosticism," 13.

Huxley's philosophy, despite all its intellectual caution, was not without its challenges. For a society grappling with the erosion of traditional values and the rise of materialism, agnosticism offered neither the comfort of faith nor the clarity of certainty. In place of the old answers, it offered only open questions, inviting individuals to accept the limits of their understanding. Huxley's agnostic worldview thus left humanity suspended in an ambiguous state, neither fully disbelieving nor fully believing, unsure whether its existential needs could be met by a philosophy that placed boundaries on human knowledge. In the absence of religious or moral absolutes, individuals found themselves tasked with navigating a world of possibility—and uncertainty—without a compass.

The effects of Huxley's agnosticism rippled through the cultural currents of the time, influencing writers, thinkers, and ordinary people alike. For those who had lost faith in the certainties of the past but could not accept atheism's bleak finality, agnosticism became a kind of intellectual refuge. It allowed for reverence without conviction, awe without assurance. Yet in this approach lay a profound tension. By acknowledging the limits of knowledge, agnosticism implicitly accepted that humanity might never truly understand its purpose or destiny. This uncertainty could foster humility, but it could also lead to a kind of spiritual paralysis, a hesitation to engage with the larger questions that, despite all doubt, continued to stir within.

In Huxley's world, there were no final answers, only provisional understandings. This recognition marked another stage in modernity's gradual unraveling, as humanity moved from theism to skepticism and from skepticism to uncertainty. The quest for knowledge had now encountered its own boundaries, revealing an existence that might be intelligible in parts yet unknowable in whole. In the age of Huxley, humanity had reached the limits of what science could offer, standing on the edge of a horizon beyond which lay only mystery.

Huxley's agnosticism underscored the profound limits of the modern project. If the cosmos was disenchanted by science and the self divided by psychology, then agnosticism placed the final boundary around human understanding, leaving the deepest questions untouched. Yet even here, on the brink of modernity's ultimate realization—that some truths would forever remain beyond reach—there remained an impulse to press on, to seek, and perhaps, to hope. The thinkers who followed would wrestle with this boundary, some crossing it in search of new beliefs, others retreating from it with a wary reverence for the unknown.

The Disenchanted World

As modernity's light penetrated the mysteries of nature, self, and belief, it cast long shadows that revealed an unexpected emptiness. The grand promises of progress had given way to a strange kind of barrenness, a sense that for all we had discovered, something essential had been lost. Science had shown us a universe governed by laws and forces but indifferent to human yearning. Psychology had uncovered hidden depths within us, only to suggest that we might never truly know ourselves. Philosophy and agnosticism, meanwhile, had placed a boundary around our understanding, leaving the ultimate questions forever unresolved. What remained was a world thoroughly mapped but curiously hollow—a disenchanted world.

This world, as Nietzsche foresaw, was one in which humanity had lost its compass, a world in which the "death of God" echoed in the deepest recesses of culture and consciousness. The absence of the divine, whether personal or abstract, left humanity adrift, uncertain of its purpose and suspicious of its own motives. Even as scientific discovery expanded our horizons, our sense of meaning shrank, reduced to fleeting goals, subjective choices, and self-made values. And yet, for all our mastery over the physical world, we found ourselves increasingly vulnerable to the existential void left by the dismantling of faith and tradition. The universe was no longer a story written with humanity at its heart; it was a machine, vast, indifferent, and silent.

In this landscape, figures like Nietzsche and Freud, Schopenhauer and Huxley, offered frameworks not of answers but of challenges, questions that would shape modernity's ongoing search for meaning. Where Nietzsche warned of nihilism, Freud diagnosed the fractured self, and Schopenhauer revealed existence as a blind, ceaseless drive. Huxley, meanwhile, called for intellectual humility, urging humanity to respect the limits of its understanding. Each voice contributed to the unraveling of the old certainties, and each in its own way underscored the precariousness of a world stripped of the sacred.

This disenchanted new world did not merely reflect a loss of belief; it signified a fundamental shift in how humanity saw itself and its place in the cosmos. In earlier times, the universe was animated by meaning—by gods, by spirits, by a divine order that gave life purpose. But now, in a world redefined by empirical certainty, life seemed governed by impersonal forces, forces that recognized neither beauty nor morality, neither love nor hope. The modern individual, equipped with knowledge but deprived of mystery, was left to navigate a reality that felt increasingly foreign, fragmented, and devoid of deeper significance.

And yet, within this disenchantment, a paradox emerged: the very loss of meaning compelled a search for something more. As Nietzsche observed, humanity could not bear to live without purpose; even in the absence of absolute truth, there remained a need to create, to believe, to hope.[8] The thinkers we will explore in the chapters ahead grappled with this very impulse. Figures like H. G. Wells imagined utopian futures and then recoiled in horror as they envisioned the dystopian outcomes of unchecked progress. Dostoevsky explored the consequences of moral relativism and spiritual emptiness, revealing a world where freedom could lead either to despair or redemption. T. S. Eliot, through poetry, captured the spiritual desolation of a post-faith society, where ancient myths lingered as faint echoes, calling out in a world seemingly deaf to their significance.

We now find ourselves on the brink of a new exploration, not into the unknowns of the cosmos or the mind but into the depths of the human condition as it confronts its own solitude. In a world stripped of divine purpose, what, if anything, remains to be reclaimed? And is there a way forward, a path that can reconcile the promises of modernity with the enduring need for transcendence?

---

8. Nietzche, *Thus Spoke Zarathustra*, 78–83.

2

H. G. Wells
The Machine, the Man, and the Meaning

"I have thought since how particularly ill-equipped I was for such an experience. When I had started with the Time Machine, I had started with the absurd assumption that the men of the Future would certainly be infinitely ahead of ourselves in all their appliances."

—H. G. Wells[1]

H. G. Wells was a man who saw the world with both the fervor of a believer and the caution of a skeptic. His vision was one in which technology and reason would lift humanity from suffering, ignorance, and want into a future built on the triumphs of scientific progress. And yet, as Wells pursued this dream, he began to see another possibility lurking behind his utopian visions: a future where machines and minds could indeed advance but perhaps only to create new forms of alienation, inequality, and despair. For Wells, science was both a shining path forward and a chasm of unanticipated consequences, a way to grasp control over nature but also a force that might control, or even destroy, humanity itself.

This chapter follows the arc of Wells's transformation from a young writer impassioned with optimism for scientific advancement to an elder

---

1. Wells, *Time Machine*, 41.

statesman of literature who could no longer ignore the shadows cast by his own visions. He was both the prophet of progress and, in time, its growing critic, grappling with questions that remain profoundly relevant today: What happens when technology outpaces our ethical and spiritual maturity? Can a world ruled by machines, bereft of meaning beyond utility, ever truly satisfy the human heart? Wells's work reflected his own struggle with these questions, a journey that paralleled modernity's struggle to reconcile the promises of science with the disillusionments of reality.

Wells's early writings are filled with the faith that science could be humanity's salvation, a means to escape the bonds of ignorance and shape society according to reason and compassion. Inspired by his mentor, T. H. Huxley, Wells saw evolution as not only a biological fact but a promise for humanity's future. A future that, in his mind, could be molded by the power of scientific knowledge. His early works, like *A Modern Utopia*, envisioned societies where technology solved hunger, disease, and conflict, freeing humanity to pursue wisdom and enlightenment. In this vision, Wells captured the high hopes of his time, a belief that progress could, and eventually would, mean human flourishing.

But, Wells, as both a thinker and an artist, would come to question the ideals he once championed. With novels like *The Time Machine* and *The War of the Worlds*, he began to probe the darker side of his scientific utopia, exploring how unchecked technological advancement could dehumanize, divide, and ultimately lead to ruin. Through these stories, he warned of a dystopian future in which the machine becomes master and humanity its obedient servant, where the drive for progress risks tearing apart the very fabric of what makes us human. Wells's life and work reveal a mind pulled between faith in human ingenuity and a dawning awareness of its limits, embodying the aspirations and anxieties of a world torn between enlightenment and estrangement. His story serves as a case study in modernity's uneasy balance between discovery and disenchantment, a journey through both the promise and the peril of progress.

As we delve into Wells's transformation, we encounter the ambitions, fears, and moral dilemmas of an age that sought to leave behind the myths of old, only to find itself haunted by new questions. Through Wells's visionary and cautionary tales, we glimpse the double-edged sword of modernity, one that both illuminates and darkens, offering knowledge that may ultimately reveal its own futility. And so, in Wells, we find not only a voice for the promises of the modern age but a prescient warning of the disenchanted future it may bring.

Scientific Enthusiasm and Utopian Dreams

Wells, as a young man, saw in science the potential to reshape humanity's fate, a tool as powerful as any myth that had ever guided human civilization. Trained under T. H. Huxley, Wells's worldview was deeply infused with the conviction that knowledge, if harnessed wisely, could liberate humanity from suffering and usher in an era of reason and justice. For Wells, science was a transformative force, a key to the future, carrying humanity beyond the limitations of its past and into a new epoch where suffering could be systematically conquered.

In these early days, Wells believed wholeheartedly in the potential of human progress. He envisioned a world governed by rational principles, shaped by social engineering, and improved by technological innovation. His early works, like *A Modern Utopia*, brim with a confidence that knowledge and technology could create societies free from poverty, disease, and war. Here, Wells imagines a parallel world where every individual's needs are met, where social and economic inequalities are minimized, and where scientific advancements are celebrated as the architects of collective well-being.[2] In these writings, Wells's enthusiasm for science as humanity's ultimate emancipator is almost palpable. It is a vision of utopia sketched with all the precision and grandeur of the greatest scientific imaginations.

This belief in progress was not limited to the material. Wells saw in evolutionary theory a promise not just of biological advancement but of social and moral improvement. Darwin's ideas had shaken the foundations of traditional belief, suggesting that humanity was not a fixed creation but a species in constant development. Wells, like many of his contemporaries, saw in evolution the thrilling possibility that humanity itself could "evolve" morally and intellectually. The process of natural selection, he believed, could be harnessed to guide society's growth, transcending the errors of history and creating a world rooted in the ideals of reason, justice, and peace. Science, in this vision, was humanity's new scripture, a foundation upon which a rational paradise could be built.

---

2. Wells, *Modern Utopia*, 9.

Wells's faith in the power of scientific and social engineering led him to imagine a world where suffering was not an inescapable fate but a problem that could be solved. His optimism mirrored the spirit of the age, an era that saw technological advancements like the steam engine, electricity, and medicine transforming daily life in ways previously unimaginable. For the first time, humanity seemed to hold the keys to a brighter future, and Wells positioned himself as a prophet of this new world. In *The World Set Free*, he imagined technology bringing an end to want and disease, allowing human beings to focus on art, philosophy, and personal growth. Here, Wells's vision of science verged on the sacred: a force that could redeem the world, if only humanity would use it wisely.

Underlying this dream was Wells's conviction that humanity's problems could be approached scientifically, that through reasoned intervention, societies could be molded toward an ideal state. It was a bold, even revolutionary idea: that human suffering could be lessened, perhaps even eradicated, by understanding and addressing its causes. This was a vision of science not just as a tool but as a moral enterprise, a means of reshaping reality itself. Wells embraced the idea of a complete scientific state. A society organized according to principles of reason and efficiency, governed by an enlightened class of thinkers and planners who would manage the social order for the collective good.

Yet even in these utopian visions, hints of Wells's growing ambivalence toward progress begin to emerge. In *The First Men in the Moon*, Wells explores the possibility of a lunar society governed by extreme rationality, one that has purged all but the most "efficient" members and roles. While the story was intended as a lighthearted adventure, it hinted at a darker side to Wells's scientific utopia: a society so bent on efficiency that it risks sacrificing individuality and compassion in the name of progress. Here, Wells seems to ask whether a world governed solely by reason might itself become a kind of machine—impressive, functional, but lacking the human warmth that makes life worth living.

For all his early optimism, Wells was not blind to the complexities of human nature. His enthusiasm for science was tempered by a quiet awareness that technology, while powerful, could only shape society insofar as human beings allowed it. The idealistic dreams in his earlier works suggest a Wells who hoped that humanity would rise to the moral challenges presented by progress. But beneath these utopian sketches lay a growing concern that science might create as many problems as it solved, that technology alone could not account for the ethical and spiritual dimensions of human life.

By exploring the possibilities of a scientifically perfected society, Wells placed himself at the heart of modernity's great experiment. He saw both the promise and peril of a world guided by knowledge, and his early writings reflect an optimism that science could not only improve life but elevate it to something grander, more meaningful. Yet, as he sketched out these dreams of a perfected world, Wells began to realize that technology, without a moral compass, could lead humanity down paths as dark as any the world had yet known. And so, from this optimism, a seed of doubt began to grow. A doubt that would deepen in his later works as Wells considered the consequences of a world governed by machines and methods, where science could not answer humanity's deepest needs.

Doubts and Dystopian Reflections

For a time, Wells's optimism seemed unshakable, fueled by a belief that science could not only improve life but elevate humanity itself. Yet, as the twentieth century dawned, shadows began to creep into his vision. The rapid march of technological progress, which had once promised enlightenment and abundance, now revealed potential dangers—new ways in which humanity's pursuit of power and control could spiral into oppression and destruction. As Wells matured, so did his reflections on what progress might cost. This shift marked a turning point in his writing, a movement from utopian dreams to dystopian warnings that would come to define his legacy. Through works like *The Time Machine* and *The War of the Worlds*, Wells began to explore the perils of unchecked advancement, questioning whether humanity's fascination with knowledge and technology might lead not to salvation but to ruin.

In *The Time Machine*, Wells's doubts find their first powerful expression. Here, his early enthusiasm for evolution as a force for progress gives way to a more complex, even haunting, portrayal of what humanity's future might hold. The protagonist—a nameless Time Traveler—journeys to the distant future only to discover a world divided between two distinct classes of beings: the Eloi and the Morlocks. The Eloi, delicate and childlike, live above ground in what appears at first to be an idyllic society, marked by peace, beauty, and leisure. Yet, as the Time Traveler soon learns, this appearance is deceptive. The Eloi are helpless, docile creatures, and their existence is only possible because of the Morlocks—brutal, subterranean beings who toil in darkness, maintaining the machinery that sustains the Eloi's paradise. The Eloi, in turn, serve as sustenance for the Morlocks, preyed upon as they wander in their idyllic fields, oblivious to their own dependence on the labor and hunger of the creatures below.

In this grim vision, Wells imagines a future where social and technological "progress" has led not to unity but to division and degeneration, where humanity has fragmented into two separate species, each trapped in its own form of suffering. Here, Wells casts a chilling light on the possible endpoint of class division and unchecked technological evolution. The Morlocks and Eloi are not merely fictional beings; they are a symbolic warning of what can happen when society values progress over people. Beneath Wells's portrayal of a future divided, we see a critique of industrial capitalism, a system that often demanded labor without regard for the humanity of the laborers themselves. In *The Time Machine*, Wells confronts the disturbing possibility that evolution, left to its own devices, might not produce a better world but a fractured, exploitative one, where even those who benefit from "progress" are rendered empty and diminished by it.

In *The War of the Worlds*, Wells's concerns deepen further. This tale of alien invasion and human vulnerability serves as both an epic of survival and a sobering parable about scientific hubris. As Martians descend upon England with devastating weaponry and overwhelming technological superiority, the fabric of human society is torn apart. Humans, once confident in their own advancements, find themselves powerless in the face of a more advanced species. Wells's message is clear: humanity's faith in its own supremacy and the protective power of technology is a dangerous illusion. The Martians, with their cold detachment and ruthless efficiency, embody a scientific worldview devoid of empathy or moral restraint. In their invasion, Wells captures his growing skepticism that technological power, when wielded without conscience, leads not to liberation but to annihilation.

The impact of *War of the Worlds* lies not only in its portrayal of a catastrophic invasion but in the unsettling parallel it draws between the Martians' treatment of humans and humanity's treatment of other species and even of its own people. The Martians observe humanity with the same detachment a scientist might bring to an experiment, indifferent to human suffering and driven solely by their own interests. This image served as a critique of colonialism and imperialism, casting the "superiority" that justified such practices in a sinister light. Through his depiction of humans as vulnerable subjects of alien indifference, Wells challenges the reader to question humanity's own sense of superiority and to consider the ethical cost of viewing others, whether people or nations, as resources to be exploited.

These dystopian works mark a profound shift in Wells's view of progress. The optimism of *A Modern Utopia* and *The World Set Free* gives way to a darker realization: technology, when unchecked by ethical considerations, can be as destructive as it is transformative. Wells's later works grapple with this paradox, portraying technology not as a guaranteed path to a better world but as a tool that could be used to dehumanize and divide. His stories echo with the fear that scientific advancements, rather than erasing suffering, might only amplify it by magnifying human flaws. The very tools that promised to uplift humanity could just as easily become instruments of oppression, creating new hierarchies, new forms of dependence, and new threats.

As Wells wrestled with these ideas, his writings began to explore the cost of a society governed by scientific rationalism alone. He imagined futures where human beings, reduced to roles and functions within a mechanical system, lose the very qualities that make them human—creativity, compassion, and the capacity for moral judgment. In his view, a purely materialistic world, focused on efficiency and progress at any cost, might eventually strip life of its intrinsic value, turning society into a cold machine and individuals into replaceable parts. Through these dystopian reflections, Wells voiced a warning to a world enraptured by its own innovations: without moral guidance, technological power could well become humanity's undoing.

In *The Island of Doctor Moreau*, Wells takes these concerns to a new depth, exploring the boundaries of science and the consequences of playing God. On this remote island, Dr. Moreau conducts experiments to transform animals into human-like creatures, a grotesque parody of evolution. Here, Wells confronts the ethical perils of unchecked scientific experimentation. Moreau's creations suffer for his ambitions, caught between animal instinct and human form, trapped in a torturous liminality. In Moreau, Wells portrays a man driven by curiosity but devoid of compassion, a figure who embodies the dangers of knowledge pursued without regard for its consequences. This novel's disturbing imagery and themes underscore Wells's realization that science, when disconnected from ethical responsibility, can lead to horrors as profound as those born from ignorance.

Through these dystopian reflections, Wells's work became a mirror to modernity's doubts, reflecting the anxieties of a world in which technology, once seen as a path to enlightenment, now loomed as a potential threat to humanity itself. His stories serve as cautionary tales, warning that while the machines we build may be powerful, they may also create worlds where people become subservient to the systems they once controlled. Wells began to see that a future defined by science alone, untempered by moral wisdom, might be a barren one—where progress would strip life of its depth and meaning, where humanity would lose itself in the pursuit of power.

In this turning point of Wells's career, we find a crucial insight into the heart of the modern project. Progress, he came to realize, is not simply a matter of knowledge or technology; it is a question of what kind of world we wish to create and what we are willing to sacrifice to achieve it. For all his early enthusiasm, Wells grew wary of a future in which humanity might gain the world but lose its soul, a world that, for all its wonders, would be disenchanted, hollow, and perhaps irreparably fractured.

Conflicted Worldview

As his view of progress dimmed, Wells began to question not only the trajectory of scientific advancement but the very worldview upon which it was built. One cannot ignore the inconsistencies between his scientific ideals and his deeper social concerns. Beneath his calls for progress lay an unresolved tension: if humanity was merely a product of blind evolutionary forces, driven by survival and reproduction, what basis could there be for values, compassion, or justice? In a materialistic universe, where meaning was reduced to mechanisms and morality to social constructs, could anything truly transcend self-interest or the cold logic of the natural order?

Wells's novels increasingly reflect this struggle. While his materialistic outlook viewed humanity as the sum of biological and social forces, his critiques of class, exploitation, and oppression revealed a moral urgency that seemed to demand more than what evolution or science alone could offer. In *The Island of Doctor Moreau* and *The War of the Worlds*, Wells critiques the human tendency to exploit others, yet his materialism offers little rationale for why such exploitation should be condemned beyond human sentiment. This conflict between Wells's social ideals and his scientific worldview created a profound ambivalence as he wrestled with the implications of a philosophy that could justify conquest as easily as compassion.

In *Doctor Moreau*, this tension reaches a disturbing intensity. Moreau's experiments—transforming animals into tortured approximations of humanity—reflect a raw embodiment of materialism's darkest potential. Here, creatures are reshaped not by evolution but by cold, scientific manipulation. The island is a grotesque caricature of the evolutionary process, where Moreau plays the role of creator without conscience. His creatures, stitched together through biological experimentation, are caught between animal instinct and human form, their suffering a byproduct of Moreau's detachment from any concept of inherent value or compassion. Through Moreau, Wells grapples with the moral barrenness of a worldview that elevates science to the highest authority while neglecting the ethical implications of its power. The novel implies that in a purely materialistic universe, where beings are shaped by survival rather than intrinsic worth, cruelty becomes not only possible but inevitable.

At the same time, Wells's critique of Moreau's heartless experiments exposes a contradiction. Take, for instance, this passage from the book:

> Had Moreau had any intelligible object, I could have sympathized at least a little with him. I am not so squeamish about pain as that. I could have forgiven him a little even, had his motive been only hate. But he was so irresponsible, so utterly careless! His curiosity, his mad, aimless investigations, drove him on; and the Things were thrown out to live a year or so, to struggle and blunder and suffer, and at last to die painfully.[3]

His moral outrage at the doctor's actions suggests that some values, such as compassion and dignity, ought to transcend mere biological drives. Yet, Wells's evolutionary framework, with its emphasis on survival, offers little justification for these values beyond pragmatic social cohesion. If humans are ultimately products of evolution, no different in essence from animals, what foundation remains for the idea that we should respect or protect one another? Moreau's laboratory, with its brutal disregard for suffering, challenges the very idea that science or evolution could offer an adequate moral framework, suggesting instead that a

---

3. Wells, *Island of Dr. Moreau*, 178.

purely materialistic worldview is not only insufficient but also dangerous when divorced from a greater transcendent responsibility.

In *The War of the Worlds*, Wells takes this ambivalence further, using the Martian invasion as a stark critique of imperialism. The Martians, with their superior technology and ruthless disregard for human life, mirror the very colonial attitudes of Wells's own society. Yet here again, Wells's criticism is fraught with contradiction. Evolutionary theory, which formed the basis of Wells's worldview, had often been used to justify imperialism by positing that stronger, more "advanced" societies had a natural right to dominate others. While Wells abhorred this mindset, the materialistic framework he embraced offered little to refute it. If evolution favors the survival of the fittest, and if life is a matter of dominance and competition, then what ethical grounds remain to critique the Martians' conquest of Earth—or, by extension, humanity's own conquests?

This philosophical conflict reflects Wells's growing discomfort with the moral implications of a purely mechanistic universe. As the Martians rain destruction upon an unprepared humanity, Wells seems to suggest that technological power, devoid of ethical guidance, leads only to devastation. Yet his evolutionary view cannot explain why this destruction should be seen as wrong beyond its effect on human survival. The very concepts of "right" and "wrong" lose substance in a world that sees humans as evolved animals rather than moral beings created with intrinsic worth. By casting humanity as both victim and aggressor, Wells grapples with the irony that evolution, the very process he had championed, might justify atrocities as easily as it could condemn them.

This ambivalence permeates Wells's later works, as he increasingly questions whether a materialistic worldview can ever truly satisfy humanity's need for meaning and moral purpose. If all human actions, from compassion to cruelty, are products of biological imperatives, then is morality itself nothing more than a social convenience? In a universe governed solely by natural laws, Wells struggled to find a basis for the justice, empathy, and accountability he so deeply valued. His critique of materialism became, in many ways, a critique of himself, as he questioned whether the ideals he cherished could survive in the very world he envisioned.

Wells's late work, *Mind at the End of Its Tether*, is perhaps his most candid reflection on this existential crisis. In the opening chapter of the book, Wells writes, "The writer is convinced that there is no way out or round or through the impasse. It is the end."[4] In this bleak meditation, Wells expresses his despair over humanity's future, grappling with the possibility that progress itself might be a hollow pursuit.

For all his early dreams of a scientifically ordered society, Wells now faced the sobering realization that knowledge and technology, while powerful, could not answer life's most pressing questions. In a world stripped of mystery, where all values are seen as constructs and all beings as products of chance, he found himself wrestling with a fundamental emptiness. Materialism, once his guiding star, now appeared to him as a cold and indifferent philosophy, unable to provide the moral vision he longed for.

In the end, Wells's exploration of a materialistic worldview exposed the profound limitations of a universe explained solely by science. He had once believed that humanity's advancement would be defined by reason and knowledge, yet he came to see that knowledge without meaning, progress without purpose, leads only to alienation. Through his characters, Wells asks a haunting question: If life has no inherent value, if we are simply products of evolution and mechanisms, then what, ultimately, are we striving for? And is there anything within us that science cannot dissect, quantify, or replicate? Wells's exploration of these ideas reflects a world struggling with the same questions.

A Mirror of Modernity's Unraveling

As H. G. Wells journeyed from youthful idealism to sobering disillusionment, he became a mirror for modernity itself—a mind both captivated and haunted by the power of knowledge, wrestling with the question of what remains when progress outruns purpose. For Wells, science was at first a bright torch illuminating the path to a rational, just society; it offered humanity the tools to conquer ignorance, to elevate civilization, and to transcend the superstitions of the past. Yet by the end of his life, this light seemed almost blinding, exposing a world made clearer but emptier, powerful but devoid of true meaning. Wells's transformation, from a prophet of scientific utopia to a critic of its pitfalls, reveals the inherent tension within the modern project: the seductive allure of knowledge paired with the ever-present shadow of disillusionment.

---

4. Wells, *Mind at the End of Its Tether*, 4.

In his final years, Wells grew increasingly skeptical that science alone could provide a foundation for a humane society. *Mind at the End of Its Tether*, reads as a stark admission of the failure of his own ideals. Here, he confronts a world where humanity, despite all its advancements, appears to him as a species adrift, lacking the moral grounding necessary to wield its newfound powers responsibly. This reflection is not merely Wells's own; it speaks to a broader cultural crisis, the creeping sense that modernity's triumphs, while dazzling, might be ultimately hollow. In a universe governed by mechanistic laws, where life is stripped of transcendent purpose, Wells finds himself in a kind of existential despair. He once envisioned a future where humanity, guided by knowledge and reason, would evolve into something greater; now he sees only a humanity potentially overwhelmed by its creations, on the brink of unraveling under the weight of its own progress.

Wells's shift from optimism to despondency captures a profound irony at the heart of modernity. The very tools that were meant to liberate humanity—science, reason, and technology—have also become potential sources of alienation and disenchantment. In his work, we see a dawning recognition that progress, while liberating, may not address the deepest needs of the human heart. Knowledge can reveal the mechanics of the cosmos, but it cannot answer why we should care for one another, why justice matters, or why life itself deserves reverence. Through his later writings, Wells seems to acknowledge that science, when divorced from any higher purpose, might ultimately strip life of depth and mystery, reducing the human experience to mere function, devoid of meaning beyond survival.

This was not simply a personal struggle for Wells; it was the struggle of an age facing the limits of the Enlightenment dream. The promise of a rational, scientific worldview was seductive, offering humanity a sense of mastery over its fate, yet Wells's life reveals the fragility of this promise when confronted with the complexities of human nature. His dystopian visions, once dismissed as fiction, increasingly took on a prophetic tone, forewarning a society where technology, in its relentless quest for efficiency, might strip away compassion, reducing individuals to roles within a mechanized system. The more Wells probed the future of a purely materialistic world, the more he sensed that humanity's aspirations required something beyond mere advancement—an ethical framework, a spiritual dimension, something that materialism alone could not provide.

In many ways, Wells's journey so clearly reveals the cultural anxiety birthed out of modernity. His life and work embody the modern paradox: a faith in human progress paired with an increasing awareness of its potential consequences. While he remained an advocate for knowledge, he began to see that wisdom lay not only in understanding but in restraint, in acknowledging the limits of what science could offer to the human spirit. By the end of his life, Wells's works reveal a desire for values that transcend empirical observation, a quiet but unmistakable yearning for a moral foundation that science could neither construct nor explain.

In his pessimism, Wells came to stand as a reluctant prophet of modernity's disenchantment. A voice calling attention to the gap between humanity's intellectual triumphs and its ethical shortcomings. His story reminds us that knowledge, though powerful, cannot fully address the questions that have haunted humanity since its beginning: Why are we here? What makes life worth living? Wells's doubts, his cautionary tales, and his ultimate disillusionment all point toward a hard-won realization: that the achievements of science, remarkable as they are, may leave humanity spiritually impoverished if they are not grounded in something beyond themselves.

In the end, Wells's legacy is not just his scientific foresight or his literary imagination but his ability to capture the modern soul's deepest conflicts. Through his transformation, we see modernity's own journey—a movement from the thrill of discovery to a sober acknowledgment of its limits, from the belief that science could redeem to the realization that knowledge, without wisdom, might lead us only to alienation. Wells's life stands as both a testament to the aspirations of modernity and a cautionary tale about its discontents. As we turn to other voices in this unfolding narrative, we carry forward the questions he raised: Can progress satisfy the human soul? Can a world explained by science alone ever truly address the longings of the human heart?

3

Fyodor Dostoevsky
Faith, Freedom, and the Abyss

"If *there is no God, all things are lawful.*"
—Fyodor Dostoevsky[1]

Fyodor Dostoevsky stood at the edge of modernity, gazing into an abyss that few of his contemporaries dared approach. Where others saw science and reason as the path to liberation, Dostoevsky perceived a dangerous emptiness, a creeping moral and existential void lurking behind humanity's turn from faith. What lay beyond this loss was a world in which freedom became unmoored from responsibility, where truth was hollowed out, and where human beings, cast adrift, struggled to find purpose in a cosmos that seemed, to many, indifferent to their existence.

Dostoevsky's works are not merely stories; they are explorations of the deepest conflicts within the human soul, prophecies of a society severed from its spiritual roots. Through characters who grapple with faith, freedom, guilt, and despair, Dostoevsky confronted questions that haunt the modern world to this day: In a society without moral absolutes, what remains to guide us? Can true freedom exist without the anchor of faith, or will it lead us only to destruction? For Dostoevsky, these were not philosophical abstractions but urgent crises. He saw that the quest for

---

1. Dostoevsky, *Brothers Karamazov*, 717.

individual autonomy, unchecked by any higher authority, could become a path toward self-destruction, not enlightenment.

In the novels of Dostoevsky, modernity's spiritual crisis finds a voice, raw and unflinching. His *Notes from Underground* introduces the "Underground Man," a figure who embodies modern nihilism and the struggle to find purpose in a godless world. *The Brothers Karamazov* presents a grand symphony of belief and doubt, with characters like Ivan and Alyosha who grapple with the paradoxes of faith and moral relativism. In *Crime and Punishment*, Dostoevsky lays bare the torment of a young man who tries to transcend morality only to be crushed by the weight of his own conscience.

This chapter journeys into Dostoevsky's profound reflections on the consequences of a disenchanted world, one in which humanity is left to wrestle with the freedom to choose without the guidance of a transcendent truth. His characters, each in their own way, inhabit the abyss of modernity, facing the horror of absolute freedom alongside the allure of redemption. As we delve into Dostoevsky's works, we find not only a critique of the modern soul's unraveling but a testament to its resilience—a call to confront the void and, perhaps, to discover that within faith, even if fragile, lies the only light strong enough to guide us through it.

The Underground Man and the Nihilistic Soul

In *Notes from Underground*, Dostoevsky introduces a figure both contemptible and pitiable, a man who is, in his own words, "a sick man . . . a spiteful man."[2] The "Underground Man" is not just a character but a portrait of modern humanity unmoored from any sense of higher purpose. He embodies the psychological and moral turmoil of a world that has turned its back on faith and, in doing so, lost its anchor. Here is the individual stripped of transcendent meaning, left to define himself in a world where definitions hold no weight. His existence is one of defiance and resentment, yet his defiance finds no purpose, and his resentment is directed at a universe that seems indifferent to his suffering. Through this character, Dostoevsky exposes the birth of modern nihilism. The worldview that, in rejecting God, also rejects transcendent meaning, coherence, and morality.

---

2. Dostoevsky, *Notes from Underground*, 3.

The Underground Man's musings are paradoxical and fragmented, capturing the psyche of someone adrift in a universe without ultimate truth. "I say let the world perish," he writes, "but I should always have my tea."[3] His voice is both scathing and self-loathing, mocking himself as much as he mocks society. He embodies the bitter fruit of individualism unbound, a man who seeks freedom at all costs yet despises the very freedom he has achieved. In rejecting society, morality, and even reason, the Underground Man believes he is affirming his autonomy. Yet, paradoxically, his autonomy leaves him only more alienated, trapped in a cycle of self-sabotage that he neither desires nor escapes. Dostoevsky reveals, through this man's tortured reflections, that without a higher purpose, freedom itself can become a form of self-imposed prison.

At the core of the Underground Man's existence is a profound distrust of rationality, an attitude that marks a sharp contrast to the Enlightenment optimism of Dostoevsky's contemporaries. Where thinkers of the nineteenth century saw reason as the key to human progress, the Underground Man views it as an instrument of oppression, one that constrains the individual by demanding conformity to the "laws" of human behavior. "What can be expected of man," he asks, "since he is a being endowed with strange qualities?"[4] His response to the modern world's insistence on rationality is to reject it altogether, favoring a perverse freedom to act against his own interests. In one particularly famous passage, he asserts, "Man is sometimes extraordinarily, passionately, attached to suffering."[5] This line captures Dostoevsky's insight that without a higher moral structure, humanity may choose irrationality and self-destruction simply to prove that it is free to do so.

The Underground Man's celebration of irrationality reflects Dostoevsky's belief that the human soul cannot be reduced to mechanistic or utilitarian principles. This is a man who suffers precisely because he refuses to conform, even to his own best interests. For him, the freedom to choose—whether it brings pain or pleasure—is more vital than the choices themselves. In this, Dostoevsky illustrates a fundamental paradox of the modern condition: the pursuit of autonomy can lead not to fulfillment but to isolation and despair. In the Underground Man's own words, "to act against reason, against your own best interest, is sometimes

---

3. Dostoevsky, *Notes from Underground*, 142.
4. Dostoevsky, *Notes from Underground*, 34.
5. Dostoevsky, *Notes from Underground*, 39.

the most real thing there is."[6] Here, freedom becomes an end in itself, a self-destructive affirmation that reveals not only the futility of a life without purpose but the inner void that such freedom uncovers.

This rejection of rationality and embrace of suffering is not an anomaly but a reflection of modernity's own struggles. The Underground Man mocks the "Crystal Palace," a symbol of the rational utopias envisioned by Enlightenment thinkers, where society would be perfected through order and reason. He sees in this vision not freedom but a cage, where humanity would be reduced to predictable patterns and stripped of its complexity. "You believe in a palace of crystal that can never be destroyed," he scoffs, "a palace at which one will not be able to put out one's tongue or make a rude gesture even on the sly."[7] For Dostoevsky, this mockery reveals the danger of a world that values progress over meaning. The Underground Man's defiance is a reminder that humanity, in its essence, craves something more than material comfort or rational stability; it longs for meaning, even if that meaning is bound up in suffering.

In the Underground Man, we see a man who, having rejected the notion of a higher purpose, exists solely to prove his own autonomy. An autonomy that brings no satisfaction, only further alienation. Dostoevsky captures the sense of nihilism that arises when humanity abandons faith and moral absolutes, leaving individuals free but unfulfilled. His freedom is absolute, yet it is the freedom of an individual who has severed himself from any connection, from any moral or spiritual community, leaving him stranded in a self-made prison of discontent.

Dostoevsky's "Underground Man" is not merely a character but a prophecy of what modernity's obsession with autonomy and rejection of moral structure might yield. Through this embittered figure, Dostoevsky anticipates the rise of a culture that values freedom above all yet fails to recognize that freedom without direction can be a kind of bondage. The "Underground" becomes a metaphor for the modern soul—hidden, resentful, and self-destructive—searching for purpose yet unable to find it in a world that offers no guide beyond personal preference.

Dostoevsky warns us that a world without faith, without a higher purpose, is not a world of freedom but of futility. The Underground Man's freedom, stripped of all meaning, drives him only further into isolation and despair, an embodiment of the existential void left by modernity's

---

6. Dostoevsky, *Notes from Underground*, 29.
7. Dostoevsky, *Notes from Underground*, 40.

rejection of transcendence. His story is not merely one of individual angst but a reflection of a broader crisis—the birth of a worldview that, in rejecting God, also rejects the very things that give human life coherence and value. In this character, Dostoevsky paints a dark vision of modernity's unraveling, a vision in which the pursuit of freedom, when detached from any higher truth, leads not to liberation but to a form of spiritual imprisonment.

Faith, Doubt, and the Abyss of Relativism

In *The Brothers Karamazov*, Dostoevsky reaches the apex of his exploration into the crisis of faith and the abyss of moral relativism that threatens to consume a world unanchored from God. This novel is not just a family saga but a profound examination of the struggle between belief and skepticism, compassion and despair, purpose and moral ambiguity. Through the lives and conflicts of the Karamazov brothers, each representing a different path in the search for truth, Dostoevsky delves into the heart of modernity's existential crisis. It is here that Dostoevsky grapples most openly with the consequences of a world that has rejected the divine and finds itself, instead, adrift in doubt and despair.

Central to this exploration is the character of Ivan Karamazov, a man whose fierce intellect and moral sensitivity draw him into a profound struggle with faith. Ivan embodies the modern skeptic, a man who cannot reconcile the suffering and injustice in the world with the idea of a loving and omnipotent God. His arguments, distilled into the unforgettable "Grand Inquisitor" parable, reveal a worldview that sees religion as a form of oppression, a system that denies human freedom in the name of a divine authority.

This "Grand Inquisitor" parable, recounted by Ivan, is Dostoevsky's most pointed critique of a world that values security over freedom and comfort over truth. In this tale, Jesus returns to Earth during the Spanish Inquisition, only to be arrested by the church, whose grand inquisitor tells him that humanity cannot bear the burden of true freedom. The Inquisitor declares, "In the end they will lay their freedom at our feet, and say to us, 'Make us your slaves, but feed us.'"[8] Through this parable, Dostoevsky exposes the dark side of human nature. A desire for security and certainty that can lead individuals to surrender their freedom and

---

8. Dostoevsky, *Brothers Karamazov*, 300.

conscience to any authority that promises comfort. Ivan, in presenting this tale, reveals his belief that religion is a crutch for the weak, a system that manipulates humanity's fears to maintain control.

Yet Ivan's skepticism is not merely intellectual; it is deeply moral. He cannot accept a God who allows the innocent to suffer, who stands silent while children endure unspeakable cruelty. In one of his most famous outbursts, Ivan declares, "I most respectfully return Him the ticket."[9] This rejection is not born of cynicism but of a profound moral revulsion. For Ivan, the price of faith—a faith that demands acceptance of suffering as part of a divine plan—is too high to bear. He sees in religion a contradiction: it promises justice yet leaves the world in turmoil. In this, Ivan reflects the modern soul torn between the desire for moral clarity and the bitter reality of a world that appears indifferent to human suffering.

However, Ivan's rebellion against God leads him not to libertarian freedom but to despair. His rejection of a divine moral order leaves him in a void where he struggles to find any reason for ethical behavior. Without God, Ivan argues, all values are subjective, and morality becomes a matter of personal choice rather than universal truth. Dostoevsky, through Ivan, warns that in rejecting divine authority, modernity risks losing not only faith but the very foundation of ethical life.

In contrast to Ivan's rebellion, Dostoevsky presents the character of Alyosha, a young novice who represents a path of faith, compassion, and humility. Alyosha is not naïve to the suffering of the world, but he chooses to confront it with love rather than anger. For Alyosha, faith is not an escape from reality but a means of embracing it with courage and compassion. He sees God not as a distant judge but as a source of hope, a force that can redeem even the darkest of human experiences. Through Alyosha, Dostoevsky suggests that faith, while difficult, provides the only true foundation for meaning and morality. Alyosha's journey is one of humility, a recognition that love and forgiveness can coexist with suffering, offering a path to redemption rather than despair.

The contrast between Ivan and Alyosha captures Dostoevsky's vision of the existential struggle at the heart of modernity. Ivan's rejection of God leaves him adrift, caught in a moral vacuum where his ideals clash with his inability to accept an indifferent universe. Alyosha, in contrast, finds meaning not in philosophical arguments but in action, in a faith that serves others and embraces suffering with a sense of purpose. This

---

9. Dostoevsky, *Brothers Karamazov*, 291.

difference between the brothers encapsulates Dostoevsky's belief that reason alone cannot satisfy the human soul; without a moral and spiritual anchor, reason descends into cynicism, while faith offers a path through the darkness.

At the heart of this contrast is the question of suffering. For Ivan, suffering is an insurmountable obstacle to faith, a reality that renders belief in a benevolent God impossible. For Alyosha, suffering is an invitation to compassion and solidarity, a way to connect with others in shared humanity. Dostoevsky does not offer easy answers to this problem but suggests that the path of faith, while fraught with difficulty, allows individuals to face suffering with dignity and purpose. In this way, Dostoevsky reveals a tension within modernity itself: a longing for justice and meaning set against a worldview that, in rejecting the divine, leaves humanity alone to confront its pain.

In *The Brothers Karamazov*, Dostoevsky reaches the depth of his critique of a godless world. Through Ivan, he presents the seductive power of doubt, the allure of rejecting God as a protest against an imperfect world. But through Alyosha, he reveals an alternative—a faith that, though tested by suffering, offers a way to endure, to find purpose, and to embrace life despite its contradictions. This tension is Dostoevsky's vision of modernity's challenge: to choose between a freedom that leads to despair or a faith that can provide hope in the midst of uncertainty.

As the novel unfolds, Dostoevsky's message becomes clear. Ivan's struggle with faith is not only intellectual but existential; his rejection of God leaves him without a foundation for moral action, leading him into a nihilism that isolates and torments him. Alyosha, by contrast, accepts the mystery of faith, finding strength not in answers but in compassion and love. Dostoevsky suggests that in a world that often seems devoid of meaning, it is faith—humble, flawed, and courageous—that offers the only hope for a life of purpose.

Through *The Brothers Karamazov*, Dostoevsky calls upon his readers to confront the abyss of relativism and despair, to see in Ivan and Alyosha the two paths available in a disenchanted world. He warns that without faith, modernity's freedom can become a form of bondage, a road to isolation and futility. Yet he also holds out a vision of redemption, a belief that faith, though demanding, can lead to a life marked by compassion and meaning. In the end, Dostoevsky offers a choice: to embrace freedom without purpose or to surrender to faith, finding within it the strength to face a world that offers no guarantees.

Freedom, Guilt, and the Burden of Conscience

If *The Brothers Karamazov* confronts the existential struggle between faith and doubt, *Crime and Punishment* plunges into the dark recesses of moral relativism, asking what happens when an individual tries to transcend traditional morality to achieve a vision of absolute freedom. In this novel, Dostoevsky dissects the psychological torment that ensues when human beings cast aside the inherent laws of conscience. At its heart, *Crime and Punishment* is the story of Raskolnikov, a young man who believes he can act as his own moral authority, only to be ensnared by a deeper truth. The fact that true freedom cannot exist without a foundation in ethical responsibility.

Raskolnikov's intellectual arrogance leads him to a belief that certain "extraordinary" individuals—men like Napoleon—possess the right to step outside society's laws if it serves a higher purpose. In his eyes, these individuals are not bound by the conventional constraints of morality; rather, they are propelled by their vision and strength to commit acts that, for ordinary people, would be unforgivable. Raskolnikov's theory leads him to justify the murder of a pawnbroker, a "louse," as he sees her, an insignificant life that he believes he can sacrifice for the greater good. "I wanted to dare," he says, "and I killed. I wanted to find out then and there whether I was a louse like everybody else or a man."[10] This idea of testing his own strength, of "stepping over" conventional morality, reflects the hubris of the modern mind that seeks liberation through the rejection of any higher moral order.

Yet as Dostoevsky reveals, Raskolnikov's attempt to claim godlike freedom is fraught with inherent contradictions. No sooner has he committed the murder than he is haunted by an unbearable sense of guilt, a visceral reminder that his soul is bound by a moral reality he cannot escape. His initial justifications—that he was eliminating a parasite, that he was sacrificing a life of little value for a "higher purpose"—quickly unravel. He finds himself trapped, not by society's laws, but by his own conscience, a force he had dismissed as irrelevant but that now reveals itself as more powerful than any intellectual rationale. "Crime? What crime?" he tries to convince himself. "My killing a loathsome, harmful louse, a filthy old moneylender woman, whom nobody would miss, who's useless to society? How is it a crime?"[11] Despite his efforts, he cannot

---

10. Dostoevsky, *Crime and Punishment*, 288.
11. Dostoevsky, *Crime and Punishment*, 288.

shake the feeling that he has crossed a boundary that runs deeper than societal norms, a boundary etched into his very being.

Raskolnikov's descent into paranoia and despair becomes a study in the failure of moral relativism to account for the depths of human experience. While he initially believes that he can construct his own moral code, his growing torment reveals Dostoevsky's belief in an objective moral order that exists independent of human invention. This sense of guilt is not merely a response to the act itself but an encounter with the limits of human autonomy. In Raskolnikov's inner conflict, Dostoevsky demonstrates that, far from liberating us, the rejection of moral absolutes can lead to profound psychological suffering. His crime has set him apart from humanity, rendering him isolated, alienated, and inwardly fractured. His attempted "freedom" becomes its own kind of prison, as his conscience condemns him more powerfully than any external authority ever could.

In this exploration of moral torment, Dostoevsky brings forth a profound insight into the nature of guilt and responsibility. Raskolnikov's punishment is not merely a matter of legal consequence; it is an existential reckoning with his own humanity. His theory of "extraordinary men" has led him not to strength but to weakness, not to transcendence but to a debilitating crisis of identity. "I didn't kill a human being, but a principle!"[12] he insists, attempting to distance himself from his crime by intellectualizing it. Yet his efforts to reduce his actions to a mere abstraction fail, as his guilt takes on a life of its own, manifesting in hallucinations, feverish dreams, and constant dread. In his suffering, Raskolnikov embodies Dostoevsky's conviction that the human soul, no matter how hardened, cannot entirely deny the voice of conscience. A voice that speaks of responsibility, humility, and the interconnectedness of all lives.

Dostoevsky's message becomes even clearer through Raskolnikov's relationship with Sonya, a young woman forced into prostitution to support her impoverished family but who embodies a self-sacrificial faith that stands in stark contrast to Raskolnikov's intellectual pride. Sonya's simple, unwavering faith and her acceptance of suffering challenge Raskolnikov's worldview at its core. She does not judge him but instead reaches out to him with compassion, offering him a glimpse of redemption that he instinctively resists. In one of the novel's most powerful scenes, Sonya reads him the story of Lazarus's resurrection, a biblical passage laden with

---

12. Dostoevsky, *Crime and Punishment*, 287.

symbolic hope for renewal. Raskolnikov is deeply moved but conflicted; the idea of redemption terrifies him because it demands that he confront his guilt rather than intellectualize it.

Sonya's presence forces Raskolnikov to face the limits of his philosophy and the emptiness of his attempt to live beyond good and evil. While he initially sees her as weak and dependent on faith and society's morality, he begins to recognize that her willingness to suffer for others embodies a strength and integrity that he lacks. Sonya's love for humanity, even in the midst of her suffering, reveals to him the power of humility and compassion, values that cannot be rationalized but must be felt and accepted. Through her, Dostoevsky suggests that redemption is possible, but only through an acknowledgment of one's own limitations and the willingness to embrace moral truth.

Raskolnikov's eventual confession marks a turning point in his journey, an act that signifies his surrender to the moral order he had once tried to escape. By confessing, he bows to a higher law, a recognition that he cannot live as an island, separate from others, immune to the consequences of his actions. His decision to seek punishment is not merely a response to external pressure but an acknowledgment of his need for atonement, a desire to reconnect with humanity by accepting responsibility for his crime. In choosing to submit to justice, Raskolnikov finds a form of freedom that his previous philosophy had denied him—the freedom that comes from humility, from recognizing one's place within a moral universe.

In *Crime and Punishment*, Dostoevsky presents a compelling critique of modernity's fascination with moral autonomy and its assumption that freedom lies in the absence of constraint. Raskolnikov's journey reveals that such freedom, when unchecked by ethical responsibility, leads only to alienation and despair. Dostoevsky's insight here is that human beings, when left to define morality solely by reason or personal ambition, are liable to fall into self-destructive patterns, unable to bear the weight of a conscience that refuses to be silenced. Raskolnikov's breakdown, his descent into guilt and eventual redemption, serves as a testament to the inescapable nature of moral law. A law that, Dostoevsky suggests, is as much a part of our humanity as our capacity to reason.

Ultimately, Dostoevsky portrays Raskolnikov's suffering as a path to redemption, a painful but necessary journey through which he confronts his limitations and reclaims his humanity. His confession is an act of surrender, not just to society's laws but to a deeper moral reality that transcends human invention. In recognizing his guilt, Raskolnikov opens himself to the possibility of grace, a concept that Dostoevsky saw as essential to human wholeness. This surrender is not a denial of freedom but a fuller realization of it—a freedom that recognizes the interconnectedness of all lives and the need for accountability to others.

Through this novel, Dostoevsky warns that the pursuit of autonomy, unchecked by moral grounding, can lead to profound spiritual emptiness. Raskolnikov's crime is not just a violation of the law; it is a rejection of the very principles that bind humanity together, principles that cannot be dismissed without consequence. In his suffering and eventual acceptance of guilt, Dostoevsky reveals the paradox of freedom. It cannot exist without responsibility, and true liberation is found not in self-assertion but in humility and the recognition of one's place within a moral order. Raskolnikov's redemption, painful though it is, embodies Dostoevsky's belief that conscience and grace are inextricable from the human condition. That in the end, we are bound by truths that transcend individual will.

Dostoevsky's *Crime and Punishment* presents a stark choice for the modern soul: to live as Raskolnikov first attempts, free but hollow, or to embrace the burden of conscience and find, within it, the only freedom worth having. True freedom does not lie in the rejection of limits but in the acceptance of them, a recognition that morality is not a restriction but a pathway to a richer, more humane existence.

A Prophet of Modernity's Abyss

In his novels, Dostoevsky stands as a prophet bearing witness to the consequences of a society that has turned from transcendent truth. He confronts the existential void left in the wake of secularism, depicting characters whose lives unravel as they grapple with freedom, moral relativism, and the search for meaning. Dostoevsky's insights reveal that without a moral and spiritual anchor, modernity's vision of self-made autonomy becomes a pathway not to enlightenment but to despair. His characters' inner conflicts and ultimate confrontations with conscience are more than individual struggles; they are mirrors to the modern soul—a soul stripped of its divine reference point and left to wander in search of purpose.

Throughout his works, Dostoevsky shows us what happens when faith is dismissed and meaning is reduced to individual preference. He understood that humanity's need for purpose runs deeper than intellectual pursuits or societal structures. In a famous line from *The Brothers Karamazov*, he writes, "What is hell? I maintain that it is the suffering of being unable to love."[13] This declaration underscores Dostoevsky's conviction that without a spiritual foundation, humanity is left in isolation, cut off from the love and connection that give life coherence. The characters who reject faith in Dostoevsky's works do not find freedom in doing so; instead, they encounter a painful solitude, a spiritual "hell" where love and meaning become unreachable.

Dostoevsky's warning to modernity is that a purely materialistic worldview, while championing human freedom, ultimately fails to satisfy the soul's deepest longings. His novels vividly illustrate the dangers of a secular, relativistic society that exalts personal autonomy over communal responsibility, purpose, and humility before something greater than the self. In *Crime and Punishment*, Raskolnikov's belief that he can act as his own moral arbiter leads him to a dark inner chaos that no amount of reasoning can resolve. In severing themselves from divine authority, Dostoevsky's characters seek purpose but only find alienation; they long for freedom but discover its weight to be crushing when detached from any higher truth.

Through characters like Ivan, Raskolnikov, and the Underground Man, Dostoevsky grapples with modernity's promise of liberation, revealing it to be fraught with paradox. The desire to be "like God," to transcend traditional morality and assert one's will as sovereign, leads not to the power or autonomy his characters seek but to spiritual exile. Their journeys reflect a universal truth Dostoevsky saw in the human experience: that without a moral and spiritual order, human beings are bound to create prisons of their own making. This struggle is not merely personal but collective, emblematic of an age that seeks meaning in self-determination while simultaneously dismantling the structures that could provide such meaning.

Yet Dostoevsky's vision does not end in despair. For all the darkness he explores, he also offers a glimpse of redemption. A path that requires humility, repentance, and the recognition of humanity's need for grace. Sonya's quiet compassion for Raskolnikov, Alyosha's resilient faith, and the Underground Man's confessions each represent a possibility for healing. Dostoevsky understood that to reject faith is not only to lose meaning

---

13. Dostoevsky, *Brothers Karamazov*, 387.

but to sever the bonds that connect us to one another, bonds rooted in shared responsibility and sacrificial love. He suggests that meaning, while elusive, is found not in intellectual achievement or absolute freedom but in humility and reverence before something greater than ourselves.

In this way, Dostoevsky stands to warn us of the dangers inherent in a world that exalts human reason and autonomy above all else. His novels are a call to return to the foundational questions of existence: What is good? What is true? What is worth living—and even dying—for? Through his characters' anguish and eventual moments of grace, he reminds us that freedom divorced from truth leads only to despair, while surrender to a higher moral order can bring redemption. His works offer us a way to confront the abyss without being consumed by it, to find hope in the depths of suffering by acknowledging the spiritual dimension of human life.

Dostoevsky's works reveal an enduring truth: that the soul cannot survive on autonomy alone. His vision calls us back to a life marked by faith, humility, and community, urging us to resist the temptation to live as if meaning can be crafted in isolation. He saw that human freedom, when coupled with responsibility to a transcendent truth, becomes a means of true fulfillment rather than self-destruction. His novels are thus a clarion call to resist the empty promises of modernity's materialism and to embrace the spiritual grounding that alone can ward off the creeping despair of a secular age.

4

T. S. Eliot
The Waste Land and the Collapse of Meaning

"I will show you fear in a handful of dust."
—T. S. Eliot[1]

By the time T. S. Eliot penned "The Waste Land" in 1922, the world had witnessed horrors that shattered its faith in progress. The promises of modernity, with its emphasis on reason, science, and unyielding faith in human advancement, had withered under the weight of a devastating world war. The Western world, once confident in its pursuit of enlightenment and material prosperity, found itself hollowed out, drifting through a spiritual and cultural desolation that Eliot captured with haunting precision. "The Waste Land" stands as a bleak mirror to the soul of modernity. It offers a fractured portrait of a civilization that had abandoned its sacred traditions, severed its connection to the divine, and discovered, as Eliot would show, that freedom without faith often leads to despair.

Eliot did not merely reflect on this cultural malaise; he immersed himself in it, bringing to life the voices, fragments, and symbols of a civilization that could no longer find unity. His poetry exposes the soul's silent scream as it searches for meaning in a world that appears indifferent, even hostile, to its most profound needs. "The Waste Land" is a

---

1. Eliot, *Waste Land*, I, line 30.

poem of brokenness. In its lines split from meaning, voices cut off mid-thought, and symbols that once held power are now rendered impotent. In its pages, we feel the disorientation of a culture adrift, untethered from its spiritual moorings and lost in a landscape of barren pursuits and shattered ideals.

If Dostoevsky's characters encountered the unraveling of meaning on an individual level, Eliot expands this despair to encompass an entire civilization, casting Western culture itself as a haunted soul stumbling through a wasteland of its own making. As we journey through Eliot's fractured world, we find glimpses of ancient wisdom. Snatches of mythology, scripture, and literary references that evoke the distant memory of a time when life was infused with purpose. Yet in Eliot's vision, these fragments of the past offer no easy answers; they are remnants of a language forgotten, a map torn and incomplete. They haunt the modern consciousness, reminding us of what has been lost and pointing, with both longing and irony, toward a sacred truth that lies just out of reach.

Eliot's genius lies in his ability to capture this tension, this aching desire for redemption in a world that seems determined to reject it. "The Waste Land" is both an elegy for a lost world and a searing critique of modernity's insistence on autonomy without transcendence. Eliot's poetry does not lament the loss of progress or the demise of empire; it mourns the death of the sacred. Through images of drought, desolation, and decay, he creates a vision of life stripped of its spiritual depth, a civilization that, in its pursuit of freedom, has relinquished its connection to the eternal and settled instead for the fleeting and the fragmented.

This chapter explores "The Waste Land" as Eliot's prophetic cry against modernity's spiritual barrenness. Through his use of fragmentation, mythology, and religious symbolism, Eliot reveals a world haunted by its abandonment of faith and tradition. His work confronts us with a critical question: Can a culture that has severed itself from its spiritual roots ever rediscover meaning? In Eliot's poetry, we find a desperate search for redemption, a longing for the sacred in a landscape that has all but forgotten it. And yet, for all its despair, this profound poem does not merely end in defeat. Beneath the bleakness, Eliot offers glimpses of hope, echoes of a renewal that may still be possible if modernity can recognize its own spiritual hunger and reach beyond the material to reclaim the transcendent.

Through Eliot's work, we encounter modernity at its breaking point, a world where the rejection of faith has led not to liberation but to a profound disorientation. Through Eliot's foresight, his work reveals the soul of a civilization in ruins, calling us to confront the high cost of a culture that has chosen autonomy over reverence. In this final chapter of Part I, we see modernity laid bare, struggling to reconcile its thirst for progress with its need for meaning, and we are invited to consider what might yet be salvaged from the ruins. As we turn each page, we follow Eliot's voices—desperate, broken, and hopeful—asking, in their own fractured way, whether there is still a path back from the wasteland.

The Wasteland

In "The Waste Land," Eliot captures the fractured psyche of a world grappling with the aftermath of war, disillusioned with progress, and struggling to find meaning in a landscape that seems barren of it. Written amidst the ruins of Western civilization's ideals, the poem mirrors the shattered hopes of a culture that had placed its faith in human achievement only to discover that progress alone could not satisfy the soul. With its haunting landscapes, disconnected voices, and enigmatic symbols, Eliot's poem unveils the spiritual void left in the wake of a world that has traded sacred traditions for material pursuits and collective memory for personal autonomy.

His depiction of this desolation begins with the opening line, "April is the cruellest month, breeding / Lilacs out of the dead land," a stark inversion of spring's traditional symbolism as a time of renewal.[2] In the poem, spring's attempts at rebirth are tinged with irony, as nature's efforts to revive a barren world seem hollow, almost mocking. This is not the lush renewal of life but a painful resurgence within a world devoid of spiritual vitality. Eliot's April does not bring hope; it stirs up fragments of life that seem to bloom out of "the dead land," as if to remind the reader of life's emptiness in a disenchanted age.

Throughout the poem, Eliot employs fragmentation to underscore the disjointed experience of modernity. Its' structure is a broken mosaic, interwoven with abrupt shifts in voices, languages, and literary allusions, reflecting the fractured consciousness of a culture that has lost its coherence. In one of the most striking transitions, the speaker abruptly shifts to a disembodied, despairing voice that echoes a disillusionment with modern relationships: "What are the roots that clutch, what branches

---

2. Eliot, *Waste Land*, I, lines 1–2.

grow / Out of this stony rubbish?"[3] This line captures Eliot's vision of a world that has become spiritually sterile, where nothing fruitful can grow because the soil (the culture's foundation) is barren. The stony rubbish, devoid of life, represents a modernity that has severed itself from its roots, attempting to flourish in an environment hostile to deeper meaning.

The fragmentation extends beyond form, permeating the characters and voices that populate Eliot's barren landscape. In "A Game of Chess," Eliot introduces a mundane and despairing conversation, capturing the emptiness of human connection in the modern age. One voice laments, "I think we are in rats' alley / Where the dead men lost their bones," conjuring an image of people existing in a lifeless maze, directionless and without purpose.[4] Here, Eliot presents the futility of relationships stripped of depth, reduced to fragments of meaningless chatter, echoing a broader cultural crisis in which individuals are disconnected not only from one another but from any larger purpose or transcendent truth.

In this poem, the people who wander through its desolate landscapes are neither fully alive nor truly dead; they are hollow, spiritually starved beings who have lost the vitality that once came from a sense of connection to the divine. As we saw in that line quoted at the beginning of the chapter, "I will show you fear in a handful of dust." Eliot's image of dust—impermanent, insignificant—becomes a metaphor for a humanity that has lost its grounding, left only with the "fear" of its own mortality and insignificance in a world where traditional sources of meaning have disintegrated.

The myths and legends that populate "The Waste Land" act as echoes of a forgotten language, one that once spoke to humanity's deeper needs for purpose and transcendence. Eliot repeatedly invokes the legend of the Holy Grail, a symbol of divine mystery and redemption, in an attempt to highlight modernity's severed connection to the sacred. But this invocation is not to revive the myth directly; rather, it serves as a haunting reminder of what has been lost. In the opening lines of "The Burial of the Dead," Eliot alludes to the Grail quest through Madame Sosostris, the fortune-teller, who pulls the "Hanged Man" card, a symbol connected to sacrifice and redemption. But here, the quest is obscured, reduced to a parlor game, degraded and misunderstood in a world that no longer comprehends its significance. Eliot's use of the Grail reminds

---

3. Eliot, *Waste Land*, I, lines 19–20.
4. Eliot, *Waste Land*, II, lines 115–16.

us that while humanity yearns for a deeper meaning, it is trapped in a culture that has forgotten how to seek it.

The Grail's symbolic promise of restoration and purity stands in stark contrast to the spiritual barrenness that defines Eliot's wasteland. The legendary quest was once a journey toward the sacred, a pursuit of a lost wholeness that held a vision of life redeemed. Yet in Eliot's world, such quests seem futile. In "What the Thunder Said," the speaker describes a bleak and hostile landscape where "there is not even solitude in the mountains, / But red sullen faces sneer and snarl / From doors of mud-cracked houses."[5] The sacred journey that once inspired reverence has become a trudge through desolation as if even the mountains, the traditional symbol of spiritual ascent, have turned away. Eliot's imagery reveals a landscape where redemption feels unreachable, where ancient symbols linger but offer no sustenance to those who encounter them. The Grail, the journey, and the myth have all become spectral remnants, haunting a world that no longer knows how to seek what it needs most.

Amidst the desolation, "The Waste Land" continually reaches back to the past, quoting works like Dante's *Inferno*, Shakespeare, and the Hindu Upanishads in a desperate attempt to recover fragments of wisdom from lost ages. These references do not provide unity; rather, they amplify the dissonance of a culture that can no longer find coherence in its heritage. When the narrator states, "These fragments I have shored against my ruins," he acknowledges that the pieces of ancient wisdom, though once vibrant, are now little more than relics, bits of meaning held together in a fragile attempt to withstand collapse.[6] For Eliot, these "fragments" are all that remain of a culture that once spoke with a unified voice, but now can only grasp at the pieces of a shattered tradition.

Perhaps the most powerful image of "The Waste Land" is its pervasive sense of drought and desolation, which extends beyond the physical into the spiritual realm. In one of the poem's most memorable passages, Eliot describes "a heap of broken images, where the sun beats, / And the dead tree gives no shelter, the cricket no relief."[7] This image of barren, broken pieces scattered under a relentless sun evokes a culture scorched by its own spiritual emptiness. The absence of "shelter" or "relief" underscores the isolation and suffering of those who inhabit this wasteland, where even the past, the "broken images" of history and tradition, offers

---

5. Eliot, *Waste Land*, V, lines 342–44.
6. Eliot, *Waste Land*, V, line 430.
7. Eliot, *Waste Land*, I, lines 22–23.

no comfort or guidance. Eliot's imagery suggests a world both scorched and abandoned, where attempts to find shade or solace are in vain.

The recurring theme of water, or the lack of it, serves as a metaphor for the soul's yearning for spiritual sustenance in a world devoid of it. In the poem, water represents not only life but also spiritual revival. "If there were water, we should stop and drink," Eliot writes, capturing the desperate thirst for meaning in a world where "there is nothing, again nothing."[8] This absence of water becomes a metaphor for the absence of faith and purpose in modern life, a condition that leaves humanity perpetually parched, seeking but unable to find satisfaction.

Throughout his work, Eliot creates not only a poem but a haunting vision of a civilization stripped of its spiritual core, left to wander aimlessly in search of something it cannot name. Through the fragmented structure, the disjointed voices, and the unyielding landscapes, Eliot exposes the hollowness that lurks beneath modernity's façade. His characters are adrift, his images are barren, and his language is fractured all to convey the profound emptiness of a world that has abandoned its roots. This is modernity laid bare: a landscape littered with the remnants of meaning, haunted by memories of a sacred past yet moving forward with no compass to guide it.

In his vision of a spiritually desolate world, Eliot invites readers to confront the bleakness of a life severed from transcendent meaning. And while his depiction of this wasteland is grim, his poem does not resign itself entirely to despair. Throughout "The Waste Land," glimmers of redemption through myth, memory, and the faint call of the sacred suggest that modernity's emptiness, though pervasive, is not beyond remedy. Beneath the fragments and dust lies a haunting question: Can a civilization that has rejected the sacred find a path back to wholeness?

Losing Tradition, Longing for Redemption

In his work, Eliot mourns not only the fragmentation of individual lives but the disintegration of a culture that has severed itself from its spiritual and mythological heritage. He portrays a civilization adrift, haunted by the loss of its once-unifying traditions and filled with a deep yet inarticulate longing for redemption. The disillusionment of modernity is not just the collapse of religious belief but the erosion of a moral and cultural

---

8. Eliot, *Waste Land*, V, lines 335.

framework that once imbued life with meaning and coherence. Through a labyrinth of mythological, literary, and religious allusions, Eliot evokes fragments of this lost tradition, offering glimpses of a world that once held sacred truths, only to reveal a profound emptiness when those truths are ignored.

The poem's disillusioned voices, drifting through broken landscapes, continually reach back to religious texts and mythological imagery as if trying to recover a wisdom that has slipped away. In "The Fire Sermon," Eliot blends references to the Buddha's sermon on renunciation with the stark sensuality of twentieth-century London, portraying a world in which even spiritual discipline has been buried under layers of hedonism and disinterest. Here, the call for self-denial and enlightenment is drowned out by the trivialities of a society focused on fleeting pleasure. "Burning burning burning," Eliot writes, echoing the Buddha's teaching on the fires of desire, hatred, and delusion.[9] Yet this fire brings no enlightenment; it consumes without purifying, leaving only ashes where there was once potential for spiritual growth. Eliot's blending of East and West reflects his belief that humanity's search for redemption is universal, yet modernity's disconnection from spiritual discipline has left it without the means to attain it.

Eliot's incorporation of diverse religious references also reflects his belief that the modern search for meaning transcends any single tradition. His inclusion of the Hindu Upanishads, for instance, suggests that humanity's hunger for the sacred is not bound to Western thought alone. The final section of "The Waste Land" ends with the Sanskrit words "Datta, dayadhvam, damyata" (Give, sympathize, control), reflecting principles that Eliot saw as essential for renewal.[10] These words, however foreign they may seem to Eliot's Western audience, resonate with a universal yearning for a peace that the fractured Western world has long lost. Eliot's invocation of this prayer suggests that redemption, though distant, is still conceivable if only modernity could open itself to wisdom beyond its own understanding.

The "longing for redemption" that runs throughout "The Waste Land" reflects Eliot's awareness that modernity has not simply forgotten its sacred myths; it aches for their return. The barren rock, where nothing can grow, becomes a symbol of the modern soul, hardened and unyielding, unable to

---

9. Eliot, *Waste Land*, III, line 308.
10. Eliot, *Waste Land*, V, line 432.

absorb the life-giving grace it so profoundly craves. Yet, even as he mourns this loss, Eliot's imagery suggests that the desire for renewal persists. The presence of these symbols, however faint or fragmented, points to an enduring human hunger for the sacred. Eliot's vision of the "wasteland" is bleak, but it is haunted by the hope that redemption might still be possible if humanity can once again learn to seek it.

This longing for redemption, though largely unfulfilled in "The Waste Land," reveals Eliot's conviction that modernity's malaise is not absolute. For all its bleakness, the poem does not end in complete despair; it closes with a whispered prayer, "Shantih shantih shantih"—a plea for peace in a world that has forgotten how to find it.[11] This final line hints that redemption may yet be attainable, that a fractured civilization might still return to its spiritual roots and rediscover a path to wholeness. Eliot's prayer suggests that the fragments of lost traditions and myths, though scattered and incomplete, might still be gathered and restored. His invocation of peace is both a lament for what has been lost and a hope for what might still be reclaimed.

Eliot's vision is one of paradox: a civilization in ruins, haunted by the memory of a sacred past, yearning for redemption yet hesitant to reach for it. He leaves us not with a conclusion but with a question: Can a society that has forsaken its traditions ever find its way back to meaning? This question, echoing through Eliot's work, calls modernity to confront its own emptiness and perhaps, just perhaps, to rediscover the sacred amidst the ruins.

The Hollow World of Secularism

As Eliot's poem unfolds, it becomes clear that he is not merely depicting a spiritually barren world; he is offering a pointed critique of the secularism that he saw as the root of modernity's crisis. In Eliot's view, the secular world has dismantled the sacred structures that once gave life coherence and meaning, leaving in their place a "hollow" society defined by moral relativism, disillusionment, and existential dread. The secularism Eliot confronts is not simply the absence of religion but the hollowing out of all those elements—faith, tradition, and collective memory—that once imbued life with significance and bound communities together. Through fragmented voices and haunting images, Eliot reveals the hollow world

---

11. Eliot, *Waste Land*, V, line 432.

of secularism as one in which humanity's spiritual needs are neglected, leaving individuals adrift in a culture that provides no answers to life's deepest questions.

Eliot's sense of a hollow society permeates "The Waste Land," but it is in his later poem "The Hollow Men" that he fully captures the essence of modern secularism's emptiness. In this work, he describes the modern individual as "shape without form, shade without colour, / Paralysed force, gesture without motion."[12] The hollow men are echoes of beings, outwardly human but devoid of inner substance. This powerful image reflects Eliot's view of a society that, having rejected its spiritual heritage, is left with only the external trappings of humanity, devoid of the vitality that once animated it. These hollow men "whisper together / Are quiet and meaningless," revealing a generation whose voices, devoid of conviction, blend into a murmur of existential despair.[13]

The line "This is the way the world ends / Not with a bang but a whimper" encapsulates Eliot's view of a world decaying not through sudden catastrophe but through gradual moral and spiritual erosion.[14] For Eliot, secularism's victory over faith does not herald a brave new world of enlightenment; instead, it marks the slow decay of meaning, the quiet descent into a world where life lacks direction, purpose, and depth. The hollow men are haunted not by the grandeur of loss but by the sheer banality of it, the way in which secularism reduces life to a series of empty gestures, leaving nothing behind but the "whimper" of a civilization that has lost its soul.

Eliot's critique of secularism extends beyond mere poetry; it is woven into his essays, where he argues that secularism strips society of its moral foundation. In *The Idea of a Christian Society*, Eliot warns that "a society has not ceased to be Christian until it has become positively something else."[15] The absence of Christian faith in the public and private lives of individuals results not in a neutral state but in a moral void where individuals, cut off from any higher truth, become vulnerable to the whims of social trends and ideological manipulation. He feared that without a spiritual anchor, society would become prey to moral relativism, a state in which the soul is divided against itself. In Eliot's view, a secular society is inherently unstable, built on a foundation that erodes

---

12. Eliot, "Hollow Men," lines 11–12.
13. Eliot, "Hollow Men," lines 6–7.
14. Eliot, "Hollow Men," lines 97–98.
15. Eliot, *Idea of a Christian Society*, 15.

the very values it purports to uphold (community, justice, and compassion), leaving in their place a society of isolated, hollow individuals.

This vision is poignantly captured in "The Waste Land," where Eliot returns to the theme of fragmentation and disillusionment, painting a portrait of a world in desperate need of redemption but unwilling to recognize it. The hollow nature of secularism is illustrated by the image of "a heap of broken images," a scene of desolation where fragments of once-sacred symbols lie scattered, unrecognizable, and unappreciated.[16] Eliot's "broken images" symbolize the secular age's inability to make sense of its inherited symbols and traditions, leaving only fragments that lack the coherence once provided by faith. This brokenness is not merely a symptom of a lost past; it is a reflection of a world where secularism, in denying the sacred, has left humanity without a framework for meaning.

The isolation and alienation that Eliot associates with secularism are reflected in his famous line from "Choruses" from *The Rock*: "Where is the Life we have lost in living? / Where is the wisdom we have lost in knowledge? / Where is the knowledge we have lost in information?"[17] Here, Eliot criticizes the modern world's obsession with knowledge and information, an obsession that, he argues, has led to the loss of wisdom and, ultimately, life itself. Secularism's focus on empirical knowledge and rationalism, he suggests, has stripped humanity of its capacity for introspection and spiritual understanding, reducing life to a series of disconnected facts rather than a unified pursuit of truth. Eliot underscores his belief that without spiritual orientation, knowledge becomes sterile, incapable of leading individuals toward a fuller understanding of life's purpose. This fixation on data and information, he warns, risks turning society into a machine-like entity, efficient but devoid of soul.

Throughout "The Waste Land," this secular obsession with progress and rationality is portrayed as a barren pursuit. Characters wander through Eliot's wasteland, seemingly in search of something, yet their actions are hollow, their words devoid of conviction. In "The Fire Sermon," Eliot contrasts the transient pleasure of physical desire with a deeper, unfulfilled longing, capturing a society driven by impulses but lacking the guidance of moral or spiritual discipline. This internal fire consumes rather than enlightens, reflecting Eliot's view that secular society, in its rejection of restraint, is driven by shallow pursuits that ultimately lead only to self-destruction.

16. Eliot, *Waste Land*, I, line 22.
17. Eliot, *Rock*, 7.

The secularism Eliot critiques is one that has reduced the sacred to a relic, a cultural artifact rather than a living reality. The fragmented allusions in "The Waste Land" to the Bible, the Buddha, and the Grail legend are presented not as cohesive narratives but as disjointed pieces, haunting reminders of a truth that modernity can no longer fully grasp. Eliot's use of these symbols is not an attempt to return to a simpler time but a lament for a world that has forgotten the sources of its own identity. The poem becomes a tapestry of lost meanings, where each reference to the sacred is like a ghost, reminding the reader of what once gave life purpose and direction but now lies discarded, misunderstood, or ignored.

Through his works, Eliot reveals the limitations and dangers of a secular society that denies its need for the sacred. He argues that without a connection to the transcendent, individuals are left hollow, societies become morally unstable, and knowledge itself is reduced to mere data, stripped of wisdom. Eliot's vision is ultimately a warning that secularism, in its attempt to liberate humanity from the constraints of faith, risks leaving us lost, isolated, and fragmented. His poetry does not offer easy solutions, but it calls us to recognize that the hollowness of modern life may be the result not of a lack of progress but of a deeper failure to engage with the spiritual realities that define us.

Eliot's critique of secularism challenges us to confront the cost of a life devoid of the sacred. His poems invite readers to see modernity not as the triumph of reason but as a world haunted by the very traditions it has discarded. In his haunting, fragmented verses, Eliot captures the spirit of a civilization that has lost its way and offers a quiet plea for redemption. A call to rediscover the depths of human experience that secularism cannot reach.

The Poetic Voice of Modernity's Unraveling

Through his works, T. S. Eliot does more than depict a disenchanted world; he becomes its voice, echoing the cries of a culture that has lost its way and a people hollowed out by the relentless pursuit of progress without purpose. His poetry captures the essence of modernity's unraveling, exposing the spiritual and moral vacancy that arises when society severs itself from its sacred traditions. His verse, fragmented yet potent, resonates with the quiet desperation of a world that, in casting off the restraints of faith, has also cast aside its anchor, drifting ever further from meaning and coherence.

Eliot's prophetic voice warns us of the dangers inherent in a society that equates freedom with autonomy, intellect with information, and secularism with progress. He invites us to see that beneath the accomplishments of modern civilization lies an unaddressed void, a yearning for something more enduring than the pleasures and distractions that secular culture offers. In the dry and barren landscapes of "The Waste Land," Eliot's poetry compels us to confront this emptiness to recognize that a society without the sacred is a society in peril, vulnerable to spiritual decay and moral confusion. He forces us to ask ourselves what might fill that void, what remnants of meaning could be salvaged from the fragments of a broken tradition.

Yet, even in his bleakest moments, Eliot's verse hints at the possibility of redemption. The faint echoes of myth, the whispered words of ancient prayers, and the call for "Shantih" (peace) suggest that the way out of this wasteland might lie not in further strides toward secularism but in a courageous return to the spiritual wellsprings of human life. Eliot does not propose a simple path; rather, he offers a vision of renewal that demands humility, a willingness to rediscover what has been lost, and an openness to seek wisdom beyond the limits of material progress.

As we leave this final chapter of Part I, Eliot's poetic voice reverberates, calling us to recognize that the modern crisis is not merely one of shifting values or social transformation. It is, at its core, a crisis of meaning, a profound disorientation resulting from the loss of purpose and the fragmentation of truth. In the chapters to follow, we will encounter thinkers who seek to reconstruct what has been dismantled, to offer new paths to coherence in a world that seems determined to erase its own past. But Eliot's haunting verses remind us that any reconstruction must grapple honestly with the spiritual depths from which modernity has turned away. The question now is whether we will listen to his call, whether we will see in the hollow world of secularism the need for something richer, something timeless, a path back to meaning that may yet lie beyond the wasteland.

Conclusion to Part I

AS WE LEAVE BEHIND the thinkers and artists who first sensed the modern world's unraveling, a vivid picture emerges: modernity, in its ardent pursuit of autonomy and progress, has severed itself from the roots that once sustained meaning and coherence. This detachment from the sacred, celebrated as a liberation of reason and individual freedom, instead led to a profound disorientation and spiritual desolation. Schopenhauer, Dostoevsky, Wells, and Eliot each serve as prophetic voices, illuminating the steady erosion of faith, identity, and purpose that accompanied the ascent of a secular worldview.

From Schopenhauer's grim perspective of a world governed by blind will, where life's ambitions are reduced to fleeting illusions, to Dostoevsky's haunting exploration of a soul lost without God, we see that secularism, far from offering clarity, introduced profound ethical and existential dilemmas. In *Crime and Punishment*, Dostoevsky shows the torment of a mind cut off from divine guidance, a tragic reminder that without a higher moral authority, freedom becomes a prison of isolation and despair.

Then, through H. G. Wells's scientific optimism turned dystopian, we glimpse the early dreams of human progress as they slip into disillusionment. *The Time Machine* and *The War of the Worlds* warned of unchecked scientific pursuits leading to unforeseen, often dehumanizing, consequences. Wells's works lay bare the conflict between modernity's promises and the unintended consequences of a purely materialistic worldview—a conflict that would only deepen with time.

Finally, T. S. Eliot, in *The Waste Land*, offers a poetic requiem for a civilization that has lost its soul. Eliot's imagery of a barren, drought-stricken world encapsulates modernity's failure to nourish the human spirit, instead leaving behind a "heap of broken images" in place of a cohesive moral and cultural order. His work captures the hollow, spiritually starved individuals who inhabit this secular landscape, grappling with the pervasive absence of meaning. Eliot does not provide answers but instead exposes the haunting reality of a world that has chosen autonomy over transcendence.

The horrors of the twentieth century—the two world wars, the rise of totalitarian regimes, and the spread of ideological violence—seemed to affirm the warnings voiced by these early critics. When the secular vision of human progress was put to the test, it gave way not to enlightenment but to mass devastation and profound moral compromise. The wars and atrocities of the twentieth century revealed that without a transcendent moral foundation, societies could rationalize almost any form of inhumanity in the name of ideology. Despite these catastrophes, modernity did not turn back to the sacred but instead moved toward a more radical disillusionment. It was not only God but truth itself that became the next casualty, leading to a deepening of the meaning crisis.

The late twentieth and early twenty-first centuries would see this crisis expand further. With the rise of postmodernity, the emergence of New Atheism, and the rejection of objective truths, the crisis of meaning would only intensify. Now, rather than facing doubt alone, society began to dismantle the very notion of meaning as something stable or universal. The postmodern turn declared that truth is relative, identity is fluid, and reality itself is a construct. What began as a loss of the sacred evolved into a crisis of reality—a world where meaning is not just questioned but fragmented, where each individual is left to construct their own reality, however tenuous, in an increasingly isolated and atomized world.

Together, these voices reveal that modernity's quest for freedom and progress, while fruitful in many respects, has failed to address humanity's deeper longings. With each step toward rationality, humanity has drifted further from the traditions and beliefs that once grounded its sense of purpose. These thinkers highlight the paradox that by embracing a purely secular world, modernity has ushered in a crisis of meaning that threatens its very foundation.

But this is only the beginning of the descent. As we move forward into Part Two, we encounter an era in which modernity's philosophical unraveling evolves into an intensified crisis. Postmodernity, along with New Atheism and cultural relativism, deepens this existential void, shifting from the questions of meaning to an outright denial of objective truth. The individual soul, once haunted by the loss of God, now faces a world where meaning itself is seen as relative, truth as negotiable, and existence as an endless array of subjective experiences.

As we continue, we will see that the edge of the abyss revealed by modernity's early prophets gives way to an era in which the abyss becomes the home of a fragmented society, grappling not only with doubt but with the elevation of doubt to a virtue. In Part Two, we venture further into the escalating despair of a world stripped bare of its certainties, embarking on a journey through the philosophical darkness of a world that, in fully rejecting the sacred, must now contend with the terrifying freedom of a universe that offers neither answers nor absolutes.

PART II

Deepening the Despair

*Postmodernity, New Atheism,
and the Growing Meaning Crisis*

5

The Shattered Mirror

Postmodernity and Deconstructionism

"We live in a world where there is more and more information, and less and less meaning."

—Jean Baudrillard[1]

The world today feels like a shattered mirror, where every fragment reflects a distorted and incomplete image. We find ourselves surrounded by countless voices, each claiming its own truth, yet the more we listen, the more elusive any semblance of certainty becomes. We are like wanderers in a house of mirrors—trapped, bewildered, each reflection more warped than the last, and yet we continue to reach out, hoping to grasp something solid, something real.

The twentieth century was a crucible that melted down many of the certainties that had once provided a framework for Western civilization. In the wake of two devastating world wars, the old ideals of progress, reason, and universal truth crumbled like ancient statues, leaving only their broken shards behind. In their place arose a new way of thinking, a philosophy that sought not to rebuild but to deconstruct, not to discover truth but to unravel it. This intellectual movement came to be known as

---

1. Baudrillard, *Simulacra and Simulation*, 55.

postmodernism, and at its heart was a profound skepticism of anything that claimed to be universally true.

The seeds of disillusionment had been sown much earlier, in the Enlightenment's relentless pursuit of reason that paradoxically paved the way for its own undoing. For if reason alone is the supreme judge, what happens when it turns inward and questions the very structures that hold it up? The result was an intellectual revolt that sought to dismantle every grand narrative, every shared story, and every trusted institution. Postmodern thinkers wielded skepticism like a sledgehammer, shattering the remaining pillars of meaning that modernity had so desperately tried to uphold.

This chapter dives into that wreckage, exploring how postmodernity's hermeneutic of suspicion and relentless deconstruction of truth, morality, and identity has left us standing amidst the broken pieces of what once was. Here, we will meet the minds who championed this intellectual revolution: Jacques Derrida, who taught us to question whether words could ever truly convey truth; Michel Foucault, who insisted that power, not truth, governs our knowledge; and Jean Baudrillard, who warned that in a world of endless simulacra, reality itself could vanish behind the curtain of its representations.

Yet, as we journey through the labyrinth of postmodern thought, a question lingers: In rejecting what they saw as the "oppressive certainties of the past," did the postmodernists throw away the very foundations upon which a meaningful life is built? Did they, in their rush to dismantle the towers of dogma, instead leave the West adrift in an endless sea of subjectivity, where every lighthouse is an illusion?

Today, we live in the aftermath of that philosophical earthquake. The world we have inherited is one where truth is treated like a relic of a bygone era, morality is seen as a matter of personal preference, and identity has become as fluid and elusive as quicksilver. And yet, deep down, we sense that something crucial has been lost. The search for meaning, once guided by faith, reason, or shared cultural narratives, now seems more like a desperate groping in the dark.

As we step into this chapter, we will trace the contours of postmodernity's impact on our world. We will see how its skepticism and deconstructionism have not merely liberated us from old dogmas but have also left us vulnerable to new forms of despair. And in the process, we will ask ourselves: Can a shattered mirror ever be made whole again?

The Birth of Postmodernity

As the dust settled on the ruins of the Second World War, the world found itself at a crossroads. The promises of the Enlightenment—reason, progress, and the inevitable triumph of human virtue—seemed hollow in the face of the atrocities humanity had witnessed. The concentration camps, atomic bombs, and ideological purges left deep scars on the collective psyche, unraveling the confident belief that humanity was marching inexorably toward a brighter future. The Enlightenment dream, which had been nurtured for centuries, now lay fractured, unable to bear the weight of its own contradictions.

The twentieth century was not merely an era of unprecedented technological advancement; it was a time when the very foundations of what it meant to be human were called into question. In Part I of this book, we explored how the modern age, with its relentless pursuit of autonomy and rationality, began to undermine its own structures. It was a time when meaning was sought apart from divine revelation as humanity attempted to construct a secular utopia. But as the horrors of war, genocide, and political oppression accumulated, so did the disillusionment. People began to doubt the grand narratives that had once provided purpose and direction, regardless of whether the narrative was religious, political, or even scientific.

By the mid-twentieth century, it became clear that the Enlightenment project had not led to the utopia it promised. Instead, the emphasis on reason and human progress resulted in a number of unforeseen consequences. The very tools that were supposed to liberate mankind—science, technology, and reason—had been turned into instruments of destruction. The blood-soaked fields of Europe, the shadow of the nuclear mushroom cloud, and the gulags of the Soviet Union were stark reminders that progress, when untethered from any moral or spiritual foundation, could easily spiral into brutality.

Into this chasm of disillusionment stepped the postmodern thinkers. They were not content to merely critique the excesses of modernity; they sought to dismantle its very foundations. If modernity had attempted to build a tower reaching the heavens, postmodernism came with a wrecking ball, questioning not just the architecture but the ground on which it was built. These thinkers were not merely reacting to historical events; they were responding to a deep existential crisis, one that had stripped away the old certainties and left a void in their place. The seeds of postmodernity first took root in the fertile soil of academia, where scholars and philosophers began to challenge the assumptions that had long been taken for granted. The early postmodernists saw themselves as liberators, freeing the world from oppressive structures of thought that, in their view, had led to the horrors of the previous decades.

One of the central figures in this movement was Jacques Derrida, whose concept of *deconstruction* became a powerful tool for questioning everything from literature to law to theology. Derrida argued that language was not a transparent medium through which reality could be clearly understood but rather a tangled web of signs, each pointing to something else, never fully capturing the essence of what it described. The implication was profound: if language itself is unstable, then so too are the truths we claim to know through it.

Jean-François Lyotard added another layer to this critique with his now-famous proclamation of the "incredulity toward metanarratives."[2] For Lyotard, the grand stories that had once unified cultures—Christianity, Enlightenment rationalism, Marxism—were no longer credible in a world that had seen how these ideologies could be twisted into instruments of oppression. In his view, the best we could hope for was a mosaic of micro-narratives, each reflecting a fragment of truth but never coalescing into a unified whole.

Michel Foucault took this a step further by suggesting that what we call "truth" is always bound up with power. In his genealogical studies, Foucault argued that knowledge is not discovered but constructed and shaped by those who hold power. He would write, "In a sense, only a single drama is ever staged in this 'non-place,' the endlessly repeated play of dominations. The domination of certain men over others leads to the differentiation of values."[3] This radical relativism undermined not only political and religious institutions but also the very concept of objective morality. If truth is simply a matter of who controls the narrative, then any claim to universal principles becomes suspect.

The academic world was quick to embrace these ideas, especially in the wake of the social upheavals of the 1960s. For a generation disillusioned with authority, whether it was the government, the church, or the nuclear family, postmodernism offered a framework to question everything. It was an intellectual rebellion against the idea that there were absolute answers to the questions of life, morality, or even reality itself.

2. Lyotard, *Postmodern Condition*, xxiv.
3. Foucault, "Nietzsche, Genealogy, History," 150.

The postmodern shift was subtle yet profound: it moved from the existentialist quest for meaning in the face of an indifferent universe to the deconstructionist claim that meaning itself is an illusion. If language is unreliable, if truth is a construct, and if power determines knowledge, then the very act of seeking meaning becomes a fool's errand. This shift did not simply question the answers; it questioned the validity of asking the questions at all.

The result was a culture that became increasingly fragmented. If there were no longer any shared stories to unite us, what was left but a cacophony of competing voices, each asserting its own version of truth? This fragmentation, as we will see, did not remain confined to the ivory towers of academia; it seeped into the broader culture, influencing everything from politics to media to the way we understand our own identities.

Deconstructionism: The Destruction of Fixed Meanings

As the philosophical wrecking ball of postmodernity swung deeper into the structures of meaning, one figure stood at its forefront: Jacques Derrida. While existentialists wrestled with the absence of inherent meaning in a "godless universe," Derrida took this a step further by questioning whether meaning could ever truly exist at all. In his hands, language once thought to be the bridge connecting human thought to reality became a slippery, unstable construct—an illusion that fragmented more than it unified.

At the heart of Derrida's thought was his concept of deconstruction. This approach was not merely a critique of individual ideas but a radical questioning of the entire process by which we understand the world. Derrida argued that every text, every belief system, and every ideology was fundamentally unstable because the language underpinning them could never be entirely trusted. Language, according to Derrida, was not a transparent medium through which truth is conveyed but rather a maze of signs pointing to other signs with no ultimate grounding.

Derrida's famous assertion that *"there is nothing outside the text"* did not imply that nothing exists beyond written words but rather that everything we perceive, understand, or know is mediated through language.[4] If language itself is a construct, then our perception of reality is always filtered, shaped, and ultimately distorted by the limitations of language.

---

4. Derrida, *Of Grammatology*, 158.

This idea was revolutionary in its implications: if words are incapable of conveying stable meanings, then how can any claim to truth be secure?

While Derrida's deconstruction revealed the hidden assumptions and biases within texts, it also unleashed a profound skepticism that extended beyond literature into theology, philosophy, and even science. For centuries, words like "truth," "justice," and "god" had served as anchors for civilization's moral and ethical compass. But under the relentless gaze of deconstruction, these anchors were revealed as mere constructs, no more secure than the paper on which they were written.

Nowhere was this more disruptive than in the realm of theology. Derrida's approach invited readers to question whether sacred texts could truly convey divine revelation. If language is inherently unstable, can Scripture, the bedrock of faith for billions, be anything more than a collection of culturally situated interpretations? This, in turn, opened the door for radical reinterpretations of Christianity, where doctrines were no longer fixed but fluid, reflecting the reader's perspective rather than an objective divine truth.

As the meaning of sacred texts became more subjective, so did the basis for ethical absolutes. If words are mere constructs, how can we assert that any moral claim is universally binding? In a world deconstructed to its linguistic atoms, nothing remains solid, not even the foundations of faith. To deny the reality of truth is not to free ourselves from it but to surrender ourselves to a chaos where nothing is fixed.

With the unraveling of language came the unraveling of meaning in other spheres as well. Derrida's deconstructionism rippled outwards, influencing the fields of ethics, politics, and even personal identity. As words lost their stability, so too did the concepts they represented. If language is arbitrary, then so are the categories of good and evil, male and female, right and wrong. This led to radical relativism, where truth became a matter of perspective rather than an objective reality.

The consequences of this shift are profound. In Part I of this book, we explored how modernity's quest for autonomy led to a crisis of meaning as individuals turned inward to find purpose. Deconstructionism only deepened this crisis. Now, even the internal compass was questioned. If there are no fixed meanings, then what is the self but a collection of shifting narratives, constantly rewritten according to the whims of the moment?

In the postmodern world, identity itself became fluid. As the boundaries blurred, so did the sense of self, leaving individuals grasping for a stable identity in a world that no longer provided one. The idea that all humans possess inherent dignity relies on the belief in an objective truth about human nature. But if truth is merely a social construct, then what basis is there for asserting that one moral claim is superior to another?

Philosopher Alasdair MacIntyre, in his work *After Virtue*, warned of the dangers of this kind of moral relativism, likening it to living among the ruins of a once-coherent moral landscape. Without a shared foundation, society risks descending into what Thomas Hobbes predicted "a time of war, where every man is enemy to every man," where power, not truth, determines what is right.[5]

Derrida's deconstructionism, while initially confined to the ivory towers of academia, soon seeped into popular culture. As scholars and intellectuals began to question the authority of language and the validity of traditional beliefs, the broader culture followed suit. The result was a widespread cultural shift toward skepticism and cynicism, where nothing was taken at face value, and every claim was met with suspicion.

This cultural shift is perhaps most evident in the way we consume information today. The rise of "fake news," the proliferation of conspiracy theories, and the deep distrust in institutions are all symptoms of a society that no longer believes in stable truths. In the postmodern world, where every narrative is filtered through the hermeneutics of suspicion and every fact is deconstructed, what remains but to doubt everything?

The fragmentation we see today is not merely the product of technological changes or political polarization; it is the fruit of a deeper philosophical crisis that began with the deconstructionists. The same spirit that questioned the authority of texts has now turned its gaze upon the very institutions that once held society together. Religion, education, government are all now viewed with a skeptical eye, seen as instruments of power rather than bearers of truth.

Derrida and his followers believed that deconstruction would liberate individuals from oppressive structures, allowing them to construct their own meanings. But instead of freedom, many have found themselves adrift. In seeking to dismantle the old certainties, postmodernism has left us with nothing solid to replace them.

---

5. Hobbes, *Leviathan*, 78.

The Rejection of Metanarratives: Lyotard's Critique

Derrida's deconstruction unraveled the fabric of language and meaning, leaving society grappling with the implications, but the critique did not stop at the level of individual texts or linguistic constructs. The very narratives that had held Western civilization together for centuries—grand stories about progress, morality, and truth—came under attack. At the forefront of this critique stood Jean-François Lyotard, who argued that the modern world could no longer sustain belief in the metanarratives that had once unified it.

These metanarratives (overarching stories that claim to explain the human experience, whether through religion, science, or politics) had provided the West with a sense of purpose and direction. The Enlightenment belief in the progress of reason, Marxism's vision of social equality, and Christianity's story of redemption had once offered cohesive frameworks through which people could understand their place in the world.

However, Lyotard argued that these narratives no longer held sway. In an age that had witnessed the atrocities of fascism, communism, and colonialism, all carried out in the name of some grand vision, society had grown suspicious of any ideology that claimed to possess universal truth. According to Lyotard, the postmodern condition is defined by a profound distrust of these totalizing stories, which were seen not as pathways to enlightenment but as tools of oppression.

While Lyotard's critique of grand narratives was, in part, a reaction to the disasters of the twentieth century, it also had profound implications for the present. If no narrative could claim to be universally true, then how could societies find the shared values needed for cohesion? In rejecting these overarching stories, Lyotard unwittingly contributed to the fragmentation of the cultural and moral landscape, leaving individuals to navigate the world with only their personal "micro-narratives" to guide them.[6]

As the influence of metanarratives waned, society became increasingly fragmented. Without shared stories to bind communities together, the focus shifted inward toward the individual. The Enlightenment had already begun this process by elevating the individual as the arbiter of truth, but postmodernism completed the turn. In this new world, meaning was no longer something that could be discovered in the cosmos, history, or divine revelation—it was something each person had to construct for themselves.

---

6. Lyotard, *Postmodern Condition*, 19–23.

This emphasis on personal narratives, however, came with a cost. While it promised freedom from the constraints of tradition and authority, it also isolated individuals in their own subjective realities. The rise of identity politics, the explosion of social media echo chambers, and the intensifying polarization in public discourse are all symptoms of this deeper fragmentation. People increasingly seek out groups that align with their personal micro-narratives, rejecting any notion of a common good or shared truth. The proverb indeed rings true: "Where there is no vision, the people perish" (Prov 29:18).

Foucault and the Critique of Power

While Lyotard revealed the collapse of grand narratives, it was Michel Foucault who dug even deeper, unearthing the mechanisms that sustained them. For Foucault, the issue was not just that metanarratives were no longer credible; it was that the very concept of "truth" was inseparably linked to the exercise of power. In his view, knowledge was not an objective discovery of reality but a construct. A construct shaped, maintained, and enforced by those in positions of power.

Foucault's revolutionary approach called into question the nature of truth itself. Unlike the Enlightenment thinkers who believed that knowledge could lead to human liberation, Foucault argued that knowledge and power were inextricably linked in ways that perpetuated social control. According to Foucault, truth is never neutral or objective but is produced by systems of power that dictate what is accepted as "true" in any given society.

Foucault's genealogical method was his way of tracing the history of ideas not to uncover their inherent truth but to reveal how they were shaped by power relations. In works like *Discipline and Punish* and *The History of Sexuality*, Foucault demonstrated how various institutions, such as prisons, hospitals, and schools, used knowledge to discipline and regulate behavior, subtly but effectively controlling society.

Foucault's famous example of the panopticon, a theoretical prison design by Jeremy Bentham, serves as a metaphor for modern society. In the panopticon, a central watchtower allows guards to observe prisoners without them ever knowing whether they are being watched. The uncertainty of surveillance ensures compliance without the need for overt force. For Foucault, modern institutions operate similarly: they do not merely impose control through physical force but through the regulation of knowledge and behavior. By internalizing societal norms, individuals become their own enforcers, perpetuating the very power structures that subjugate them.

Foucault coined the term *power-knowledge* to emphasize that knowledge is never detached from power but is instead a tool used to shape behavior and maintain control.[7] This idea is evident in how societies establish norms and define what is considered "normal" or "abnormal." For example, Foucault's analysis of psychiatry demonstrated how the concept of mental illness was used to marginalize and control those who deviated from societal norms. Similarly, his exploration of sexuality revealed how so-called scientific "truths" were wielded to regulate bodies and enforce moral standards.

By applying this genealogical critique, Foucault sought to dismantle the idea that institutions like the church, the state, or academia were simply neutral custodians of knowledge. Instead, he argued that they were enforcers of social order, using the guise of objective truth to justify their authority. This radical insight led to a new skepticism toward all forms of institutional power, prompting a reexamination of everything from medicine to education to religion.

One of Foucault's most provocative assertions was that truth is a construct produced by systems of power. According to him, every society has its own *regime of truth*—a set of beliefs that are enforced not because they are objectively true but because they serve the interests of those in power.[8] For instance, during the Middle Ages, the church's control over what constituted truth served to maintain its dominance over European society. In the modern era, scientific discourse has taken on a similar role, not as a neutral pursuit of knowledge but as a means of shaping behavior and justifying social policies.

This radical relativization of truth has profound implications for how we understand authority. If all knowledge is shaped by power, then every claim to truth becomes suspect. This perspective leads to a profound cynicism about the motivations behind any assertion of fact. Whether it is the church proclaiming moral truths, the state implementing policies, or scientists advocating for public health measures, Foucault's critique prompts us to ask: Whose interests are being served?

---

7. Foucault, *History of Sexuality*, 98.
8. Foucault, *Discipline and Punish*, 23.

This cynicism has only deepened in the decades since Foucault's death, as public trust in governments, media, and even science has eroded. The assumption that institutions operate for the common good has been replaced by a pervasive suspicion that they are driven by hidden agendas. This erosion of trust has given rise to conspiracy theories, which thrive in an environment where people no longer believe in the objectivity of knowledge. As institutions are seen not as bearers of truth but as instruments of control, society fractures into isolated groups, each with its own version of reality.

One of the most paradoxical aspects of Foucault's philosophy is his view on resistance. Although he acknowledged that power is omnipresent, he also believed that it is not monolithic. Where there is power, there is always resistance, often subtle, dispersed, and unpredictable. True freedom did not lie in overthrowing power structures but in recognizing and resisting the ways in which power shapes our thoughts and behaviors.

However, Foucault's vision of resistance is problematic. If all knowledge is a product of power, then what basis is there for meaningful resistance? How can we critique power without appealing to some higher standard of truth or justice? In rejecting the possibility of objective truth, Foucault leaves us in a paradox: we can recognize the oppression inherent in power structures, but we have no solid ground upon which to stand in resisting them. This leads to a nihilistic conclusion, where all that remains is the struggle for power itself, devoid of any overarching moral framework.

Foucault's critique of power is, in some ways, paradoxically liberating and paralyzing. On the one hand, it has opened our eyes to the subtle ways in which institutions shape our thoughts and behaviors. On the other hand, it has fostered a deep cynicism that undermines our ability to trust even those who genuinely seek the common good. By denying the existence of any objective truth, Foucault's philosophy leaves us with little more than a battlefield where competing power structures vie for dominance.

Foucault and Lyotard both sought to free individuals from the constraints of "oppressive systems," but in doing so, they removed the very foundations upon which trust and community could be built. The collapse of metanarratives and the suspicion of power have left individuals unmoored, unable to find common ground with those who do not share their personal narratives. The result is a culture where polarization, distrust, and fragmentation are the new norms.

In dismantling the grand narratives that once provided a cohesive sense of meaning, postmodernism did not merely reject outdated ideas; it undermined the very possibility of meaning itself. Without a shared story to guide us, what remains is a world of competing voices, each asserting its own version of reality. This fragmentation has profound implications for society, as the bonds that once held us together—shared values, common beliefs, and collective goals—have frayed.

The current social landscape is a testament to the consequences of this philosophical shift. The rise of relativism, the spread of conspiracy theories, and the deepening polarization in politics all point to a culture that has lost its bearings. In a world where everyone has their own truth, what hope is there for finding common ground? The pursuit of individual freedom, once the highest ideal, has left us isolated and disconnected, longing for the very sense of meaning we sought to escape.

Hyperreality and the Displacement of the Real

As the philosophical landscape shifted under the weight of postmodern skepticism, it was not only truth and grand narratives that were deconstructed. The very concept of reality itself began to blur. Enter Jean Baudrillard, one of the most provocative thinkers of the late twentieth century, who argued that in the postmodern world, we no longer experience reality directly but instead live within a realm of *hyperreality*—a world where simulations and representations replace the real until the line between fiction and reality is no longer discernible.[9]

Baudrillard's theory of *simulacra* and *hyperreality* is, in many ways, the logical extension of the postmodern project. While Derrida questioned the stability of language and Lyotard rejected overarching narratives, Baudrillard went further by challenging the very existence of a stable, objective reality. According to him, we now live in an era where signs and symbols do not merely represent reality; they replace it.

Baudrillard famously illustrated this idea through the metaphor of the map that becomes so detailed it eventually covers the entire territory it represents. In the end, the map becomes the reality, and the actual territory is lost beneath it. In today's world, the "maps" are the endless images, screens, and simulations that mediate our experience. Reality, as

---

9. Baudrillard, *Simulacra and Simulation*, 47.

Baudrillard argued, has been consumed by its representations, leading to a state where "the real is no longer real."[10]

Baudrillard's critique is especially relevant in the age of the internet, social media, and virtual reality. In a world saturated with screens, we are bombarded by images, videos, and narratives that shape our perception of reality. Social media platforms, for instance, present carefully curated versions of life that have little connection to the raw, unfiltered experiences of actual existence. The distinction between what is real and what is represented has become so blurred that, for many, the simulation is more compelling than reality itself.

This concept of hyperreality is not just an abstract philosophical idea; it is a reality we inhabit daily. Consider how news, entertainment, advertising, and social media have all merged into a single stream of content. The boundaries between fact and fiction, news and entertainment, have become so fluid that it becomes increasingly difficult to discern what is genuine from what is manufactured.

In the hyperreal world, reality is mediated through layers upon layers of representations—images edited, stories spun, narratives controlled to generate emotional responses. Reality TV shows, which present themselves as unfiltered glimpses into "real life," are often scripted and staged. Even our interactions with the physical world are mediated through screens, as we view life through the lens of our smartphones and devices.

This phenomenon has profound implications for how we understand truth, trust, and authenticity. If everything we experience is filtered, edited, and manipulated, then what is left that is real? The rise of "deepfakes" and AI-generated content further complicates our ability to trust what we see. In a hyperreal world, appearances become the new reality, and substance takes a backseat to spectacle.

The implications of living in a hyperreal world are far-reaching. As our lives become increasingly mediated by screens and simulations, our understanding of ourselves and our place in the world begins to change. The curated images of success, beauty, and happiness presented on social media become the standards by which we measure our own lives, leading to a profound sense of inadequacy and alienation. The reality of one's own life pales in comparison to the hyperreal perfection seen online, resulting in an epidemic of anxiety, depression, and loneliness.

---

10. Baudrillard, *Simulacra and Simulation*, 56.

The more we immerse ourselves in simulations, the more disconnected we become from the tangible, embodied reality of human existence. This disconnection has led to what philosopher Guy Debord describes as a "society of the spectacle," where appearances, not authenticity, are what matter.[11] Our sense of self is no longer rooted in genuine experiences or relationships but in how we are perceived by others. Identity becomes a performance, a collection of images curated for public consumption.

As hyperreality becomes the norm, the ability to discern truth from illusion becomes increasingly difficult. People grow distrustful not only of media but also of institutions, governments, and even each other. If everything is a performance, then nothing can be taken at face value. This pervasive cynicism corrodes the fabric of society, as trust, once the bedrock of social cohesion, becomes a scarce resource.

In the earlier chapters, we discussed how the erosion of belief in transcendent meaning led to the fragmentation of modern society. Hyperreality represents the final stage in this process, where even the material world is overshadowed by its representations. The longing for something real and meaningful grows more desperate in a world where reality itself seems to vanish behind layers of simulation. Charles Taylor, in his *The Secular Age*, would ultimately argue that one of the greatest challenges of the age would not be the search for knowledge but the search for authenticity.[12]

Amidst this deluge of images and simulations, the human soul is left yearning for something real, something tangible. The irony is that, in a world where everything is curated for effect, the desire for authenticity has become a commodity in itself. The search for the "real" is commodified, packaged, and sold back to us through the very mediums that perpetuate the illusion. Baudrillard's insights, while often bleak, point to a deeper longing that remains unresolved. The more we immerse ourselves in the hyperreal, the more we crave something beyond it. A reality that cannot be reduced to pixels on a screen or signs in a system.

Societal Consequences of Postmodern Thought

As we have traversed through the intellectual terrain of postmodernity, from Derrida's deconstructionism to Baudrillard's hyperreality, one thing

---

11. Debord, *Society of the Spectacle*, 21.
12. Taylor, *Secular Age*, 473.

has become clear: the cumulative impact of these ideas has not simply been the dismantling of outdated structures but a profound erosion of the social fabric itself. By questioning the legitimacy of truth, morality, and shared narratives, postmodern thought has left society in a state of fragmentation and disarray.

Postmodern thinkers aimed to liberate individuals from the constraints of inherited moral systems, but in doing so, they also unraveled the very foundations upon which ethical behavior is built. If, as Derrida suggested, words and concepts have no stable meaning, then the very idea of "good" and "evil" becomes relative, subject to endless reinterpretation. Michel Foucault's assertion that truth is merely a construct wielded by those in power further eroded confidence in any objective basis for morality.

The result is a society where ethical decisions are increasingly made on the basis of personal preference rather than shared moral principles. In the absence of a common moral framework, individuals are left to navigate ethical dilemmas on their own, often guided more by emotions than by reasoned principles. This moral relativism, while celebrated as a form of liberation, has led to widespread confusion. We are now living among the ruins of a once-cohesive moral landscape.

Consider the contemporary debates on issues such as free speech, justice, and human rights. Where once there was a common understanding of fundamental rights and wrongs, these discussions have become battlegrounds where opposing sides wield competing narratives, each claiming to represent the "truth." In this climate, the objective pursuit of justice is replaced by power struggles, where the loudest voices often prevail. The collapse of ethical absolutes has not led to a more just society but rather to one where moral confusion reigns.

The rejection of grand narratives has not only affected our ethical frameworks but has also deeply impacted how we understand ourselves. Without shared stories to anchor our identities, we are left adrift, constructing and reconstructing who we are based on the latest cultural trends, social movements, or personal feelings. The rise of identity politics can be seen as a symptom of this deeper crisis. When overarching narratives no longer provide a unifying sense of purpose, people retreat into smaller, more insular communities based on race, gender, or ideology. These micro-narratives, while offering a sense of belonging, are often defined more by what they oppose than by what they stand for.

Nowhere is this fragmentation more evident than on social media platforms, where algorithms amplify content that aligns with our existing beliefs, creating echo chambers that reinforce our personal narratives while isolating us from opposing viewpoints. The result is a society that is more connected than ever before but also more divided. The search for meaning, which once drove people towards shared ideals and collective goals, now pushes individuals further into isolated bubbles where dissenting voices are not simply challenged but silenced. The turn inward, initially seen as a path to self-discovery, has instead led to increased loneliness, anxiety, and a pervasive sense of existential dread.

The Shattered Mirror and the Quest for Wholeness

Postmodernism, with its focus on deconstruction, skepticism, and the rejection of metanarratives, was born out of a genuine desire to liberate individuals from the oppressive structures of the past. And to some extent, it succeeded. It challenged the complacency of old institutions and exposed the hidden power dynamics that shaped knowledge and belief. However, in its zeal to dismantle, postmodernism lost sight of what would replace those structures. The result is a world where meaning is constantly questioned but never found, where identities are fluid but unstable, and where truth is elusive, always just beyond our grasp.

The consequence of living in a world without stable truths is a pervasive sense of meaninglessness. If there is nothing to anchor our beliefs, if all is relative and constructed, then what can we trust? The search for meaning becomes a desperate groping in the dark, with each individual left to construct their own reality from the fragments that remain. This is the existential vacuum that postmodernism has left in its wake: a crisis not of reason but of purpose.

In Part I, we demonstrated how modernity's quest for autonomy and self-determination led to the erosion of shared beliefs. Postmodernism, instead of filling that void, has only deepened it. The rejection of metanarratives, the embrace of relativism, and the turn toward hyperreality have left individuals more isolated than ever before, surrounded by reflections that cannot offer any lasting comfort.

The story of our age is not just one of deconstruction but of a desperate search for something real and lasting. As we move forward in this book, we will explore how, despite the intellectual dismantling of the past, the human heart continues to long for meaning, purpose, and truth. The shattered mirror of postmodernity may have left us with only fragments, but within those pieces lies the glimmer of something deeper. A longing that cannot be silenced by skepticism or relativism.

In the next chapter, we will explore how the New Atheist movement, despite its confident rhetoric, failed to address this fundamental human need. The collapse of faith was supposed to free us, but instead, it has left us yearning for something beyond the material, something that speaks to the deepest parts of our being. The journey is far from over, and the question remains: Can we find a path back to wholeness in a world that has lost its way?

6

The Failed Horsemen
New Atheism and Its Attack on Faith

"Faith is the great cop-out, the great excuse to evade the need to think and evaluate evidence."

—Richard Dawkins[1]

The New Atheist movement burst onto the global stage in the early twenty-first century, its champions wielding science and reason like swords against what they saw as the darkness of religious belief. Figures like Richard Dawkins, Christopher Hitchens, Sam Harris, and Daniel Dennett, often referred to as the "Four Horsemen" of New Atheism, declared war on faith, casting it as not merely outdated but dangerous. With books like *The God Delusion* and *God Is Not Great*, they sought to dismantle religion's hold on society, arguing that belief in God was irrational and that science could provide all the answers humanity needed to progress as a species.

To many people, especially young men, their arguments seemed compelling. In an age marked by religious extremism, political division, and cultural disillusionment, New Atheism offered a vision of liberation from the so-called "illusions" of faith. It promised a future grounded in

---

1. Dawkins, "Speech at the Edinburgh International Science Festival," April 15, 1992.

evidence and reason, where science replaced superstition and secular humanism provided a moral compass. For a time, it seemed as though this movement might fill the void left by the collapse of traditional narratives explored in the previous chapter.

But beneath the surface of its confident rhetoric lay a troubling truth: New Atheism was a movement dominated by objections rather than answers. It was excellent at tearing down but inept at building up. While it attacked the foundations of religion with vigor, it offered nothing substantive to replace the meaning, purpose, and hope that faith had provided for millennia. In its zealous critique of religion, it amplified the very crisis of meaning it sought to solve, leaving individuals and societies more fragmented and disenchanted than before.

This chapter will examine how New Atheism arose from the cultural debris of modernity and postmodernity, amplifying the skepticism and relativism that already permeated the age. We will analyze the core arguments of its leading figures, the shortcomings of its vision, and its failure to address the deeper existential questions that have haunted humanity since the dawn of time. Ultimately, we will see how New Atheism, for all its zealous confidence, deepened the despair of an already disenchanted world, proving to be another voice in the cacophony of modern skepticism rather than a solution to the crises it decried.

The Intellectual Roots of New Atheism

The New Atheist movement did not emerge in a vacuum. Its rhetoric, arguments, and methods were deeply rooted in a longer intellectual tradition that sought to dismantle religious belief and elevate reason and science as humanity's ultimate guides. By the time the Four Horsemen of New Atheism—Richard Dawkins, Christopher Hitchens, Sam Harris, and Daniel Dennett—stepped onto the stage, the intellectual groundwork for their critique of faith had been well-established.

The roots of New Atheism can be traced back to the Enlightenment, an era that placed reason and empirical evidence at the center of human inquiry. Enlightenment thinkers, skeptical of religious authority and dogma, began to question the foundations of faith, often using philosophy and emerging scientific discoveries as their tools. David Hume, one of the most influential forerunners of New Atheism, challenged the rationality of belief in miracles and the existence of a divine creator. In *An*

Enquiry Concerning Human Understanding, Hume argued that miracles were violations of natural laws and, thus, inherently improbable.[2] His critique laid the foundation for a naturalistic worldview, one that relied on observable phenomena rather than metaphysical claims. For Hume, religion was not only philosophically untenable but also a product of human fear and ignorance.

Denis Diderot, another Enlightenment figure, took a more confrontational approach. As one of the editors of the *Encyclopédie*, Diderot used his platform to undermine the church's intellectual authority, presenting religion as an obstacle to human progress. His writings framed faith as a relic of a less enlightened past, perpetuated by those who sought to control society through fear and superstition. Diderot's scorn for religious institutions would resonate centuries later in the fiery rhetoric of Christopher Hitchens.

As the Enlightenment gave way to the scientific revolution, figures like Charles Darwin and Carl Sagan further challenged religious narratives. Darwin's theory of evolution, articulated in *On the Origin of Species*, provided a naturalistic explanation for the diversity of life, undermining the traditional argument for a divine designer. For many, Darwin's work marked a turning point, demonstrating that complex phenomena could be explained without recourse to the supernatural.

Carl Sagan, though less confrontational than the New Atheists, played a crucial role in popularizing a naturalistic worldview. Through works like *Cosmos*, Sagan celebrated the wonder of the universe while emphasizing the sufficiency of science to answer life's great questions. Sagan's poetic approach to atheism and his ability to evoke awe without invoking a deity provided a blueprint for figures like Sam Harris, who sought to ground ethics and meaning in a purely materialistic framework.

By the late twentieth century, the stage was set for a more aggressive critique of religion. The events of 9/11, when Islamic extremists hijacked planes and flew them into the Twin Towers and the Pentagon, acted as a catalyst that galvanized public discourse on the dangers of religious extremism. It was in this climate that New Atheism emerged, taking the skepticism of Hume, the confrontational tone of Diderot, and the naturalistic vision of Sagan and channeling them into a movement that sought not only to critique religion but to eradicate it from public life.

New Atheism distinguished itself from its intellectual predecessors by its tone and scope. Where Sagan had celebrated science, the New

---

2. Hume, *An Enquiry Concerning Human Understanding*, 79.

Atheists weaponized it, using evolutionary biology, neuroscience, and cosmology to argue not just that religion was false but that it was harmful. Where Hume and Diderot had critiqued specific doctrines, the New Atheists expanded their target to include the entire concept of faith itself. For them, faith was not merely a mistake to be corrected but a moral failing to be condemned.

This evolution from skepticism to outright hostility marked a significant shift. New Atheism's mission was not just to question religious claims but to discredit the entire enterprise of faith, positioning science and reason as humanity's only hope for progress and enlightenment. In doing so, the movement became what one might even call "missional" in its outreach and "religious" in its devotion.

While New Atheism inherited its naturalism and critique of religion from these earlier thinkers, it also carried forward its limitations. Hume's skepticism offered no replacement for the moral and existential frameworks provided by religion. Diderot's dismissal of faith as mere superstition failed to account for its enduring significance. Even Sagan, with his emphasis on wonder, acknowledged that science could not answer every human longing.

New Atheism repeated and amplified these critiques without addressing their gaps. Its reliance on materialism left it ill-equipped to grapple with the deeper questions of meaning and purpose. Its scientism, while seeking to discredit religious claims, failed to provide a vision for how humanity might navigate the existential crises that would arise in a disenchanted world. Its hostility toward faith alienated not only the devout but also anyone who would even seek to give credence to the ancient stories of faith (consider the discussions between Sam Harris and Richard Dawkins with Jordan Peterson). New Atheism, for all its intellectual pedigree, ultimately inherited the same weaknesses as its forerunners: it could deconstruct faith but not replace it. It could critique religion but not resolve the crises it claimed to address. This fragility would prove to be its undoing.

The Four Horsemen

The New Atheist movement was led by Richard Dawkins, Christopher Hitchens, Sam Harris, and Daniel Dennett, four intellectuals who saw themselves as champions of reason in a world they believed to be shackled by the oppressive chains of religion. They attacked faith not only as intellectually vacuous but as actively harmful to human progress, ethics, and freedom. Each approached the subject from their own field—science, moral criticism, neuroscience, and philosophy—but collectively, their project was marked by a shared animosity toward religion and a promise that reason and science could replace it.

Yet, for all their confidence and rhetorical strength, their arguments frequently faltered. They mischaracterized the depth and complexity of religious belief, their critiques often lacked philosophical rigor, and their proposed alternatives failed to grapple with the existential crises that faith addresses. In their zeal to dismantle religion, the Four Horsemen demonstrated that they could destroy but not rebuild. Their attacks amplified the despair of a meaning-starved age, offering no substantive answers to the deeper questions of human existence.

Richard Dawkins, a biologist and author, quickly became the most recognizable face of New Atheism with the publication of *The God Delusion*. Dawkins argued that belief in God was not merely unnecessary but irrational, claiming that religion operates as a mental virus that infects the minds of the faithful. In one of his most memorable passages, he described the God of the Old Testament as "arguably the most unpleasant character in all fiction," calling him "jealous and proud of it; a petty, unjust, unforgiving control freak; a vindictive, bloodthirsty ethnic cleanser; a misogynistic, homophobic, racist, infanticidal, genocidal, filicidal, pestilential, megalomaniacal, sadomasochistic, capriciously malevolent bully."[3]

This polemic captures the tone of Dawkins's approach: scornful, combative, and often unrestrained. Dawkins's scientific background underpins his arguments, particularly his reliance on Darwinian evolution as an explanation for the complexity of life. In his earlier work *The Blind Watchmaker*, he attacks the argument for God from design, contending that evolution provides a sufficient mechanism for the diversity of life without requiring a divine designer.[4] This forms the basis for his dismissal of God's necessity. However, Dawkins's arguments reveal a fundamental misunderstanding of the nature of theological inquiry. The teleological argument, for example, is not merely about complexity but about contingency—why anything exists at all rather than nothing. Evolutionary theory, as profound as it may seem, does not, and I would submit, cannot answer this question.

---

3. Dawkins, *God Delusion*, 51.
4. Dawkins, *Blind Watchmaker*, 162.

Further, Dawkins's dismissal of religion as a "delusion" betrays a reductive view of faith. He treats belief in God as equivalent to belief in Santa Claus or the Tooth Fairy, ignoring the existential and philosophical dimensions of faith. Religion is not simply about explaining the natural world; it is about grappling with questions of meaning, morality, and purpose. Questions that, despite his objections, Dawkins's materialism leaves unanswered.

Christopher Hitchens's *God Is Not Great: How Religion Poisons Everything* is perhaps the most rhetorically polished of the New Atheist texts, driven by Hitchens's biting wit and deep cynicism toward faith. Hitchens claimed that religion is not only untrue but actively malevolent, accusing it of fostering violence, repression, and ignorance. He wrote, "Religion spoke its last intelligible or noble or inspiring words a long time ago: either that or it mutated into an admirable but nebulous humanism."[5]

Hitchens excoriated religious institutions for their historical and contemporary failures, pointing to the Crusades, the Inquisition, and the sexual abuse scandals within the Catholic Church as evidence of religion's inherent corruption. While these criticisms are not without merit, they are also selective. Hitchens failed to address the vast contributions of religious institutions to art, education, and social justice. The same church that he decried for its failings also birthed the modern university system, pioneered scientific inquiry, laid the foundation for benevolence societies, and inspired some of the greatest artistic achievements in human history.

Moreover, Hitchens offered no meaningful alternative to the moral framework provided by religion. His claim that humanism can serve as a sufficient basis for ethics is undercut by his own admission that secular ideologies, such as communism, have been just as destructive as religion. Hitchens frequently critiqued religion for its moral failures but failed to justify why his own moral standards should be considered binding. His reliance on Enlightenment ideals, such as individual liberty and human dignity, rests on a foundation of Judeo-Christian values that he refuses to acknowledge.

Hitchens's writing is captivating, but his arguments often sacrifice nuance for rhetorical flourish. While he excels at pointing out religion's flaws, he does little to address the existential longings and ethical dilemmas that faith seeks to resolve. His critiques were loud but ultimately hollow.

---

5. Hitchens, *God is Not Great*, 7.

Sam Harris, a neuroscientist, positioned himself as the New Atheist most concerned with morality. In *The Moral Landscape*, Harris argued that science could provide an objective foundation for ethics, claiming that questions of right and wrong could be determined by measuring human well-being. Harris also critiqued religious violence, asserting that faith is a primary driver of global conflict.

Harris's approach is ambitious but deeply flawed. While science can inform moral decisions by providing empirical data about consequences, it cannot determine values. For example, science can measure the effects of certain actions on human well-being, but it cannot explain why human flourishing should be prioritized over other goals. Harris attempts to sidestep this problem by asserting that well-being is self-evidently valuable, but this is a philosophical claim, not a scientific one.

Harris's critique of religious violence is similarly reductive. By blaming faith as the root cause of extremism, he overlooks the complex social, political, and economic factors that contribute to conflict. Moreover, Harris's reliance on neuroscience to explain morality strips ethics of its narrative and existential dimensions. Religious and moral systems are not merely sets of rules; they are embedded in stories that provide meaning and purpose. Harris' framework, by contrast, is thin and uninspiring, failing to capture the depth of human moral experience.[6]

Daniel Dennett, in *Breaking the Spell: Religion as a Natural Phenomenon*, takes a more analytical approach, treating religion as a cultural artifact shaped by evolutionary pressures.[7] Dennett argues that faith, while once useful for fostering social cohesion, is now an outdated relic. Dennett's reduction of religion to evolutionary utility ignores its spiritual and existential dimensions. Faith is not merely a mechanism for survival; it is a response to humanity's deepest questions about existence, suffering, and transcendence. By focusing on religion's evolutionary origins, Dennett sidesteps its enduring appeal and transformative power.

Dennett's approach is also self-defeating. If religion is simply a product of evolution, then so too are all other beliefs, including atheism. Dennett's critique undermines his own position, as it reduces all truth claims to evolutionary constructs with no inherent validity.

The Four Horsemen of New Atheism succeeded in sparking public debate, but their arguments were deeply flawed. They critiqued

---

6. Harris, *Moral Landscape*, 3.
7. Dennett, *Breaking the Spell*, 17.

religion but failed to engage with its depth and complexity. Their proposed replacements—science, reason, and humanism—were insufficient to address the crises of meaning, morality, and purpose that faith has historically engaged. In their effort to dismantle religion, they left nothing substantial in its place, deepening the despair of a disenchanted age. Their movement, for all its confidence, proved to be a loud but hollow response to humanity's enduring spiritual questions.

Modernistic Fundamentalism and the Capstone of Disenchantment

The New Atheist movement, in its crusade against religion, sought to embody the final triumph of reason and science over the ancient specters of faith. Richard Dawkins, Christopher Hitchens, Sam Harris, and Daniel Dennett presented themselves as torchbearers of a new secular Enlightenment, one that would free humanity from the supposed chains of superstition and lead to an age of clarity, morality, and progress. Yet, in their zealous rejection of religion, they unwittingly mimicked the evangelical fervor of the Christianity they despised, adopting its rhetorical tools while hollowing out its substance. Their movement, rather than liberating humanity, became the capstone of an age of disenchantment. An era marked by the fragmentation of meaning, the erosion of shared narratives, and the deepening despair of a society unmoored from its spiritual roots.

The New Atheist project, for all its confidence, failed on philosophical, practical, and existential levels. It borrowed the zeal and certainty of the religious traditions it opposed but offered no compelling answers to the crises of meaning and morality that modernity and postmodernity had already laid bare. In its inability to construct anything substantive, New Atheism became both a symptom and a contributor to the very despair it sought to overcome. New Atheism, far from being a liberating force, deepened the crisis of the modern age and ultimately catalyzed a renewed search for the metanarratives of old.

While New Atheism prided itself on its rejection of faith, its rhetorical style and approach often mirrored the evangelical fervor of Christian fundamentalism. Richard Dawkins famously declared that teaching religion to children was tantamount to child abuse, a claim that echoes the fire-and-brimstone moral certitude of fundamentalist preachers.[8] This ironic parallel was no coincidence. Like the fundamentalist movements they opposed, the New Atheists framed their worldview as a binary struggle between truth and error, light and darkness.

Religion was not merely misguided; it was evil. Science was not merely a method; it was salvation. This dualistic framework, combined with their combative rhetoric, betrayed an underlying dependence on the very structures of thought and persuasion that religion has long employed. New Atheism, for all its claims to intellectual superiority, borrowed deeply from the emotional and rhetorical playbook of the Christianity it sought to dismantle.

Yet, unlike the Christian narratives it mocked, New Atheism offered no positive vision of the human condition. Where evangelical Christianity calls individuals to repentance and redemption, providing a narrative arc of fall and restoration, New Atheism's message began and ended with negation. It sought to dismantle faith but offered no compelling replacement for the meaning, hope, and moral vision that faith provides.

At its core, New Atheism was characterized by a profound misunderstanding of the philosophical and existential dimensions of religion. By reducing faith to a set of empirical claims about the natural world, the New Atheists missed the deeper currents that have sustained belief throughout human history. Religion is not merely a collection of propositions about the universe; it is a response to the human condition, an attempt to grapple with questions of meaning, morality, and mortality that science, for all its worth, cannot answer.

Central to the New Atheist worldview is the philosophy of scientism, the belief that science is not only the best but the only legitimate means of acquiring knowledge. While science is an invaluable tool for understanding the natural world, it is ill-equipped to address the metaphysical and moral questions that lie at the heart of human existence. By insisting that science alone could answer humanity's deepest questions, the New Atheists ignored the profound limitations of their own framework.

Neuroscience can map the brain's activity, but it cannot explain consciousness or the subjective experience of love, beauty, or grief. These are not failures of science but reminders that some aspects of human existence transcend empirical measurement. Yet the New Atheists treated these transcendent questions with disdain, dismissing them as relics

---

8. Dawkins, *God Delusion*, 18.

of a bygone era. In doing so, they failed to recognize that the human longing for meaning and purpose is not a weakness to be overcome but a fundamental part of what it means to be human. Their scientism, far from elevating humanity, reduced it to a mechanistic process, stripping existence of its depth and mystery.

One of the most glaring inadequacies of New Atheism was its inability to provide a coherent foundation for morality. While the Four Horsemen were united in their critique of religion's moral failings, they offered no substantive alternative to the ethical frameworks they sought to dismantle. Sam Harris, in *The Moral Landscape*, attempted to ground morality in human well-being, arguing that science could determine what actions promote or diminish flourishing. Yet Harris's framework rested on a fundamental philosophical assumption: that human well-being is an objective good. This assumption, while intuitively appealing, is not self-evident and cannot be derived from empirical observation alone.

Christopher Hitchens, for his part, argued that humanistic ethics could replace religious morality. Yet Hitchens's own rhetoric often betrayed a reliance on the very Judeo-Christian values he sought to discard. His appeals to human dignity, justice, and equality were rooted in a moral vision that emerged from the religious traditions he decried. By rejecting the metaphysical foundation of these values, Hitchens undermined the very ethics he sought to uphold.

The problem for New Atheism was not simply that it failed to ground morality; it was that its critiques of religion presupposed a moral framework that its worldview could not sustain. Without an objective basis for good and evil, the New Atheist's denunciations of religious violence and oppression became mere expressions of personal preference, lacking the universal authority they claimed.

If New Atheism failed philosophically, it fared no better practically. Its strident critiques of religion alienated not only the devout but also those who might have been sympathetic to its goals. By framing faith as an unmitigated evil, the New Atheists created a false dichotomy: one could either embrace reason and science or remain mired in ignorance and superstition. This oversimplification ignored the vast middle ground where faith and reason coexist, alienating countless individuals who found value in both.

Moreover, New Atheism's emphasis on negation rather than construction left its followers with little to hold onto. Religion, for all its flaws, provides communities of meaning, rituals of comfort, and narratives of hope. By dismantling these structures without offering a replacement, New Atheism deepened the loneliness and fragmentation of a disenchanted age. It stripped away the illusions of faith but left the human soul naked and unprotected against the existential void.

This failure was not merely an intellectual oversight; it was a profound abdication of responsibility. In an era marked by rising rates of anxiety, depression, and suicide, the New Atheists offered little more than the cold comfort of materialism. Their vision of humanity, reduced to a collection of atoms and evolutionary processes, failed to address the deeper questions that give life meaning. In this sense, New Atheism was not the solution to modernity's crises but their culmination.

A Catalyst for Renewal

In its failure, however, New Atheism may have inadvertently sown the seeds of renewal. By exposing the inadequacies of a purely materialistic worldview, it forced many to confront the limitations of disenchantment and seek alternatives. The movement's stridency, while alienating, also highlighted the enduring human need for transcendence, community, and meaning.

In the years since New Atheism's peak, a growing chorus of voices has emerged to challenge its narrative. Thinkers like Jordan Peterson, Tom Holland, Louise Perry, and Mary Eberstadt have called for a reexamination of the religious traditions that the New Atheists sought to discard. These voices, while diverse, share a common conviction: that the metanarratives of old, for all their imperfections, speak to something enduringly true about the human condition. They argue that religion is not merely a vestige of the past but a vital part of what it means to be human and a source of meaning, morality, and hope that no secular philosophy has yet to replace.

In this sense, New Atheism may have been a necessary chapter in the story of modernity. A final attempt to sever humanity from its spiritual roots. Its failure, however, has opened the door for a new conversation, one that seeks to recover the wisdom of the past while addressing the challenges of the present. The collapse of New Atheism is not the end of the story but a turning point, a moment that invites us to rediscover the narratives that have sustained humanity for millennia.

New Atheism was not the triumphant liberation its proponents envisioned. It was the final expression of an age of disenchantment, the culmination of a modern project that sought to reduce humanity to its material components and strip the universe of its mystery. In its failure to construct a meaningful alternative to faith, New Atheism deepened the despair it sought to overcome. Yet, in this failure lies an opportunity. A remarkable chance to rediscover the narratives, rituals, and communities that give life its depth and meaning. The door that New Atheism sought to close on religion may, in the end, have been a surprising doorway back to faith.

Conclusion to Part II

PART II OF THIS book has taken us through the desolate landscape of modernity and postmodernity's attempts to sever humanity from its transcendent roots. Chapter 5 examined the deconstructionist project of postmodernism, led by thinkers like Derrida and Lyotard, whose skepticism of truth and rejection of grand narratives fractured the cultural and intellectual foundations upon which society once stood. Chapter 6 turned to the New Atheist movement, which, rather than offering a substantive alternative, amplified the despair of disenchantment. Together, these chapters reveal how modernity's quest for autonomy and postmodernity's relentless critique of truth culminated in a profound crisis of meaning.

Together, postmodernism and New Atheism represent what I believe are the final stages of an intellectual project that sought to reduce humanity to its material components and strip the universe of its mystery. Both movements deconstructed the frameworks of meaning that had sustained civilizations for centuries but neither succeeded in constructing anything capable of filling the void they created. The result is an age of profound disenchantment, where individuals are left isolated, fragmented, and longing for a deeper connection to the transcendent.

And yet, even amid the despair of this disenchanted age, there remains a spark of hope. Long before the postmodernists and New Atheists proclaimed the end of God and the obsolescence of faith, other voices were rising to meet the fractured world of modernity. These voices were often quieter than the boisterous proclamations of secularism, but they carried a weight that could not be ignored. They reminded us that the human longing for meaning, beauty, and transcendence could not be eradicated by philosophical skepticism, scientific materialism, or the deconstruction of postmodernity. Far from being defeated, the voices of truth, beauty, and goodness persisted like a melody that remains audible even amid the cacophony of doubt and despair.

For centuries, poets, theologians, philosophers, and novelists have offered a counternarrative to the empty promises of a world stripped of the sacred. A number of voices would rise to stand against the tide of reductionism and dare to proclaim that life's deepest questions cannot be answered by man's reason alone. These thinkers illuminated paths to meaning that modernity could not obliterate, showing that the human soul, far from being a mere byproduct of evolutionary mechanisms, is irreducibly connected to the transcendent.

Their voices carried forward the wisdom of traditions that modernity sought to discard. They explored how ancient truths could speak to modern crises, how beauty could rekindle wonder in a disenchanted world, and how the search for goodness could lead us back to the ultimate source of morality. Even as secular ideologies declared the inevitability of a godless future, these thinkers recognized that the human spirit would always hunger for what materialism and rationalism could not provide.

Part III of this book will shed light on some of those voices. It will focus on thinkers, writers, and artists who resisted the despair of disenchantment and sought to restore coherence, meaning, and hope to a fragmented world. These figures did not offer mere nostalgia for a lost age but a profound reimagining of ancient truths for the modern context. They show us that the narratives of faith, far from being relics of the past, remain vital to the human experience.

This next part is a journey into the counterrevolution, a return not to a naïve past but to eternal truths that speak powerfully to the present. From writers who reclaimed beauty as a reflection of the divine, to philosophers who argued for the necessity of moral absolutes, to theologians who reconciled ancient wisdom with modern challenges, these voices offer a way forward. They remind us that the longing for meaning, goodness, and truth is not a weak vestige of a superstitious past but a testament to the human soul's connection to something greater. The despair of disenchantment, though pervasive, is not the end of the story. Beyond the ruins of modernity's and postmodernity's failed projects lies the enduring call of faith. A call to truth, beauty, and goodness that beckons us toward a deeper, richer understanding of what it means to be human.

PART III

Voices of Restoration
Messengers of Meaning in the Modern Age

7

G. K. Chesterton

Wonder, Tradition, and the Sacredness of the Ordinary

"The world will never starve for want of wonders; but only for want of wonder."
—G. K. Chesterton[1]

With these words, G. K. Chesterton offers a piercing diagnosis of modernity's spiritual malaise. In a world increasingly captivated by scientific achievement, industrial progress, and technological marvels, humanity seemed to have lost its capacity to marvel at life itself. For Chesterton, this loss of wonder was not merely an aesthetic tragedy; it was a profound spiritual crisis. Without wonder, the world became mechanical, predictable, and devoid of meaning. It was a closed system in which the sacred was replaced by the sterile.

Chesterton lived at a time when industrialization had reshaped society, skepticism was celebrated as intellectual sophistication, and relativism threatened to erode moral absolutes. Yet, in the face of these cultural shifts, he remained steadfast in his rebellion against cynicism. His rebellion, however, was not fueled by anger or bitterness but by joy, humor, and a relentless affirmation of life.

Through works such as *Tremendous Trifles*, *Orthodoxy*, *Heretics*, and *The Everlasting Man*, Chesterton championed wonder, tradition, and

1. Chesterton, *Tremendous Trifles*, 6.

the sacredness of the ordinary as antidotes to disenchantment. He sought to reawaken humanity to the mystery and majesty of existence, reminding his readers that even the most mundane aspects of life were infused with divine significance. Chesterton's vision was not merely nostalgic; it was revolutionary, a countercultural call to embrace eternal truths in a fragmented and forgetful age.

The Case for Wonder

Chesterton viewed the loss of wonder as one of the greatest tragedies of modernity, and he diagnosed this ailment with remarkable clarity. In a culture increasingly obsessed with progress and innovation, Chesterton saw a dangerous irony: the very advancements that should have filled humanity with awe—scientific discovery, technological breakthroughs, and artistic achievement—had instead dulled the collective imagination. The problem was not that the world lacked marvels but that modern people had grown too accustomed to marveling only at the superficial.

Chesterton's critique of modernity revolved around its reductionist tendencies, particularly its reliance on materialism. A materialist worldview, he argued, strips life of its enchantment by explaining everything in purely mechanical terms. He writes in *Heretics*: "The modern world is filled with men who hold dogmas so strongly that they do not even know they are dogmas."[2] One such dogma, for Chesterton, was the belief that empiricism could explain the ultimate mysteries of existence. Empiricism was a tool for investigating how the world works, but it could never answer why the world exists or why it operates with such intricate order. This was the tragedy of modern skepticism: it refused to bow before the unexplainable beauty of creation, opting instead for a cold, clinical detachment.

To combat this, Chesterton believed that paradox was the gateway to wonder. Life itself, he argued, was paradoxical: it was both intensely fragile and remarkably resilient, both fleeting and eternal, both ordinary and extraordinary. In *Orthodoxy*, he writes, "It is exactly this balance of apparent contradictions that has been the whole buoyancy of the healthy man. The whole secret of mysticism is this: that man can understand everything by the help of what he does not understand."[3] For Chesterton, contradiction was not a flaw in reasoning but a window into deeper truths.

---

2. Chesterton, *Heretics*, 304–5.
3. Chesterton, *Orthodoxy*, 47.

One of his most famous uses of paradox is his description of Christianity itself: "Christianity got over the difficulty of combining furious opposites, by keeping them both, and keeping them both furious."[4] He saw the Christian faith as uniquely equipped to hold seemingly contradictory truths in tension: divine sovereignty and human responsibility, justice and mercy, transcendence and immanence. This, Chesterton believed, was not a sign of inconsistency but a reflection of a world too complex to be flattened by human logic. Paradox, in Chesterton's view, was not merely a rhetorical device; it was a way of reclaiming mystery. By embracing the paradoxical nature of life and faith, Chesterton invited his readers to step beyond the limits of human understanding and into the boundless wonder of God's creation.

Along with his love of paradox, few writers have defended the importance of fairy tales as passionately as Chesterton. In his chapter "The Ethics of Elfland" in *Orthodoxy*, he argues that fairy tales are not merely stories for children but profound reflections of moral and spiritual truths. Fairy tales, he explains, teach us to see the world as enchanted, a place where good triumphs over evil, courage is rewarded, and the impossible becomes possible.

Chesterton wrote what I consider to be one of his most profound statements when he declared, "What fairy tales give the child is his first clear idea of the possible defeat of bogey. The baby has known the dragon intimately ever since he had an imagination. What the fairy tale provides for him is a St. George to kill the dragon."[5] This is more than a whimsical observation; it is a profoundly theological statement. For Chesterton, fairy tales embody the Christian imagination, which sees the world as a battleground where good and evil are locked in a cosmic struggle. The stories of knights slaying dragons or princes rescuing sleeping princesses mirror the deeper narrative of Christ's victory over sin and death.

He also saw fairy tales as a critique of modern relativism. In fairy tales, there is no ambiguity about what is right and wrong, good and evil. The hero's journey is always directed toward truth, even if it involves suffering or sacrifice. Within fairy tales there is the idea of a definite and attainable joy and a vision of how the world can be altered by a hero's unalterable will. For Chesterton, this moral clarity was a stark contrast to the relativistic and nihilistic narratives of his own time.

---

4. Chesterton, *Orthodoxy*, 172.
5. Chesterton, *Tremendous Trifles*, 101–8.

Moreover, Chesterton believed that fairy tales preserved the sense of wonder that modern life often erodes. The fantastical elements of these stories—talking animals, magical forests, and miraculous interventions—remind us that the world is far more mysterious and miraculous than we often realize. Fairy tales, then, are not an escape from reality but an invitation to see reality more clearly.

Paradox and fairy were all, for Chesterton, tools to help rebuild the rediscovery of wonder. But wonder was not an end in itself but a pathway to worship. To marvel at the beauty of creation, he argued, is to be drawn toward its Creator. Worship, in Chesterton's view, begins with gratitude. In his *Short History of England*, he wrote that "gratitude is happiness doubled by wonder."[6] It was through gratitude that one could transform even the most mundane aspects of life into acts of worship.

Wonder is also an antidote to pride. Modern humanity, Chesterton argued, had become arrogant in its pursuit of knowledge and control. By rediscovering wonder, people could regain a sense of humility: a recognition that life is a gift, not a possession. Worship, for Chesterton, was the natural response to this recognition. It was an act of surrender, an acknowledgment that God is the source of all that is good, beautiful, and true.

Tradition as a Form of Renewal

G. K. Chesterton's defense of tradition begins with a striking phrase: "Tradition means giving votes to the most obscure of all classes, our ancestors. It is the democracy of the dead."[7] This quip, found in *Orthodoxy*, is more than clever wordplay: it encapsulates his deep conviction that the wisdom and values of the past are indispensable for navigating the present. Chesterton saw modernity as dangerously arrogant. So enamored with its own progress that it dismissed the collective insights of generations before it. Tradition was not a fossilized relic of the past but a living conversation in which the voices of the dead speak to and inform the living.

Chesterton's concept of tradition pushes back against what he would consider the small and arrogant oligarchy of those who merely happen to be walking about. This oligarchy, he argued, tends to assume that modern thought is inherently superior to that of the past simply because it is newer. In response, Chesterton asserted that human nature is remarkably

---

6. Chesterton, *Short History of England*, 59.
7. Chesterton, *Orthodoxy*, 83.

constant across time, and the challenges and questions faced by past generations are often the same as those we face today. To ignore their solutions, observations, and experiences is to impoverish ourselves.

For Chesterton, tradition serves as a defense against cultural and intellectual hubris. By grounding our understanding in the wisdom of the past, we tether ourselves to truths that transcend fleeting fads. He believed this was particularly critical in a world increasingly driven by novelty for its own sake. Tradition could stand as a bulwark against chaos, a means of rooting ourselves in eternal truths rather than ephemeral trends.

Chesterton's commitment to tradition is most vividly illustrated in his intellectual sparring with his friend and ideological rival H. G. Wells. As noted back in chapter two, Wells championed progress as humanity's highest ideal. For Wells, the future held endless potential for human evolution, scientific discovery, and societal improvement. Wells's vision was grounded in a materialist worldview that rejected the necessity of moral absolutes or divine guidance. Humanity, he believed, could define its own destiny through reason and innovation.

Chesterton's response to Wells was not merely theoretical; it was profoundly practical. He pointed to the ways in which unchecked notions of progress had led to social and moral disintegration. Wells's faith in human ingenuity, Chesterton argued, ignored the reality of human fallibility. In *The Everlasting Man*, Chesterton offered a direct rebuttal to Wells's evolutionary view of history, which depicted humanity's development as a purely material process.[8] Chesterton argued instead that history is best understood as the unfolding story of divine intervention. Humanity's progress, in Chesterton's view, is not a straight line of increasing enlightenment but a series of moral and spiritual struggles, guided and redeemed by the hand of God.

Chesterton rejected the caricature of tradition as blind adherence to the past, arguing instead that tradition is a means of renewing and rediscovering eternal truths. "A dead thing can go with the stream," he wrote, "but only a living thing can go against it."[9] In this sense, tradition is not about passive conformity but about active engagement with the wisdom of those who have gone before us.

Chesterton's defense of tradition was deeply tied to his understanding of the human condition. He believed that humanity's greatest need

---

8. Chesterton, *Everlasting Man*, 26–28.
9. Chesterton, *Everlasting Man*, 297.

was not for novelty but for a return to the fundamental truths about God, creation, and morality. Chesterton, in this vision, fully lays out what one would define as classical Christian conservatism. He believed that tradition was a necessary prerequisite upon which humanity could build a meaningful and coherent existence. He argued that the shared values and practices handed down through generations create a sense of continuity and belonging that is vital for societal cohesion. In a world increasingly fragmented by individualism and relativism, tradition provides a common foundation upon which relationships and cultures can flourish.

Chesterton's view of tradition was deeply intertwined with his Catholic faith. His conversion to Catholicism was, in many ways, a declaration of allegiance to the tradition of the church as the custodian of divine truth. He saw the church not as an institution trapped in the past but as a living body that carries the wisdom of Christ into every age. While modernity often framed tradition as a barrier to freedom, Chesterton argued that true freedom comes from living within the bounds of divine truth. "To have a right to do a thing is not at all the same as to be right in doing it," he remarked, highlighting the moral responsibility that tradition imposes upon the individual.[10]

For Chesterton, far from being restrictive, tradition liberates the human spirit by connecting it to the eternal. In embracing the traditions of the church, Chesterton found a richness and fullness of life that modernity could not provide. "The Christian ideal," he wrote, "has not been tried and found wanting. It has been found difficult; and left untried."[11] Tradition, for Chesterton, is the means by which the Christian ideal is preserved and passed on, offering hope and renewal to every generation.

The Sacredness of the Ordinary

For G. K. Chesterton, the ordinary was not mundane; it was miraculous. Beneath the surface of the seemingly trivial, he saw the hand of God at work, infusing even the most mundane moments with divine majesty. To Chesterton, the world's great tragedy was humanity's inability to recognize this sacred dimension. Modernity, even in its earliest forms with its obsession for innovation and spectacle, had dulled the capacity for wonder, leaving people blind to the treasures of the everyday. Chesterton's

---

10. Chesterton, *Short History of England*, 120.
11. Chesterton, *What's Wrong with the World*, 39.

reflections on the sacredness of the ordinary called back to a deeper way of seeing. They challenge the modern insistence on extraordinary experiences, reminding us that true holiness and meaning are often found in the smallest and simplest aspects of life.

Chesterton's starting point for rediscovering the sacredness of the ordinary is his assertion that the seemingly trivial details of life are not accidents but intentional gifts from God. As his famous quote from *Tremendous Trifles* states, "The world will never starve for want of wonders; but only for want of wonder."[12] For Chesterton, the gift of existence itself is nothing short of a miracle, and daily life is a canvas on which divine artistry is continually displayed.

Chesterton often drew analogies between creation and storytelling. Just as a good story captures attention with its twists and turns, the story of everyday life is full of mysteries waiting to be uncovered. A sunrise is not merely a natural phenomenon; it is the climax of a divine narrative that unfolds each morning. The ordinary rhythms of life—waking, working, eating, and resting—are, in Chesterton's view, sacred rituals that reflect the order and generosity of God. This vision of life's holiness extends even to the repetitive tasks that many find tedious. Chesterton famously wrote:

> Because children have abounding vitality, because they are in spirit fierce and free, therefore they want things repeated and unchanged. They always say, 'Do it again'; and the grown-up person does it again until he is nearly dead. For grown-up people are not strong enough to exult in monotony.[13]

Chesterton believed that what we dismiss as monotonous is, in fact, a reflection of God's own joy in creation. "It may be," he wrote, "that God makes every daisy separately, but has never got tired of making them."[14] Modern people, Chesterton argued, often seek meaning in extraordinary moments: grand achievements, exotic adventures, or dramatic spiritual experiences. Yet Chesterton insisted that the most profound truths are often found in the seemingly insignificant. The holiness of life is not something we must chase; it is already present in the bread we eat, the laughter we share, and the work we do.

---

12. Chesterton, *Tremendous Trifles*, 6.
13. Chesterton, *Orthodoxy*, 106.
14. Chesterton, *Orthodoxy*, 107.

Much of Chesterton's understanding of the sacredness of the ordinary was deeply shaped by his faith, particularly regarding Catholicism's sacramental theology. The sacraments—baptism, communion, marriage—are tangible signs of invisible grace, connecting the material and spiritual realms. For Chesterton, this sacramental worldview extended beyond formal church practices to encompass all of creation. To love the ordinary is to recognize its divine origin and to defend its sanctity against modernity's tendency to dismiss or exploit it.

Chesterton was a master at finding majesty in the mundane. He demonstrated the majesty within the mundane by seeing within it echoes of a deeper reality, signs of God's generosity and love. The ordinary is sacred precisely because it is undeserved. A free gift from a loving Creator. The essay "A Piece of Chalk" offers one of his most striking illustrations of his sacramental imagination. In this story, he reflects on the humble beauty of a piece of white chalk, tracing its origins to the depths of the earth and marveling at its potential to create art. One might articulate this "sacramental imagination" as what Jesus referred to as "becoming like little children" (Matt 18:3). Chesterton in *Orthodoxy* expounded on this when he wrote:

> A mere unmeaning wilderness is not even impressive. But the garden of childhood was fascinating, exactly because everything had a fixed meaning which could be found out in its turn. Inch by inch I might discover what was the object of the ugly shape called a rake; or form some shadowy conjecture as to why my parents kept a cat.[15]

Chesterton placed the family at the center of his vision of the sacred ordinary. At a time when industrialization was eroding traditional family structures, he passionately defended the home as a holy institution. "The home is not the one tame place in a world of adventure," he wrote, "it is the one wild place in a world of rules and set tasks."[16]

The family, for Chesterton, is where the sacredness of the ordinary is most profoundly experienced. The daily tasks of cooking, cleaning, and caring for one another are not burdens to be avoided but opportunities to practice love and grace. Chesterton often described the family as a training ground for virtue. It is in the home that we learn patience,

---

15. Chesterton, *Orthodoxy*, 287.
16. Chesterton, *What's Wrong with the World*, 58.

forgiveness, and self-sacrifice. Virtues that are essential for both personal growth and societal flourishing.

Chesterton also saw the family as a countercultural force in a world increasingly dominated by consumerism and individualism. While contemporary culture often treats the family as a mere social construct, Chesterton viewed it as a reflection of divine order. The bonds of love that unite parents, children, and siblings are sacred because they mirror the love of God. The family is a cell of resistance against the tyranny of the state and the marketplace. The defense of the sanctity of the family is the first line of defense in defending the sanctity of human relationships altogether.

However, in order to fully embrace the beauty and the wonders of everyday life in the world and the family, Chesterton saw a heart of gratitude as a prerequisite. In *Orthodoxy*, he wrote: "The test of all happiness is gratitude."[17] To be grateful is to acknowledge that life is a gift, not something we have earned or created for ourselves. This humility stands in stark contrast to the modern ethos of self-sufficiency and entitlement. Gratitude is the foundation of true happiness because it shifts our focus from what we lack to what we have been given.

Chesterton's own life was a testament to this philosophy. Despite facing personal challenges, including physical ailments and financial difficulties, he maintained an irrepressible joy that sprang from his deep sense of wonder and thankfulness. His writings are filled with examples of his gratitude for the simplest things: a glass of wine, a walk in the countryside, a moment of laughter with friends. He would write:

> You say grace before meal, Alright. But I say grace before the play and the opera, and grace before the concert and pantomime, and grace before I open a book, and grace before sketching, painting, swimming, fencing, boxing, walking, playing, dancing; and grace before I dip the pen in the ink.[18]

Chesterton did not shy away from the more difficult aspects of daily life. He understood that the sacredness of the ordinary includes not only its joys but also its trials. In *Orthodoxy*, he writes: "The Christian optimism is based on the fact that we do not fit in to the world."[19] For Chesterton, suffering is not meaningless; it is a means of grace. He saw

---

17. Chesterton, *Orthodoxy*, 96.
18. Catholic Quotations, "Chesterton."
19. Chesterton, *Orthodoxy*, 144.

the struggles of daily life—financial hardships, personal failures, and relational conflicts—as opportunities for growth and sanctification. These moments of difficulty, far from detracting from the sacredness of life, enhance it by drawing us closer to God. Chesterton believed that endurance is a form of worship, a way of affirming the goodness of creation even in the face of adversity.

Chesterton's reflections on the sacredness of the ordinary are a powerful antidote to modernity's disenchantment. He reminds us that the true majesty of life is not found in extraordinary experiences but in the faithful and joyful embrace of the everyday. Through his sacramental imagination, his celebration of the family, and his unwavering gratitude, Chesterton offers a vision of the world as a place where every moment is charged with divine purpose.

In a culture that often overlooks the ordinary in its pursuit of the extraordinary, Chesterton's message is both a challenge and an invitation: to see the world with new eyes, to find joy in the mundane, and to recognize the sacredness of the life we have been given. For those willing to embrace this vision, the ordinary becomes extraordinary, and the world itself becomes a sanctuary of grace.

Chesterton's Counterrevolution

As we conclude our exploration of G. K. Chesterton's life and thought, it becomes clear that his vision was nothing less than revolutionary. In a world increasingly dominated by despair, cynicism, and disenchantment, Chesterton's response was to rebel, not with anger or violence, but with joy and gratitude. His writings offer a blueprint for a counterrevolution, one that confronts modernity's bleak outlook with an unyielding affirmation of life's beauty, meaning, and purpose. For Chesterton, joy and gratitude were not mere sentiments; they were acts of defiance against the nihilism of his age.

Chesterton's view of joy was deeply rooted in the Christian faith's, celebration of life's ultimate goodness. He writes: "Man is more himself, man is more manlike, when joy is the fundamental thing in him, and grief the superficial."[20] In a culture that often equates seriousness with intellectual sophistication, Chesterton's insistence on joy is profoundly countercultural. He recognized that modernity's skepticism had drained

---

20. Chesterton, *Orthodoxy*, 294.

life of its wonder, leaving many to believe that joy was naïve or out of reach.

Joy is not the result of ideal circumstances but of a rightly ordered heart. It is not merely a private emotion; it is a public witness to the goodness of God. To live with joy in a disenchanted world is to challenge its assumptions, to testify that life is not random or meaningless but brimming with divine purpose. "The worst moment for an atheist is when he feels a profound sense of gratitude and has no one to thank." In contrast, the Christian can live with an abiding sense of gratitude, knowing that every good thing ultimately comes from God.

Gratitude, for Chesterton, is inseparable from joy. He believed that the modern world's dissatisfaction stemmed not from a lack of blessings but from a failure to appreciate them. Chesterton's gratitude was radical because it embraced not only life's pleasures but also its difficulties. He understood that even hardships have a place in the divine economy. This posture of gratitude has profound implications for how we live. It calls us to slow down, to notice the beauty that surrounds us, and to cultivate a sense of wonder in the face of even the smallest blessings. Chesterton's example invites us to move beyond entitlement and self-centeredness, embracing instead a life of humble appreciation. His words challenge us to see every moment, every meal, and every breath as an opportunity to give thanks.

Chesterton's counterrevolution did not end with his life. His ideas have inspired generations of thinkers, writers, and believers who continue to carry forward his vision of joy, gratitude, and wonder. Among his most notable admirers are C. S. Lewis and J. R. R. Tolkien, both of whom credited Chesterton with shaping their own imaginations and faith. Lewis, for example, described *The Everlasting Man* as one of the most influential books he ever read, remarking that it profoundly shaped his understanding of Christianity.[21] Tolkien, too, shared Chesterton's sacramental vision of the world, which found its expression in the richly imaginative landscapes of Middle-earth and hero hobbits. Both men carried forward Chesterton's belief that the ordinary is infused with the extraordinary and that the stories we tell reflect deeper truths about God and creation.

In more recent years, Chesterton's writings have found new audiences among those seeking a response to the disenchantment of modern

---

21. Hooper, *Collected Letters of C. S. Lewis*, 72.

life. His critique of materialism, his defense of tradition, and his celebration of the ordinary resonate with readers who long for meaning in an increasingly fragmented world. Chesterton's counterrevolution remains as relevant today as it was in his own time, offering a way forward for those who refuse to accept the despair of modernity.

As Chesterton saw it, the ultimate goal of his counterrevolution was not merely to critique modernity but to inspire a renewed vision of life. He called his readers to a life of wonder and worship, a life that acknowledges the sacredness of creation and the goodness of its Creator. "The world is a wild and startling place," he wrote, "which might have been quite different, but which is quite delightful."[22] Chesterton's call to action is both simple and profound: to live with joy, to give thanks, and to see the world through the eyes of faith. This is not an easy task in a culture that often prioritizes cynicism and self-interest. Yet his life and writings demonstrate that it is possible, and deeply rewarding, to embrace this countercultural way of being.

To live as Chesterton envisioned is to participate in a quiet but powerful revolution. It is to challenge the narrative that life is meaningless and instead proclaim that every moment, every object, and every person is charged with divine significance. It is to choose joy over despair, gratitude over entitlement, and faith over doubt. Chesterton's counterrevolution reminds us that meaning is not something to be invented; it is something to be rediscovered. The joy and gratitude he espoused are not superficial remedies but profound answers to the crisis of disenchantment. By rooting our lives in wonder and worship, he shows us how to reconnect with the eternal truths that modernity so often overlooks. His legacy is an invitation to look at the world anew, not through the lens of skepticism and self-interest but with the eyes of a child and the heart of a worshiper.

Yet Chesterton's vision, while luminous, does not stand alone. The challenge of reclaiming meaning in a disenchanted world requires not just wonder and gratitude but also a deeper understanding of how to navigate the profound mysteries of existence. Chesterton's celebration of the sacredness of the ordinary draws our attention to the gifts of creation, the bonds of family, and the joy of simple pleasures. But his vision also prepares the way for the next step: a deeper engagement with the mystery of being itself and the sacredness found in human relationships.

---

22. Chesterton, *Orthodoxy*, 103.

As we transition to the next chapter, we turn to a thinker who moves us from marveling at the world to participating in its mysteries. Gabriel Marcel, a philosopher of mystery and hope, offers a profound vision of what it means to encounter others not as objects but as sacred participants in the drama of existence. While Chesterton invites us to rediscover the wonder of creation, Marcel challenges us to embrace the mystery of relationality, hope, and fidelity. He shows us that meaning is not merely something we observe but something we participate in. A dynamic act of being that calls us into deeper relationships with others and with God.

Together, Chesterton and Marcel form a complementary vision: Chesterton inspires us to see the extraordinary in the ordinary, while Marcel invites us to explore the depths of the human experience and the mysteries of love, faith, and hope. Both thinkers challenge the fragmented and reductionist tendencies of modern life, pointing us instead toward a reality rich with sacred interconnectedness. With Chesterton's celebration of the ordinary still fresh in our minds, we now turn to Marcel's exploration of mystery and relational wholeness, delving further into what it means to live a life infused with meaning, hope, and divine encounter.

8

Gabriel Marcel

Mystery, Hope, and Relational Wholeness

"I almost think that hope is for the soul what breathing is for the living organism. Where hope is lacking, the soul dries up and withers."
—Gabriel Marcel[1]

Gabriel Marcel is a lesser-known figure than many of the other thinkers found throughout this work. For Marcel, life's deepest truths could not be reduced to equations or explained away through rational analysis. Instead, they were to be embraced, experienced, and participated in. Marcel, a French philosopher, Christian existentialist, and playwright, lived at a time when the world's focus on technical solutions and material progress often overshadowed questions of meaning and purpose. In response, he presented a vision of existence that rejected reductionism and celebrated the sacred dimensions of life.

Marcel critiqued the modern tendency to approach all parts of life as a set of problems to be solved. While problem-solving has its place in the practical aspects of existence, he argued that treating mysteries like love, faith, and being as such only leads to alienation and despair. Marcel defines problems as those things that are external and solvable, while

---

1. Marcel, *Homo Viator*, 11.

mysteries are those things that are participatory and inexhaustible. Mysteries, he insisted, cannot be understood from a distance; they invite us into a relationship that changes both the participant and the mystery itself.

Marcel's philosophy also addressed the growing fragmentation and isolation of modern life. In an age of individualism, he reminded us that true meaning arises not from detached analysis but from relational wholeness. To encounter another person is to engage with a sacred mystery, one that reflects the divine. This emphasis on relationality is central to Marcel's response to the meaning crisis, offering a vision of human connection that counters the loneliness and objectification of the modern world.

Finally, Marcel called for the recovery of hope and fidelity as practices of meaning. Hope, for Marcel, is not mere optimism about the future but a profound trust in the unseen and the eternal. Fidelity, meanwhile, is the commitment to remain engaged with life's mysteries even when answers seem elusive. Hope and fidelity offer a path forward for those seeking meaning in a fragmented and disenchanted world.

As we turn from Chesterton's celebration of the ordinary to Marcel's philosophy of mystery and hope, we take another step in the journey toward reclaiming meaning in a fragmented world. While Chesterton focused on finding the divine in creation, Marcel pushed us to see life itself as an unfathomable mystery in which we are called to participate, not merely observe. Let us now enter Marcel's vision of a life deeply lived, charged with mystery, and rooted in the sacred.

Problems vs. Mysteries

Gabriel Marcel diagnosed the modern age as one beset by a reductionist impulse, which is the tendency to treat every aspect of life as a problem to be solved. This impulse, born out of the Enlightenment and accelerated by technological and industrial revolutions, prioritizes analysis, control, and functionality at the expense of depth, meaning, and relationality. Marcel argued that this approach to life leads to a profound alienation, as it strips existence of its sacred and participatory dimensions.

Marcel observed that modernity often conflates problems and mysteries, treating both as if they were objects of intellectual mastery. This, he argued, is a fundamental error. In his work *The Mystery of Being*, he writes:

> A problem is something that I find and see fully before me, and therefore can control and reduce, can define with a technique.

> But a mystery is something in which I myself am involved, and which transcends all conceivable technique—leading to action based on an intuition I did not know I possessed.[2]

For Marcel, modernity's failure lies in its inability to see life's greatest questions—love, faith, and existence—as mysteries. When we approach these realities as problems to be solved, we reduce them to abstractions. Love becomes a matter of compatibility; faith is reduced to doctrine or ritual; existence itself is treated as a series of measurable milestones. This reductionistic approach dehumanizes and ultimately alienates us from the very truths that give life meaning. Marcel was, in many ways, building on the ideas of Søren Kierkegaard, another Christian existentialist, who similarly critiqued the tendency to prioritize objectivity over subjectivity. Kierkegaard emphasized that truth is not merely something to be understood but something to be lived, which is echoed in Marcel's belief that mysteries require personal involvement.

Marcel's distinction between problems and mysteries is one of his most significant contributions to philosophy. Marcel often used the example of death to illustrate this distinction. When approached as a problem, death becomes an event to be studied—its biological processes cataloged, its inevitability quantified. But when experienced as a mystery, death challenges us to confront our own finitude, the meaning of life, and the hope of what lies beyond. A mystery is not something that can be entirely resolved; it is something that is constantly revealing itself, something that is both accessible and inexhaustible. This understanding of mystery aligns with Marcel's belief that certain truths, such as the nature of God or the resurrection, are not problems to be dissected but mysteries to be embraced in faith. Marcel's philosophy thus resonates deeply with Christian theology, offering a framework for navigating life's deepest questions without reducing them to mere puzzles.

A key consequence of treating mysteries as problems is the objectification of human beings and relationships. Marcel critiqued the modern tendency to treat others as "things" rather than persons, reducing relationships to transactions or functions. The man who sees others as objects to be manipulated is himself diminished, for he loses sight of their sacred worth.

This objectification is evident in various aspects of modern life, from the commodification of relationships in dating apps to the dehumanization of labor in industrial systems. When people are treated as problems

---

2. Marcel, *Mystery of Being*, 211.

to be managed or resources to be optimized, the richness of human connection is lost. Marcel argued that this objectifying gaze not only harms those it is directed toward but also impoverishes the one who employs it. The consequences of this mindset are not limited to interpersonal relationships. Marcel believed that the objectification of mysteries leads to a broader cultural disenchantment, in which meaning is replaced by efficiency and depth is sacrificed for convenience.[3] This crisis, he argued, can only be remedied by reclaiming a sense of mystery. A recognition that not all aspects of life can or should be mastered.

This requires a shift from control to openness, from detachment to involvement. Mysteries are not meant to be solved; they are meant to be lived, explored, and continually revisited. This participation in the mystery involves a fundamental humility, a willingness to acknowledge that some truths transcend human understanding. This humility is not a weakness but a strength, as it opens us to deeper experiences of love, faith, and meaning. Marcel's emphasis on participation also serves as a critique of the modern obsession with certainty, reminding us that ambiguity and uncertainty are not barriers to meaning but pathways to it.

By reclaiming the participatory nature of mystery, he challenges us to move beyond the detached analysis of life's deepest questions and to engage with them in a way that transforms both ourselves and the mysteries we encounter. This foundational understanding sets the stage for Marcel's exploration of relationality in the next section, where he delves into the sacred nature of human connection and the role of love in restoring meaning to a fragmented world.

Being and Relational Wholeness

Marcel's philosophy begins with a foundational assertion: human existence is inherently relational. He would write, "I am constituted by my relations with others. It is the 'we' which creates the 'I.'"[4] He viewed the modern world's increasing focus on individualism as a dangerous misstep, one that isolates people from one another and from the deeper mysteries of life. For Marcel, to be fully human is to live in connection with others, with oneself, and ultimately with the divine. Relationality, he believed, is not an optional or secondary aspect of existence but its very essence.

---

3. Marcel, *Mystery of Being*, 185.
4. Marcel, *Philosophy of Gabriel Marcel*, 28.

Modernity often promotes the idea of the autonomous individual, a self-contained being whose value is determined by personal achievements or possessions. Marcel rejected this notion outright, arguing that the self cannot exist meaningfully apart from relationships. In other words, I am not only who I am but who I am in relation to others. Marcel emphasized that human identity is formed and fulfilled through interaction, through the recognition of others as subjects rather than objects. In his concept of "availability," which he referred to as "*disponsibilité*," Marcel articulated what it means to live relationally.[5] Availability is a willingness to be fully present to others and to open oneself to their needs, joys, and struggles. As one Marcel scholar describes it, "The disponible person is hospitable to others; the doors of his soul are ajar."[6] It stands in stark contrast to the detached, distracted tendencies of modern life. Marcel warned against the dangers of where relationships are reduced to transactions or utility, stripping them of their sacred depth. Instead, availability calls us to approach others with reverence, seeing them as mysteries to be encountered rather than problems to be managed.

Both Marcel and the Christian tradition affirm that love requires presence, attention, and sacrifice. Yet Marcel's philosophy also challenges us to consider how modern distractions, such as the overuse of technology, might inhibit our ability to be truly available to one another. His insights anticipate concerns raised by contemporary thinkers like Sherry Turkle, whose work on the alienating effects of digital communication echoes Marcel's critique of functionalized relationships. Turkle, using extensive interviews and half a lifetime of research, suggests with reference to the birth of the environmental movement in the 1960s that we are at a "Silent Spring" moment in our infatuation with life on screens rather than life in the real world, never wholly in one or the other.[7]

For Marcel, every encounter with another person is an encounter with a sacred mystery. In relationships, we are confronted with the reality of another being who is both familiar and unknowable. This interplay between proximity and mystery, Marcel argued, is where relational meaning is found. He famously wrote, "To love someone is to say to them: You will never die."[8] This statement reflects his belief that love affirms the eternal significance of the other person, recognizing their value as more

---

5. Marcel, *Mystery of Being*, 163.
6. Gallagher, *Philosophy of Gabriel Marcel*, 26.
7. Turkle, *Reclaiming Conversation*, 4.
8. Marcel, *Homo Viator*, 147.

than mere flesh and function. Marcel's vision of relationality challenges people to move beyond surface-level interactions and to embrace the vulnerability and depth required to truly know and love others.

Marcel's understanding of love transcends the emotional or romantic; it is fundamentally participatory and spiritual. To love, in Marcel's view, is to partake in something eternal, something that points beyond the immediate relationship to a transcendent reality. It involves a willingness to embrace the mystery of the other person without attempting to control or fully comprehend them. This stands in contrast to the modern tendency to define relationships in terms of compatibility, predictability, or convenience. True love, Marcel argued, requires faith in the unseen and the unknowable, trusting that the relationship itself is part of a larger, divine mystery.

This idea connects with Chesterton's vision of the sacredness of the ordinary. Just as Chesterton found holiness in the simple, Marcel found the divine in the depths of human relationships. Both thinkers challenge modern assumptions about where meaning is found, urging us to seek it not in grand gestures but in the faithful, day-to-day encounters that shape our lives.

While Marcel celebrated the sacredness of relationality, he was deeply aware of the barriers that modern life places between individuals and the higher cases of relational isolation it creates. He critiqued the alienation caused by consumerism, industrialization, and technology, arguing that these forces prioritize efficiency over connection. One of Marcel's most compelling critiques of isolation is found in his work *Creative Fidelity*. There, he explores how the breakdown of trust and commitment in modern relationships leads to a sense of existential loneliness. Fidelity, for Marcel, is the antidote to this fragmentation. It is the act of remaining present and committed to another person, even when challenges arise. He writes, "The fact is that when I commit myself, I grant in principle that the commitment will not again be put in question."[9] In a world that often prioritizes convenience over commitment, Marcel's emphasis on fidelity calls us to a deeper, more intentional way of living.

A philosophy of relational wholeness offers a powerful response to the modern meaning crisis. By emphasizing availability, sacred encounter, and fidelity, Marcel challenges the isolation and superficiality that characterize much of contemporary life. His insistence that relationships

---

9. Marcel, *Creative Fidelity*, 162.

are sacred mysteries invites us to see others not as objects to be used but as subjects to be loved.

Marcel's vision is deeply countercultural, calling us to resist the forces of functionalization and disposability and to embrace the vulnerability and beauty of true relationality. In doing so, he offers not only a critique of modernity but also a hopeful path forward, a path where meaning is found not solely in individual achievement but in the sacred connections that bind us to one another and to God. This relational vision lays the foundation for Marcel's broader response to modern despair: hope and fidelity.

Hope and Fidelity—The Practices of Meaning

If mysteries invite us into participation and relationality binds us to the sacredness of others, Gabriel Marcel believed that it is hope and fidelity that empower us to live meaningfully within these realities. For Marcel, hope and fidelity are not abstract virtues but dynamic, lived practices, disciplines of the heart and soul that sustain us in a world that often feels fragmented, alienating, and despairing. These practices transcend mere optimism or duty; they are acts of spiritual courage grounded in a trust that meaning can be found even when it is not fully seen or understood.

Marcel distinguished between hope, which is rooted in the unseen, and optimism, which depends on favorable circumstances. Hope is thus an act of faith that rises above the tangible, trusting in a reality beyond what we can immediately perceive. In *Homo Viator*, he writes: "I almost think that hope is for the soul what breathing is for the living."[10]

Marcel's hope is not naïve; it acknowledges the presence of suffering, uncertainty, and loss. Yet it refuses to let these realities define the human experience. Instead, hope draws its strength from a sense of transcendence. A belief that existence is not self-contained but oriented toward something greater. This aligns closely with Christian existentialist ideals, particularly those of Kierkegaard, who described hope as a "passion for the possible."[11] Both thinkers see hope as essential for navigating life's trials, not by erasing them but by transforming how we endure them. This echoes the Christian concept of faithfulness, particularly as described in the book of Hebrews: "Now faith is the assurance of things hoped for, the conviction of things not seen" (Heb 11:1).

---

10. Marcel, *Homo Viator*, 10.
11. Kierkegaard, *Fear and Trembling*, 171–72.

As noted earlier, hope is not just an individual virtue for Marcel; it has a profoundly relational dimension. To hope is to trust that our relationships with others and with God are meaningful and enduring, even in the face of betrayal or suffering. This relational hope counters the isolation and despair that often accompany modernity's fragmented view of existence.

Marcel's philosophy of hope and fidelity finds its fullest expression in the context of Christian faith. While his existentialism is deeply personal, it is also profoundly theocentric. For Marcel, hope and fidelity are not abstract virtues; they are rooted in the presence of God, who is both the source and the fulfillment of meaning. In *Homo Viator*, he writes: "Hope is only possible on the level of the us, or we might say of the agape, and that it does not exist on the level of the solitary ego, self-hypnotized and concentrating exclusively on individual aims."[12]

This hope is grounded in the Christian narrative of redemption, where meaning is not merely constructed by the individual but revealed by God. Fidelity, likewise, reflects God's own nature. Just as God remains faithful to his promises, so too are we called to remain faithful to the mysteries of life, trusting that they will lead us closer to him. Marcel's philosophy resonates with the biblical understanding of covenant, where faithfulness is both a divine attribute and a human responsibility.

Marcel's emphasis on hope and fidelity also provides a practical response to the modern meaning crisis. In a world characterized by uncertainty and transience, these practices offer stability and purpose. They remind us that meaning is not always immediately apparent but must often be pursued with patience and trust. For Marcel, this pursuit is not a burden but a joy, as it draws us into deeper communion with others and with God.

The ultimate power of hope and fidelity lies in its orientation toward transcendence. Marcel believed that life's mysteries point beyond themselves to a greater reality, a divine presence that undergirds all of existence. To hope and to remain faithful is to participate in this transcendent order, trusting that meaning is not something we create but something we receive. This vision of transcendence is profoundly redemptive. It transforms suffering into an opportunity for growth, isolation into a call to community, and despair into a pathway toward hope. Marcel's philosophy invites us to see life not as a series of disconnected

---

12. Marcel, *Homo Viator*, 10.

events but as a coherent narrative, where even the darkest moments have purpose and meaning.

By anchoring us in transcendence and calling us to remain engaged with life's mysteries, they offer a path toward meaning that is both deeply personal and inherently relational. Marcel challenges us to move beyond the fleeting comforts of optimism and the shallow commitments of convenience, inviting us instead to embrace the beauty of endurance, trust, and relational presence. These virtues—hope and fidelity—are not merely individual practices but communal ones. They call us into deeper relationships with God and others, reminding us that meaning is not something we achieve alone.

Mystery, Hope, and Relational Wholeness

Marcel's philosophy stands as a beacon in a world often overwhelmed by fragmentation, alienation, and despair. His invitation to engage with life as mystery, to encounter others as sacred, and to live in hope and fidelity calls us to transcend the reductionist tendencies of modernity. Marcel does not offer easy answers or quick solutions; instead, he provides a framework for living deeply, embracing the tensions and uncertainties that make life meaningful.

At the heart of Marcel's thought is the conviction that life cannot be controlled or fully understood; it must be lived. Mysteries, unlike problems, do not yield to mastery; they demand humility and participation. By reclaiming this participatory view of existence, Marcel reawakens our capacity for wonder, reminding us that the search for meaning is not a task to be completed but a journey to be undertaken. This journey unfolds not in isolation but in relationship. A relationship with others, with the world, and with God.

Marcel's ideals of hope and fidelity are particularly poignant in addressing the meaning crisis of the modern world. Hope is not passive or blind; it is an active trust in the unseen, an affirmation that there is more to life than what can be immediately grasped. Fidelity, similarly, is not a mere adherence to duty but a profound act of staying present, of refusing to abandon the search for meaning even when it seems elusive. These virtues empower us to live courageously in the face of uncertainty, grounding us in the transcendent while calling us to engage with the immanent.

The beauty of Marcel's vision lies in its relational depth. To live meaningfully, he teaches, is to be available to others, to see in them the reflection of the divine. It is to embrace the sacredness of every encounter, knowing that love, hope, and fidelity are not merely human endeavors but echoes of eternal truths. This understanding transforms the mundane into the miraculous, the fleeting into the eternal, and the broken into the beautiful.

Marcel's thought also carries a profound ethical dimension. In an age of increasing objectification and commodification, his insistence on the sacredness of relationality serves as a prophetic critique of modernity's dehumanizing tendencies. By calling us to see others not as objects to be used but as mysteries to be revered, Marcel invites us into a way of life that honors the image of God in every person. His philosophy not only challenges us to think differently but also to live differently. To cultivate practices of presence, gratitude, and trust that restore meaning to a fragmented world.

As we conclude this chapter, it is clear that Marcel's vision is both deeply rooted in the Christian tradition and strikingly relevant to the challenges of the present age. His work reminds us that meaning is not something we achieve through control or calculation; it is something we receive through openness and participation. It is found in the spaces where mystery and relationality intersect, where hope and fidelity take root, and where the presence of God quietly but profoundly transforms the ordinary into the extraordinary.

In turning to Reinhold Niebuhr in the next chapter, we step from Marcel's celebration of relational and participatory meaning into a more explicit confrontation with the realities of history and power. Where Marcel illuminates the sacredness of mystery and the practices of hope, Niebuhr challenges us to grapple with the complexities of human fallibility, societal sin, and moral responsibility. Together, these thinkers offer complementary visions of what it means to live meaningfully in a broken but deeply sacred world. Marcel has called us to embrace mystery and relationality; Niebuhr will now call us to confront history and engage the tension between faith and the realities of life in a fallen world. In doing so, both lead us further into the quest for meaning that lies at the heart of this journey.

9

Reinhold Niebuhr
Christian Realism and Moral Responsibility

"In religion all the higher moral obligations, which are lost in abstractions on the historic level, are felt as obligations toward the supreme person. Thus both the personality and the holiness of God provide the religious man with reinforcement of his moral will and a restraint upon his will-to-power."
—REINHOLD NIEBUHR[1]

AS THE SHADOWS OF World War II receded and the Cold War loomed over the horizon, America found itself in a precarious cultural and moral position. The confidence born of victory, economic growth, and technological progress ran parallel with a growing anxiety about the nature of humanity, the potential for global catastrophe, and the integrity of American ideals. Reinhold Niebuhr emerged during this period as one of the most perceptive and influential voices grappling with the crisis of modernity in the American context. He saw the allure of optimism that promised a straightforward march toward progress and the reality of a human condition fraught with complexity and moral contradiction.

Niebuhr was no stranger to the American inclination toward triumphalism. Yet he resisted the narrative that humanity's destiny could

---

1. Niebuhr, *Moral Man and Immoral Society*, 54.

be shaped solely by its ingenuity or moral virtue. He exposed the tension between the lofty ideals proclaimed by societies and the self-interest lurking behind their actions. For Niebuhr, history was marked by paradox: humanity's capacity for extraordinary creativity and self-transcendence was matched only by its propensity for selfishness and destruction. His seminal works, including *Moral Man and Immoral Society* and *The Irony of American History*, reflect a theology that sought to confront this paradox head-on, providing a framework for understanding the role of faith in the messy and often tragic realities of history.

At the core of Niebuhr's thought is a sharp critique of both liberal optimism and fundamentalist simplicity. He challenged the utopianism that naively trusted in human progress and the rigid dogmatism that refused to engage with the complexities of the modern world. Instead, Niebuhr offered a vision of *Christian realism*, a theological approach that acknowledges the depth of human sin while affirming the hope of divine redemption. He wrote, "Man's capacity for justice makes democracy possible, but man's inclination to injustice makes democracy necessary."[2] This dual recognition of human potential and human fallibility became the cornerstone of his philosophy, a guiding principle for navigating the tensions of history and morality.

Niebuhr's insights remain strikingly relevant in our own time. The crises of the twentieth century that shaped his theology—economic inequality, political polarization, the specter of war—are still with us today. His work offers a sobering yet hopeful perspective, calling us to grapple with the reality of sin, the complexity of power, and the necessity of moral responsibility. This chapter explores Niebuhr's response to the meaning crisis of modernity, tracing the contours of his Christian realism and its implications for faith, politics, and ethics. We will examine his critique of idealism, his analysis of sin and power in history, and his theology of hope and redemption. Niebuhr's vision does not flinch from the brokenness of the world; instead, it offers a way to engage with it faithfully and responsibly.

Niebuhr's Background and the Birth of Christian Realism

Born in 1892 in Wright City, Missouri, Reinhold Niebuhr was deeply shaped by his upbringing in a devout German immigrant family. His

---

2. Niebuhr, *Children of Light and the Children of Darkness*, xi.

father, Gustav Niebuhr, was a pastor in the Evangelical Synod of North America, a context that instilled in Niebuhr a lifelong commitment to the integration of faith and moral action. These early experiences profoundly influenced his later theological reflections, particularly his insistence that genuine faith must manifest itself in ethical responsibility and engagement with social issues.

Niebuhr pursued his theological education first at Elmhurst College and Eden Theological Seminary, institutions associated with the German Evangelical Synod, before completing his studies at Yale Divinity School. At Yale, Niebuhr encountered liberal Protestant theology, which emphasized human progress, moral uplift, and social reform. Initially drawn to this optimistic framework, Niebuhr admired theologians like Albrecht Ritschl and Adolf von Harnack, who viewed Christianity primarily as a moral and ethical force capable of improving society through reason and collective effort.

However, Niebuhr's early optimism was soon challenged during his pastoral tenure in Detroit, Michigan, from 1915 to 1928. The harsh realities of industrial capitalism and the stark economic disparities he witnessed in Detroit deeply undermined his faith in the liberal Protestant ideal of continual human progress. Niebuhr observed firsthand the exploitation of factory workers, unsafe working conditions, and rampant inequality, which stood in sharp contrast to liberal theology's utopian aspirations.

As Niebuhr engaged with these social realities, he grew increasingly critical of the prevailing idealism and the belief that rationality and moral goodwill could eradicate social evils. He contended that such optimism grossly underestimated the depth and persistence of human sin. In *Moral Man and Immoral Society*, he articulated this skepticism: "Individuals have a moral code which makes the actions of collective man an outrage to their conscience. They therefore invent romantic and moral interpretations of the real facts, preferring to obscure rather than reveal the true character of their collective behavior."[3] He argued that while individuals might demonstrate moral restraint, groups driven by collective interests frequently fail to act ethically.

Niebuhr's critique extended to utopian visions that sought to create perfect societies through social reform. He recognized the significance of striving toward justice but emphasized the futility and danger inherent in utopianism. In other words, the tragedy of man is that he can conceive

---

3. Niebuhr, *Moral Man and Immoral Society*, 9.

self-transcending ideals but cannot achieve them. Niebuhr warned that utopian dreams ignore the corrupting potential of power and the persistent reality of human imperfection.

His skepticism toward idealism also informed his views on pacifism, particularly evident during the rise of Nazi Germany. While respecting pacifists' moral convictions, Niebuhr believed that moral persuasion alone was insufficient against aggressive evil. He saw pacifism as another instance where idealistic principles failed to grapple realistically with human depravity and power dynamics. This perspective led Niebuhr to support military intervention during World War II, affirming that moral responsibility sometimes necessitates the use of force to resist injustice.

Rejecting both idealism and cynicism, Niebuhr developed what has been termed "Christian realism," a theological stance acknowledging human sinfulness yet affirming the redemptive possibilities through divine grace. Christian realism calls for humility in recognizing human limits while persistently pursuing justice. This framework insists on "proximate justice," the concept that while ultimate justice belongs to God alone, humanity remains responsible for working toward achievable justice within its flawed historical conditions.[4]

Niebuhr's Christian realism also informed his critique of American exceptionalism. In "The Irony of American History," he cautioned, "The pretensions of virtue are as offensive to God as the pretensions of power," highlighting how nations, including the United States, often rationalize questionable actions under virtuous guises.[5] His insights remain deeply relevant, resonating with contemporary geopolitical discourse and individual ethical dilemmas alike, offering guidance to those who navigate complex moral landscapes with an awareness of human limitations and reliance on divine grace.

The Nature of Sin and Power in History

At the heart of Niebuhr's Christian realism is a foundational understanding of sin as a universal and inescapable reality, shaping both personal lives and the structures of society. Niebuhr saw sin not as an abstract theological concept but as a lived and observable force that influences every human endeavor. While sin is often viewed in individual terms,

---

4. Niebuhr, *Moral Man and Immoral Society*, 118.
5. Niebuhr, *Irony of American History*, 160.

Niebuhr's insights broaden its scope, illustrating how sin operates collectively and is magnified in systems of power. In this way, Niebuhr provides a critical lens for understanding the paradoxical nature of history: humanity's ability to achieve remarkable progress while simultaneously perpetuating injustice and suffering.

Niebuhr's doctrine of sin draws heavily from Augustine of Hippo's understanding of original sin and human fallibility. For Niebuhr, sin is not merely a series of moral failings but a condition of estrangement: alienation from God, others, and even ourselves. This alienation is rooted in pride, or the human tendency to place oneself at the center of existence. In *The Nature and Destiny of Man*, Niebuhr writes, "The pretension that they are not is, in the view of Christian faith, one of the primary proofs of the sinfulness of the human spirit which, in its pride, claims unconditioned validity for its systems of logical coherence and rational unities."[6]

Niebuhr viewed pride as the root of all sin, leading humanity to overreach its limits in a misguided quest for control and self-justification. This pride is evident in everything from personal ambition to nationalistic fervor. Yet Niebuhr also recognized sin's subtler forms, such as complacency and sloth, which prevent individuals and communities from addressing injustice. A reflection on Niebuhr's view of sin might consider the ways in which pride manifests in everyday life. For example, a person striving for professional success might unintentionally harm relationships or neglect ethical considerations in pursuit of their goals. Niebuhr's insights challenge us to examine these tendencies critically, acknowledging both their destructiveness and their pervasiveness.

Niebuhr pointed to systemic inequalities as evidence of collective sin. Historical examples of economic exploitation, political corruption, and human injustices are not simply the result of personal failings but the cumulative effect of self-interest embedded within social structures. This understanding anticipates later discussions of systemic sin in liberation theology and civil rights movements. For instance, Niebuhr's critique of collective sin resonated with the reflections of Martin Luther King Jr., who, in *Letter from Birmingham Jail*, described segregation as a systemic injustice requiring not just personal repentance but structural change. King, deeply influenced by Niebuhr, shared his conviction that social reform must address the broader dynamics of power and sin embedded in institutions. King would write, "History is the long and tragic story of

---

6. Niebuhr, *Nature and Destiny of Man*, 30.

the fact that privileged groups seldom give up their privileges voluntarily. Individuals may see the moral light and voluntarily give up their unjust posture, but, as Reinhold Niebuhr has reminded us, groups are more immoral than individuals."[7]

Niebuhr's exploration of power lies at the heart of his Christian realism. He acknowledged that power is necessary for maintaining order and achieving justice, yet he warned that it is inherently corrupting. His reflections on power are particularly relevant in the context of geopolitics. In *The Irony of American History*, he warns that the United States, despite its democratic ideals, is not immune to the temptations of empire. Niebuhr saw the tendency of nations to justify their actions, however unjust, by appealing to their moral superiority.[8] His insights help us see how power, even when used for seemingly noble purposes, often carries unintended consequences. This applies not only to nations but also to smaller-scale power dynamics, such as those within organizations or communities. A connection can be made here with George Orwell's *Animal Farm*, which demonstrates how power, once obtained, often corrupts even the most idealistic movements. Like Orwell, Niebuhr recognized that the pursuit of power, however justified, requires constant vigilance against the lure of self-interest and domination.

One of Niebuhr's most profound insights is the paradox of progress: the idea that human achievements often carry the seeds of their own destruction. Technological advancements, for example, can improve life while simultaneously creating new dangers. The invention of nuclear weapons exemplifies this paradox. While they may deter conflict, they also threaten humanity with unprecedented devastation. He writes, "Our dreams of a pure virtue are dissolved in a situation in which it is possible to exercise the virtue of responsibility toward a community of nations only by courting the prospective guilt of the atomic bomb."[9]

Man has always been his own worst enemy because his most impressive achievements are so often transformed into instruments of his own undoing. This paradox reflects the tension between human creativity and human sinfulness. Progress, while valuable, is never an unqualified good; it must be tempered by humility and moral responsibility. For example, technological conveniences often come at the cost of deeper human connection, as seen in the overuse of smartphones and social media.

7. King, "Letter from Birmingham Jail," 2.
8. Niebuhr, *Irony of American History*, 42.
9. Niebuhr, *Irony of American History*, 2.

Niebuhr's analysis reminds us that progress is not inherently virtuous and must always be evaluated in light of its broader implications.

For Niebuhr, the persistence of sin means that no human system of justice can fully eradicate injustice. Even the most well-intentioned efforts are tainted by partiality and self-interest. This does not absolve us of the responsibility to pursue justice, but it requires us to do so with humility. Justice is a balance of power between rival forces within a community. It is never absolute and always relative when levied by men.

Hope in Divine Redemption

Niebuhr's Christian realism, while grounded in a sobering view of human sin and power, does not end in despair. Instead, it points toward a profound hope rooted in God's redemptive work in history. For Niebuhr, hope is not abstract optimism but a theological virtue, a trust in God's unseen and ultimate purposes. It is this hope that enables individuals and communities to engage meaningfully with a broken world, embracing the tension between the realities of sin and the promises of redemption.

Niebuhr believed that humanity's greatest need is for divine grace, which alone can address the depth of human sinfulness. While human efforts at justice and progress are necessary, they are inevitably flawed by pride and self-interest. In *The Nature and Destiny of Man*, Niebuhr concludes that the only final hope for man is to live in relation to God which transcends all these relativities of time and place and nation and race.[10] This relationship with God, rooted in grace, provides the foundation for meaningful action in history.

Niebuhr's theology of grace is deeply personal yet profoundly social. Grace does not absolve humanity of responsibility; rather, it empowers individuals and communities to pursue justice and reconciliation in the face of imperfection. A helpful analogy is the relationship between a mentor and a struggling student. The mentor's grace, offering guidance without condemnation, motivates the student to strive for improvement, even when progress feels slow or incomplete. Similarly, divine grace inspires and sustains human efforts toward goodness, even in a world marred by sin. This emphasis on grace finds resonance with the works of Flannery O'Connor, whose fiction often portrays grace as a disruptive but transformative force. Like Niebuhr, O'Connor understood that

---

10. Niebuhr, *Nature and Destiny of Man*, 294–97.

grace does not negate human brokenness but works through it, revealing glimpses of redemption amid the chaos of life.

Central to Niebuhr's theology of hope is the eschatological tension between the "already" and the "not yet." God's kingdom has already broken into history through the life, death, and resurrection of Christ, but its fullness has not yet been realized. This tension shapes the Christian's engagement with the world, calling for active participation in God's work while acknowledging that ultimate redemption lies beyond human achievement. History is not meaningless because it is not self-sufficient. Its meaning is fulfilled only in the divine purposes which transcend it. This perspective allows Christians to confront the brokenness of history without succumbing to despair. It affirms that while the world's injustices may persist, they are not the final word.

Martin Luther King Jr's "I Have a Dream" speech embodies the tension of the already and the not yet: the vision of racial equality is grounded in the biblical promise of justice, but its full realization requires persistent struggle in the present. As he declared:

> The marvelous new militancy which has engulfed the Negro community must not lead us to distrust all white people, for many of our white brothers, as evidenced by their presence here today, have come to realize that their destiny is tied up with our destiny. No, no, we are not satisfied, and we will not be satisfied until justice rolls down like waters and righteousness like a mighty stream.[11]

Niebuhr's theology provides the framework for this kind of hope, which is active yet humble, grounded in God's sovereignty rather than human efforts alone. Hope calls for faithful action in the face of imperfection. Christians are not absolved from the responsibility to work for justice and peace, even though their efforts will always fall short of perfection. In *The Irony of American History*, he wrote, "We must be saved by the final form of love which is forgiveness, and yet there is no salvation without justice."[12] This dual emphasis on love and justice reflects Niebuhr's conviction that faith must engage with the world's complexities. Niebuhr's perspective resonates with Dietrich Bonhoeffer's concept of "costly grace," similarly emphasizing the need for sacrificial action in the pursuit of justice. Both thinkers reject the idea that grace allows

11. King Jr., "I Have a Dream."
12. Niebuhr, *Irony of American History*, 63.

Christians to retreat from the world; instead, grace demands engagement with the suffering and brokenness of others.

In a world often dominated by cynicism and disillusionment, Niebuhr's theology offers a powerful counternarrative. Hope, he argued, is an act of resistance against the despair that comes from recognizing humanity's limitations. It is a declaration that, despite sin's pervasive influence, God's purposes will ultimately prevail. Niebuhr writes, "Nothing worth doing is completed in our lifetime; therefore, we are saved by hope."[13] This "saving hope" is a moral force rooted not in the likelihood of success but in the conviction that something is worth doing regardless of the outcome. It is a sustaining virtue, empowering individuals to act with courage and integrity even when results are uncertain.

Niebuhr believed that the church plays a critical role in fostering and sustaining hope. As a community of faith, the church bears witness to God's redemptive work in history, offering a vision of justice and reconciliation that transcends human limitations. At the same time, Niebuhr was keenly aware of the church's imperfections. He critiqued both liberal Christianity, which often diluted the gospel's radical message, and fundamentalist Christianity, which withdrew from the world's complexities. The church, Niebuhr argued, must embrace its prophetic role, challenging injustice while embodying the hope of God's kingdom. Niebuhr's theology of hope and redemption offers a profound response to the brokenness of history. By grounding hope in God's sovereignty and eschatological purposes, he provides a framework for faithful action that resists both cynicism and utopianism. This hope is not a passive waiting but an active participation in God's work, sustained by grace and oriented toward a future that transcends human limitations.

Niebuhr's Response to the Meaning Crisis

Reinhold Niebuhr understood that modernity, for all its promises of progress and liberation, had left humanity with a profound void born out of disillusionment with the grand ideals of reason, scientific advancement, and material prosperity. The twentieth century, marked by global conflict, economic turmoil, and existential despair, exposed the inadequacies of these ideals to address the deepest questions of human existence. Niebuhr's response to this crisis was both theological and

---

13. Niebuhr, *Irony of American History*, 63.

existential, offering an alternative vision rooted in the Christian understanding of sin, redemption, and grace.

At the heart of Niebuhr's response to the meaning crisis was the Christian narrative of the cross. For Niebuhr, the cross of Christ was the ultimate symbol of both human brokenness and divine love. He saw it as the axis upon which human history turns. A paradoxical event that exposes humanity's sin while also revealing God's redemptive purposes. Niebuhr wrote in *Christ and Culture*, "Through his cross and resurrection, he [Christ] redeemed them from their prison of self-centeredness."[14] The cross dismantles the illusions of human greatness, showing that even the best among us are capable of complicity in violence and oppression. At the same time, it offers a transformative vision of grace, demonstrating that God's love enters into the depths of human suffering to bring reconciliation and hope.

This understanding of the cross resonates deeply with Fyodor Dostoevsky's reflections in *The Brothers Karamazov*. Like Niebuhr, Dostoevsky saw the suffering and sacrifice embodied in Christ as the only response to the paradoxes of human existence. Both figures understood that meaning is not found in escaping suffering but in confronting it with faith, hope, and sacrificial love.

Niebuhr's critique of modernity often focused on its tendency to place ultimate hope in finite things—whether technological advancements, political ideologies, or human ingenuity. He referred to this as idolatry, the elevation of created things to the status of ultimate meaning. Such misplaced hopes inevitably lead to disappointment and despair, as they cannot bear the weight of humanity's deepest longings.

Niebuhr believed that the modern emphasis on individual autonomy had deepened the meaning crisis, isolating people from the relational contexts in which true meaning is found. He argued that humanity is inherently social, created for relationships with God and with others. That we find our highest meaning not in what we achieve alone but in the grace we experience together. It is through grace that individuals recognize their own limitations and the need for forgiveness, creating the conditions for genuine community. This relational vision stands in contrast to modernity's ideal of the self-sufficient individual, offering instead a picture of humanity as interdependent and bound by shared moral responsibility.

---

14. Niebuhr, *Christ and Culture*, 161.

For Niebuhr, the ultimate meaning of history is not found in human achievements or progress but in the redemptive work of God. This perspective allows individuals to engage with the world's brokenness without being overwhelmed by it, trusting that God's sovereignty ultimately governs even the most chaotic moments of history. Niebuhr's understanding of hope as a theological virtue offers a powerful counternarrative to modern nihilism. Where modernity placed its faith in progress and found itself disillusioned, Niebuhr pointed to a deeper source of meaning, a hope grounded not in human success but in the unchanging character of God.

Niebuhr's theology does not call for withdrawal from the world but for faithful engagement with its challenges. He acknowledged that the pursuit of justice would always be imperfect, marred by human sin and frailty. Yet he argued that this imperfection does not absolve individuals or communities from responsibility or the need for said justice. He writes regarding this, "Christian faith sees in the Cross of Christ the assurance that judgment is not the final word of God to man; but it does not regard the mercy of God as a forgiveness which wipes out the distinctions of good and evil in history and makes judgment meaningless."[15]

Niebuhr's response to modernity's unraveling of meaning was both deeply theological and profoundly practical. He addressed the intellectual disillusionment of his time by offering a vision of humanity that takes seriously both its grandeur and its fallenness. He confronted existential despair with the hope of the cross, which speaks to the reality of suffering while pointing to the possibility of redemption. And he called for a recovery of grace and community, recognizing that true meaning is found in relationship both with God and with others.

Niebuhr's vision offers a powerful counternarrative to the meaning crisis, reminding us that meaning is not dependent on human achievement but on God's unchanging love and grace. In a fragmented and alienated world, Niebuhr's call to Christian Realism and moral responsibility provides a path toward hope and purpose, challenging us to embrace the paradoxes of history with faith and courage. As we transition to Viktor Frankl in the next chapter, we turn from Niebuhr's engagement with collective sin and historical paradoxes to Frankl's exploration of individual suffering and the search for meaning in the darkest of circumstances.

---

15. Niebuhr, *Nature and Destiny of Man*, 152–53.

10

Viktor Frankl

The Will to Meaning

> *"Life's meaning is an unconditional one, for it even includes the potential meaning of suffering."*
>
> —Viktor Frankl[1]

NAZI IDEOLOGY REPRESENTS ONE of the most chilling examples of modernity's promises turned to ashes. Rooted in the ideals of progress, efficiency, and scientific rationalism, the Nazi regime sought to construct a utopia by applying technological and bureaucratic precision to the machinery of genocide. The horrors of the Holocaust—an event meticulously planned and executed under the guise of modernist logic—exposed the depths of human depravity when progress is divorced from moral restraint. Auschwitz, Dachau, and Treblinka became symbols of the complete embrace of modernity's tools and methods, wielded in the service of unimaginable cruelty.

Amidst the systematic dehumanization and unspeakable suffering of the Holocaust, Viktor Frankl endured. A Jewish psychiatrist from Vienna, Frankl survived Auschwitz, but he lost nearly everyone: his wife, his parents, his brother, and countless friends. Yet, in the darkness of the

---

1. Frankl, *Man's Search for Meaning*, 181.

concentration camps, he discovered a profound truth, one that would shape his philosophy and inspire millions. Stripped of every material possession, denied every freedom, and surrounded by death, Frankl realized that the one thing no oppressor could take from him was his freedom to choose his response. It was this freedom, this capacity to find meaning even in suffering, that sustained him through the darkest hours of his life.

The Holocaust was not only a historical atrocity but also a philosophical crisis. It shattered the modern belief in unending progress and revealed the moral void left by the abandonment of traditional ethical and spiritual frameworks. In its aftermath, humanity was forced to confront the question: How can life have meaning in the face of such overwhelming suffering? For Frankl, this question was deeply personal. His experiences in the camps became the foundation of his *logotherapy* and his seminal work, *Man's Search for Meaning*.

Unlike the despair of nihilism or the resignation of absurdism, Frankl's philosophy offered a way forward. He argued that even in the most horrific circumstances, meaning could be found. "Everything can be taken from a man but one thing," he wrote, "the last of the human freedoms—to choose one's attitude in any given set of circumstances, to choose one's own way."[2] This radical belief in the human capacity for meaning, even amidst suffering, became the cornerstone of his response to the modern crisis.

In an age increasingly marked by existential anxiety, alienation, and the collapse of shared values, Frankl's message resonates deeply. He saw suffering not as something to be avoided but as a pathway to meaning. Where modernity sought to eliminate hardship through technological progress, Frankl embraced hardship as an opportunity for growth and transformation. His insights challenge us to confront the difficulties of life with courage and purpose, discovering meaning not in spite of suffering but because of it.

Through his reflections on suffering, his philosophy of logotherapy, and his emphasis on the will to purpose, Frankl provides a roadmap for navigating life's challenges. His voice complements those of thinkers like Gabriel Marcel and Reinhold Niebuhr, who similarly grappled with the complexities of human existence. Together, they remind us that meaning is not something we construct but something we discover, even in the most unlikely places. As we delve into Frankl's philosophy, we are invited

---

2. Frankl, *Man's Search for Meaning*, 104.

to see life not as a problem to solve but as a journey to embrace. Even in the shadow of Auschwitz, Frankl's message shines: meaning is always within reach, waiting to be uncovered, even in the depths of suffering and despair.

Searching for Meaning in a Fractured World

The decline of traditional religious and moral frameworks, paired with the relentless pursuit of material advancement, created a void where humanity struggled to find purpose. Viktor Frankl observed that this "existential vacuum" was one of the great afflictions of his time. He identified the existential vacuum as a condition unique to modernity. The shift from religious and communal life to an emphasis on individualism and scientific rationalism severed many from traditional sources of meaning. As old frameworks collapsed, individuals were left adrift, often compensating with superficial pursuits of wealth, status, or hedonistic pleasure. While these pursuits might temporarily dull the sense of purposelessness, they could never fully satisfy the deeper human longing for meaning.

In *Man's Search for Meaning*, Frankl noted that this vacuum manifests in feelings of boredom, apathy, and anxiety. He wrote, "Man is no longer told by traditions what he has to do, and no longer told by values what he ought to do; soon he will not know what he wants to do."[3] This disconnection from purpose was, for Frankl, a central cause of the despair and alienation so characteristic of the modern age.

Unlike other existential thinkers who focused on the absurdity or futility of life, Frankl offered a hopeful and constructive response. Drawing from his own experiences in Auschwitz, he argued that the search for meaning is the most fundamental human drive, surpassing even the desire for pleasure or power. Frankl's logotherapy (his psychotherapeutic method) rests on this insight, which he called the "will to meaning."[4]

This concept stands in stark contrast to Friedrich Nietzsche's "will to power." While Nietzsche viewed the pursuit of power as the ultimate driver of human action, Frankl saw meaning as the higher and more enduring motivator. He wrote, "Man's main concern is not to gain pleasure or to avoid pain but rather to see a meaning in his life."[5] This shift from

---

3. Frankl, *Man's Search for Meaning*, 168.
4. Frankl, *Man's Search for Meaning*, 154–55.
5. Frankl, *Man's Search for Meaning*, 179.

power and pleasure to purpose offered a transformative lens through which individuals could reframe their suffering and reclaim their agency.

Frankl was deeply critical of both hedonism, which seeks meaning in transient pleasures, and nihilism, which denies the possibility of meaning altogether. He saw these as two sides of the same coin, both rooted in a failure to engage with life's deeper questions. Hedonism, Frankl argued, is ultimately hollow; it reduces life to the pursuit of gratification while ignoring the existential questions that make life worth living. Nihilism, on the other hand, offers no answers, only despair.

This critique echoes the observations of T. S. Eliot in *The Waste Land*, where Eliot depicts a post-World War I society consumed by distractions and disconnected from transcendent truths. Both Frankl and Eliot grappled with the emptiness of modernity, though Frankl's response was more directly therapeutic and hopeful. He called individuals to confront their despair, not avoid it, and to see it as a gateway to deeper meaning. Frankl writes, "Each man is questioned by life; and he can only answer to life by answering for his own life; to life he can only respond by being responsible."[6]

This responsibility to find meaning, even in the midst of suffering, became the foundation of Frankl's philosophy. He believed that meaning is unique to each individual and must be sought in the specific circumstances of one's life. By embracing this search, individuals can move beyond despair and reclaim a sense of purpose, even in the most trying situations. The fractured world of modernity left many searching for meaning in the wrong places, trapped by the illusions of pleasure or the despair of nihilism. Viktor Frankl's insights into the existential vacuum offered a powerful critique of these modern tendencies while pointing toward a hopeful alternative. By elevating the search for meaning as humanity's highest calling, Frankl provided a framework for navigating the complexities of the modern age.

The Practice of Logotherapy

Logotherapy, which Frankl described as "meaning-centered therapy," is both a philosophical vision and a practical method.[7] Rooted in his experiences in Auschwitz and his observations of human behavior in

---

6. Frankl, *Man's Search for Meaning*, 172.
7. Frankl, *Man's Search for Meaning*, 153.

extreme circumstances, logotherapy empowers individuals to confront suffering, reframe their challenges, and uncover purpose in their lives. Where psychoanalysis delves into the subconscious and existentialism often dwells on absurdity, logotherapy stands apart in its forward-looking approach. It is not concerned primarily with past traumas or abstract despair but with the question Frankl considered essential: "What does life expect of me?"

At the heart of logotherapy is Frankl's conviction that the search for meaning is humanity's primary drive. This stands in contrast to Freudian psychoanalysis, which centers human motivation on the pursuit of pleasure, and Adlerian psychology, which emphasizes the pursuit of power. Frankl argued that neither pleasure nor power could ultimately satisfy the human soul.

Logotherapy begins with the assumption that life has meaning under all circumstances, even the most difficult. It challenges individuals to discover that meaning by confronting their unique situations with responsibility and courage. Frankl often used the metaphor of life as a question posed to each person, writing, "Life is not something vague, but something very real and concrete, just as life's tasks are also very real and concrete. They form man's destiny, which is different and unique for each individual."[8] This emphasis on individuality and responsibility connects Frankl to existentialist thinkers like Søren Kierkegaard and Martin Buber, who emphasized the significance of personal choice and relationality. However, Frankl distinguishes himself by rooting his philosophy in practical application, providing a framework for individuals to act meaningfully within their specific contexts.

One of the most profound insights of logotherapy is its emphasis on the freedom to choose one's attitude, even in the most unbearable circumstances. Frankl saw this as the ultimate expression of human dignity. While individuals cannot always control their external circumstances, they can control their inner response to those circumstances.

Frankl's reflections on this freedom are deeply personal. Amidst unimaginable suffering, he observed that those who could find meaning in their pain were often able to endure with greater resilience. He described moments when prisoners found solace in small acts of kindness, a shared memory, or a vision of hope for the future. These moments demonstrated that even in the face of extreme oppression, the human spirit could

---

8. Frankl, *Man's Search for Meaning*, 122–23.

remain free. This idea resonates with the work of Aleksandr Solzhenitsyn, whose reflections in *The Gulag Archipelago* similarly emphasize the power of inner freedom. Solzhenitsyn, like Frankl, endured the horrors of imprisonment and found that meaning and moral integrity could persist even in the most dehumanizing environments.

Logotherapy identifies three primary ways in which individuals can discover meaning in their lives. First, meaning can be found in the act of creating or accomplishing something valuable, such as professional success, artistic endeavors, or contributions that leave a lasting impact. Frankl provides an example of a fellow prisoner who found purpose in planning a scientific manuscript he hoped to complete after liberation. Though his circumstances were dire, his mental engagement with meaningful work helped him endure. Second, meaning is often discovered in connection with others. For Frankl, love was one of the most profound sources of meaning, transcending physical suffering and offering a glimpse of the eternal. Reflecting on his own experience, Frankl wrote, "Love is the only way to grasp another human being in the innermost core of his personality."[9] He found solace in the memory of his wife, imagining her face and presence during moments of despair. Lastly, meaning can be found in how one confronts suffering. While suffering itself is not inherently meaningful, the attitude with which it is faced can transform it into a source of growth and purpose. Frankl frequently cited examples of patients who found meaning in their final days by focusing on their relationships, legacy, or spiritual reflections.

A hallmark of logotherapy is its ability to reframe suffering as an opportunity for meaning. Frankl often recounted the story of a grieving mother who had a crippled son. While the woman's pain was immense, Frankl helped her see that his suffering could become meaningful by having her think about what life would be like without her son. By reframing her sorrow, the woman found purpose in the quality of life she was able to provide for her son and the time she had with him. This principle of transformation connects Frankl's work to that of Dietrich Bonhoeffer, who wrote of the importance of "costly grace" in *The Cost of Discipleship*. Both thinkers emphasize that meaning is not found in avoiding hardship but in embracing it with faithfulness and courage.

Logotherapy offers a powerful and practical response to the crisis of meaning in the modern world. By emphasizing the will to meaning, the

---

9. Frankl, *Man's Search for Meaning*, 176.

freedom of attitude, and the transformative potential of suffering, Frankl provides a framework for individuals to navigate life's challenges with purpose and resilience. His philosophy is not a denial of life's difficulties but a call to engage with them meaningfully, discovering in them the seeds of hope and transformation.

Suffering as a Stage for Transformation

For Frankl, suffering was not merely an inevitable part of life but a profound opportunity for growth and transformation. In his writings, he frequently emphasized that meaning is not contingent upon a life free from hardship. Instead, suffering can become a pathway to purpose if faced with the right attitude. When we are no longer able to change a situation, we are challenged to change ourselves. This idea, forged in the crucible of his own experiences, became one of the central tenets of his philosophy. His reflections on suffering extend beyond his seminal work, *Man's Search for Meaning*, and into his later writings, including *The Doctor and the Soul*, where he expanded on the transformative potential of suffering and its role in human flourishing.

Like so many other thinkers in this part of the book, Frankl's understanding of suffering is rooted in a paradox: while suffering is inherently negative, it can also become a source of the deepest meaning. He argued that suffering, when faced without purpose, leads to despair. But when suffering is imbued with meaning, it ceases to be merely a burden and becomes an opportunity for transcendence. He wrote, "If there is meaning in life at all, then there must be meaning in suffering. Suffering is an ineradicable part of life, even as fate and death. Without suffering and death, human life cannot be complete."[10]

This paradox finds resonance in other philosophical and spiritual traditions. For instance, the Christian understanding of the cross parallels Frankl's insights. Just as the crucifixion represents both immense suffering and ultimate redemption, Frankl's philosophy posits that human suffering can serve as a means of transformation and renewal. Both frameworks affirm that suffering is not the final word but a stage through which meaning and hope can emerge.

Frankl's reflections on suffering were deeply shaped by his experiences in the concentration camps. Stripped of all material possessions,

---

10. Frankl, *Man's Search for Meaning*, 106.

denied even the basic dignity of freedom, and surrounded by death, Frankl discovered that the human spirit could endure even the most unimaginable circumstances if it was anchored in meaning. He observed that prisoners who had a reason to live—a loved one waiting for them, a project to complete, or a spiritual belief—were more likely to survive. As he regularly repeats Nietzsche here, "Those who have a 'why' to live, can bear almost any 'how.'"[11]

One of Frankl's most poignant accounts from Auschwitz illustrates this principle. He described a fellow prisoner who found solace in the thought of reuniting with his daughter after the war. Though his physical circumstances were dire, the prisoner's mental engagement with the future gave him strength to endure. Similarly, Frankl himself found meaning in imagining his wife's face and in the thought of completing his manuscript on logotherapy. These acts of mental resistance demonstrated that even in the face of extreme oppression, the human spirit could remain free.

Frankl's approach to suffering is deeply tied to his concept of responsibility. He argued that suffering poses a question to the individual: How will you respond? In *The Doctor and the Soul*, he expanded on this idea, stating that individuals are not passive recipients of suffering but active participants in how it shapes their lives. He writes, "Suffering establishes a fruitful tension in that it makes an emotional awareness of what ought not to be."[12] This awareness is what drives man to act against the "what ought not to be." Such a sense of responsibility is crucial to Frankl's philosophy. He believed that individuals must not only endure suffering but also strive to transform it into something meaningful.

Frankl was deeply critical of modern society's tendency to avoid or suppress suffering rather than confront it meaningfully. He observed that the pursuit of comfort and pleasure, while alluring, often leads to emptiness when it becomes a substitute for grappling with life's deeper questions. In a society that suffers from an existential vacuum, the realities of boredom and apathy are symptoms of the failure to confront life's ultimate concerns. This critique resonates with the work of Jacques Ellul, who warned against the dehumanizing effects of modern technological culture. Like Frankl, Ellul observed that modernity's obsession with efficiency and convenience often comes at the expense of deeper, more

---

11. Frankl, *Man's Search for Meaning*, 127.
12. Frankl, *Doctor and the Soul*, 108.

meaningful engagement with life's challenges. Both thinkers called for a return to authenticity, urging individuals to confront suffering as an integral part of the human experience.

For Frankl, the ultimate lesson of suffering is its redemptive potential. He believed that suffering could be transformed into a source of profound meaning when individuals approached it with courage, faith, and a willingness to grow. This redemptive vision is illustrated in countless acts of heroism and resilience. Frankl frequently recounted the story of Edith Weisskopf-Joelson, a psychologist and Holocaust survivor who used her experiences to help others confront their own suffering. By reframing her pain as a source of empathy and wisdom, Weisskopf-Joelson demonstrated how suffering could be transformed into a gift for others.[13]

Frankl's philosophy is not an endorsement of suffering but an affirmation that meaning can be found even in the most challenging circumstances. It is a call to see suffering not as an obstacle to life but as an integral part of its purpose. These reflections on meaning in suffering challenge modern assumptions about comfort and avoidance, offering instead a vision of life that embraces hardship as an opportunity for transformation—turning one's pain into a source of profound purpose and hope.

Purpose and Flourishing

Viktor Frankl's philosophy is not only about finding meaning in suffering but also about cultivating a life oriented toward purpose and flourishing. The will to meaning is not confined to moments of crisis or hardship; it is a constant call to align one's life with values and goals that transcend the self. Flourishing, in Frankl's vision, is not defined by material success or the absence of adversity but by a life lived intentionally, with purpose at its center.

Frankl writes, "What man actually needs is not a tensionless state but rather the striving and struggling for a worthwhile goal."[14] He argued that meaning and purpose are found not by looking inward, as modern individualism often suggests, but by orienting oneself outward—toward work, relationships, and contributions to the world. This outward

---

13. Another great example of this is Corrie Ten Boom, whose incredible story can be found in her work, *The Hiding Place*.
14. Frankl, *Man's Search for Meaning*, 166.

orientation connects Frankl's philosophy to classical ideals of virtue and self-transcendence. Aristotle's *Nicomachean Ethics*, for example, emphasizes that human flourishing, or *eudaimonia*, is achieved through the cultivation of virtue and the pursuit of higher goals. Similarly, Frankl believed that individuals flourish when they dedicate themselves to causes or tasks that go beyond their immediate desires.

A powerful literary example of this principle can be found in George Eliot's *Middlemarch*. The character of Dorothea Brooke, though initially naïve in her aspirations, discovers true purpose by dedicating herself to the betterment of others. Her selflessness and commitment to meaningful work illustrate Frankl's assertion that "self-actualization is possible only as a side-effect of self-transcendence."[15] Purpose, in this sense, is not about achieving personal gratification but about contributing to something larger than oneself.

Frankl saw creativity and responsibility as central to living a purposeful life. He believed that individuals are called to create, whether through art, work, or relationships, and that this creative process is a profound expression of human freedom. As he notably wrote, "The point is not what we expect from life, but rather what life expects from us."[16] This perspective reframes life as a dialogue, where individuals respond to its challenges and opportunities with their unique gifts and contributions.

This idea resonates with the philosophy of Albert Schweitzer, whose "reverence for life" emphasizes the ethical responsibility to contribute positively to the world.[17] Like Schweitzer, Frankl believed that human flourishing is inseparable from the responsibility to act in ways that honor and uplift life itself. Creativity, for both thinkers, is not merely an artistic endeavor but a moral imperative, a way of participating in the ongoing creation of meaning.

For Frankl, relationships are among the most profound sources of meaning and purpose. He viewed love not merely as an emotion but as a way of seeing and affirming the intrinsic value of another person. Through love, individuals transcend their own egocentric concerns and participate in something eternal. This perspective aligns with Gabriel Marcel's emphasis on relationality and the sacredness of encounter.

One of the great aspects of good literature is its ability to provide countless examples of the redemptive power of relationships. In Leo

---

15. Frankl, *Man's Search for Meaning*, 175.
16. Frankl, *Man's Search for Meaning*, 122.
17. Schweitzer, *Reverence for Life*, 25.

Tolstoy's *Anna Karenina*, the character of Konstantin Levin finds purpose and peace not through his intellectual pursuits but through his relationships: first with his wife, Kitty, and later with his community and faith. Levin's journey reflects Frankl's insight that true flourishing is deeply intertwined with love and connection.

In a world often characterized by distraction and superficiality, living a life of purpose becomes an act of resistance. Frankl writes, "What matters is not the meaning of life in general but the specific meaning of a person's life at a given moment."[18] This focus on the present moment underscores the urgency of living purposefully, even amidst a culture that often prioritizes convenience and escapism.

Frankl's vision of flourishing is not confined to the individual but extends to the community. He believed that meaning is most fully realized in the context of relationships and shared purpose. This communal dimension of flourishing resonates with Reinhold Niebuhr's emphasis on moral responsibility within the collective sphere. Where Frankl focuses on the individual's search for meaning, Niebuhr reminds us that flourishing also requires engagement with the broader struggles of justice and reconciliation. A powerful, real-world example of this principle can be seen in the Civil Rights Movement, where leaders like Martin Luther King Jr. drew on their faith and sense of purpose to inspire collective action. King's vision of the "Beloved Community" reflects Frankl's belief that human flourishing is achieved not in isolation but through acts of service, solidarity, and love.[19]

An Enduring Response

Viktor Frankl's life and work stand as a profound testament to the resilience of the human spirit in the face of unimaginable suffering. In an age fractured by the failures of modernity's promises and haunted by the shadow of the Holocaust, Frankl offered a path toward redemption, not through the denial of suffering but through its transformation into meaning. His philosophy of logotherapy, forged in the crucible of Auschwitz, provides a response to the meaning crisis that is both deeply personal and universally relevant.

---

18. Frankl, *Man's Search for Meaning*, 171.
19. King, "Facing the Challenge of a New Age."

Frankl challenges us to confront life not as a puzzle to be solved but as a question demanding our answer. He reminds us that meaning is not something imposed from the outside but something discovered in the unique circumstances of our lives. Whether through work, love, or suffering, the search for meaning becomes the essence of human existence. It calls us to responsibility, creativity, and courage, even when the path forward is obscured by pain or uncertainty.

One of Frankl's most enduring contributions is his affirmation of human freedom, not the external freedom of circumstance, but the inner freedom to choose our response. He shows us that even in the most oppressive conditions, we retain the ability to shape our attitudes, to rise above despair, and to discover meaning in the midst of suffering. This message is a powerful antidote to the modern tendency to view hardship as meaningless or avoidable. Instead, Frankl teaches us that suffering, when embraced with dignity and purpose, can become the fertile ground for profound growth and transformation.

At the heart of Frankl's response to the meaning crisis is his belief in the transcendence of love. For Frankl, love is the ultimate affirmation of life's value, the lens through which we see both ourselves and others as bearers of meaning. His reflections on the redemptive power of love remind us that true flourishing is found not in isolation but in relationship. In this, Frankl echoes the timeless wisdom of traditions that affirm the sacredness of human connection, challenging the alienation that so often defines modern existence.

Frankl's philosophy does not promise easy answers or shallow optimism. It does not deny the harsh realities of life, nor does it seek to escape them. Instead, it invites us to engage deeply with the complexities of existence, trusting that meaning can always be found even in the darkest of times. His response to the meaning crisis is both a call to action and a source of profound hope: life's challenges are not obstacles to be avoided but opportunities to discover who we are and why we exist. As we leave Frankl's world and turn to J. R. R. Tolkien in the next chapter, we transition from the individual's search for meaning to the collective power of myth and imagination. Frankl teaches us to endure suffering with purpose, while Tolkien offers a vision of beauty and storytelling that serves to restore hope and wonder.

11

J. R. R. Tolkien
Myth, Beauty, and the Restoration of Hope

"We have come from God, and inevitably the myths woven by us, though they contain error, will also reflect a splintered fragment of the true light, the eternal truth that is with God."

—J. R. R. Tolkien[1]

IN A WORLD INCREASINGLY dominated by materialism and disenchantment, where myth and wonder have often been relegated to childish fancy, J. R. R. Tolkien stands as a towering figure of restoration. His works, particularly *The Hobbit*, *The Lord of the Rings*, and *The Silmarillion*, have captivated millions, not merely for their intricate storytelling but for their profound truths about humanity, hope, and the divine. For Tolkien, myth was far more than entertainment; it was a means of uncovering eternal truths, a way to glimpse the transcendent through the veil of the ordinary.

Tolkien created a richly layered world through his legendarium. It was deeply moral and profoundly human. He did not simply write stories; he constructed an entire cosmos—one that reflected his understanding of good and evil, power and corruption, friendship and loyalty, hope and despair. Through this vast tapestry, Tolkien sought to provide an antidote

---

1. Carpenter, *J. R. R. Tolkien*, 198.

to the nihilism and fragmentation of modernity, using myth not just to entertain but to heal.

In his seminal essay *On Fairy-Stories*, Tolkien defended myth and fantasy as vital to human flourishing. He argued that these stories offer more than escapism; they provide glimpses of profound truth and beauty, reminding us that the world is more wondrous and meaningful than it often appears. He wrote:

> Fantasy is a natural human activity. It does not destroy or even insult Reason; and it does not blunt the appetite for, nor obscure the perception of, scientific verity. On the contrary. The keener and the clearer is the reason, the better fantasy will it make.[2]

For Tolkien, myth reflects divine truthlike a splintered fragment of light that points to the eternal reality of God's story. This is a take that stands as a powerful critique of modernity's cynicism. In an age that often dismisses beauty and wonder as irrelevant or naive, Tolkien reminds us that these are not luxuries but necessities. Myth, in his view, helps us navigate the complexities of existence by grounding us in narratives that speak to the deepest parts of the human soul. By drawing on the themes of sacrifice, redemption, and the triumph of good over evil, Tolkien's works transcend their genre to offer a vision of hope that resonates with readers across cultures and generations.

This chapter explores Tolkien's response to the modern crisis of meaning through his celebration of myth, beauty, and hope. It examines his philosophy of sub-creation, the concept of eucatastrophe, and the profound interplay between light and shadow in his stories. In doing so, it reveals how Tolkien's imaginative world offers not only an escape from disenchantment but also a pathway back to wonder and belief. As we journey through his works, we will see how Tolkien's vision of myth as a bridge to truth, beauty as a reflection of divine glory, and eucatastrophe as the restoration of hope can re-enchant a world that has grown weary and cynical.

---

2. Tolkien, *On Fairy Stories*, 27.

The Seeds of Myth—Language, Legend, and Early Inspirations

To understand J. R. R. Tolkien's monumental contribution to the re-enchantment of the modern world, we must begin by tracing the roots of his fascination with language, myth, and storytelling. Unlike many of his contemporaries, whose spiritual and creative journeys often veered into disillusionment, Tolkien's life was marked by a remarkable continuity. He held an unwavering faith, a deep-seated reverence for tradition, and an enduring passion for the myths and languages of the past. From his early years, Tolkien was drawn to the beauty and depth of ancient stories, and these early influences would ultimately converge in the creation of Middle-earth, a world that continues to captivate the imagination of readers worldwide.

Tolkien was born in 1892 in Bloemfontein, South Africa, but his early years in the English countryside left the deepest mark on his soul. After his father's death, Tolkien's mother, Mabel, moved her two sons to England, where she instilled in them a love of learning and a profound sense of faith. Mabel's conversion to Catholicism during Tolkien's childhood was a defining moment in his life, as it brought with it both spiritual richness and social isolation. Tolkien later described his mother as a martyr for her faith, recalling how her sacrifices laid the foundation for his own spiritual resilience. This devotion to faith became a cornerstone of Tolkien's worldview, subtly shaping the moral fabric of his mythology. Middle-earth is imbued with this sense of providence and grace, though Tolkien famously avoided overt allegory, believing that stories should allow truth to emerge naturally rather than through didacticism.

Alongside his faith, Tolkien's fascination with languages emerged early. By the time he was a child, he had an uncanny aptitude for picking up languages, delighting in Latin and Greek as well as the more exotic sounds of Gothic and Finnish. He didn't merely learn languages; he inhabited them. Tolkien recognized that language was more than a tool for communication—it was a vessel for culture, myth, and the human soul. He once remarked, "The invention of language is the foundation. The 'stories' were made rather to provide a world for the language than the reverse."[3] This principle became the lifeblood of his creative work. The languages he invented for Middle-earth, such as Quenya and Sindarin, were not decorative details but the beating heart of his world-building. Each language bore

---

3. Tolkien, *Letters of J. R. R. Tolkien*, 219.

the weight of its people's history, culture, and values, reflecting Tolkien's belief that language and myth exist in a symbiotic relationship.

Tolkien's academic path reflected this passion for language. As a philologist, he dedicated his career to studying the historical evolution of languages, first at the University of Leeds and later at Oxford, where he served as a professor of Anglo-Saxon. This work was not merely academic for Tolkien; it was an act of cultural and spiritual preservation. His deep immersion in the literary treasures of Northern Europe—*Beowulf*, the *Elder Edda*, and the Finnish *Kalevala*—ignited his imagination and inspired his creative endeavors. He was particularly captivated by *Beowulf*, which he described as a story that combines the heroic and the elegiac. For Tolkien, this tension—celebrating fleeting beauty even as it fades—became a defining theme in his work, as seen in the noble yet tragic struggles of characters like Frodo, Aragorn, and the Elves of Middle-earth.

Another profound influence on Tolkien's mythic vision was his experience of war. Like so many of his generation, Tolkien served in World War I, witnessing firsthand the horrors of trench warfare and the mechanized destruction of human life. The war claimed many of his closest friends, leaving a scar on his soul that never fully healed. Yet, rather than succumbing to the despair and cynicism that marked much postwar literature, Tolkien turned to myth as a source of hope and resilience. The themes of sacrifice, loss, and the corrupting power of evil that permeate *The Lord of the Rings* were shaped by his wartime experiences. However, Tolkien's response to these themes was uniquely redemptive. He rejected the nihilism of modernity, creating instead a world where courage, friendship, and perseverance could triumph over darkness.

Tolkien's desire to create an entirely new mythology began during the war, as he recovered from trench fever in 1917. It was then that he started writing the early stories that would later become *The Silmarillion*. These tales were born of a longing to provide England with a mythology of its own, one as rich as the legends he so admired. In Tolkien's view, modern England had lost its connection to the myths that once gave shape and meaning to its culture. His mythopoeic project sought to fill that void, offering a vision of wonder and transcendence that could counter the disenchantment of industrialized society. Through Middle-earth, Tolkien sought to restore the sense of awe and mystery that he believed modernity had eroded.

Underlying Tolkien's myth-making was his Catholic faith, which informed his concept of "sub-creation." In his essay *On Fairy-Stories*, Tolkien articulated his belief that humans, made in the image of a Creator, are called to imitate God's creative work. Storytelling, for Tolkien, was not a mere pastime but a sacred act, a way of glimpsing and participating in divine truth. "We make still by the law in which we're made," he wrote, suggesting that the creative impulse is an echo of God's own creativity.[4] This understanding of myth as a reflection of divine truth permeates his legendarium. Though Tolkien avoided explicit religious symbolism, his stories are suffused with Christian themes of redemption, providence, and grace.

Tolkien's early inspirations formed the foundation of his mythic vision. From these roots grew Middle-earth, a world that reflects both the sorrow and splendor of existence. In a time when many of his contemporaries responded to modernity with cynicism and despair, Tolkien chose instead to celebrate the enduring power of beauty, courage, and hope. Through his myths, he offered a response to the meaning crisis of his age, reminding readers that the stories we tell can lead us back to the eternal truths that sustain us.

Sub-Creation and the Mythic Vision

J. R. R. Tolkien's concept of "sub-creation" is one of the most profound elements of his mythic vision and serves as the philosophical underpinning of his entire legendarium. The idea is that human beings, made in the image of the Creator, have a natural calling to create worlds of their own. This is a key to understanding the intent and the enduring impact of Tolkien's work. Tolkien sought to reclaim a sense of wonder and enchantment through the process of sub-creation, which allowed him to communicate truth in a way that resonated with the soul as much, if not more, than the mind.

Tolkien articulated this vision in his 1939 essay "On Fairy-Stories," which remains an essential document for understanding his work. In this essay, Tolkien argued that myths, fairy tales, and other works of imaginative fiction are not merely escapist fantasies or idle entertainment. Instead, they serve a vital purpose in human culture by providing glimpses of deeper truths, truths that often lie beyond the reach of pure reason

---

4. Tolkien, *On Fairy Stories*, 46.

or scientific inquiry. Tolkien believed that human beings are naturally inclined to create stories because they are made in the image of God, the Creator. Through the act of storytelling, humans participate in a form of divine creativity, echoing the original act of creation and imbuing the world with a sense of meaning and purpose.

Tolkien used the term "sub-creation" to describe the artistic process by which human beings create secondary worlds. These are self-contained realities that reflect the beauty, complexity, and moral order of the primary world. For Tolkien, sub-creation was a way of capturing the truths of existence in a form that was both beautiful and accessible. He believed that myths and fairy stories could provide what he called "eucatastrophe," which describes a sudden and miraculous grace that brings about a joyful and redemptive ending. In contrast to the tragedy and despair that often characterized the narratives of modernity, Tolkien sought to create stories that affirmed hope and the ultimate triumph of good over evil. In Tolkien's view, eucatastrophe was not merely a narrative device but a reflection of the Christian understanding of redemption: the idea that even in the darkest moments, there is a light that cannot be extinguished.

Tolkien's Middle-earth was his most significant act of sub-creation. This world was not only richly detailed and internally consistent but also imbued with profound spiritual and moral meaning. Through the creation of Middle-earth, Tolkien offered his readers a vision of a familiar and transcendent world in which the timeless themes of heroism, sacrifice, grace, and redemption played out against the backdrop of a vast and intricately crafted mythology. Middle-earth was a place where beauty coexisted with danger, where even the smallest individuals could play a decisive role in the struggle against evil and where hope persisted even in the face of overwhelming darkness.

One of the most remarkable aspects of Tolkien's sub-creation is the depth of its mythology. Unlike many works of fantasy, which rely on simplistic worldbuilding or superficial magic systems, Tolkien's Middle-earth is underpinned by a complex and cohesive mythos. At the heart of Tolkien's legendarium is *The Silmarillion*, a collection of stories that form the cosmogony and early history of Middle-earth. *The Silmarillion* serves as the foundational mythology for Tolkien's entire body of work, providing the context for the events of *The Hobbit* and *The Lord of the Rings*. It tells the story of the creation of the world by the god-like being Eru Ilúvatar, the subsequent rebellion of Melkor (later known as Morgoth), and the tragic history of the Elves, Men, and other races of Middle-earth.

Through *The Silmarillion*, Tolkien sought to create a mythology that reflected his understanding of the human condition, a condition that, for him, was marked by both beauty and brokenness, by the longing for the divine, and by the tragic reality of sin and corruption. The story of the Silmarils, the three jewels crafted by the Elven prince Fëanor, encapsulates many of the themes that run throughout Tolkien's work: the desire for beauty, the danger of pride, the corrupting influence of power, and the possibility of redemption through sacrifice. The quest for the Silmarils drives much of the action in *The Silmarillion*, and the consequences of that quest ripple through the ages, affecting the events of *The Hobbit* and *The Lord of the Rings*.

The Hobbit, published in 1937, was Tolkien's first foray into the world of Middle-earth for a general audience, and it introduced readers to a world that was both enchanting and deeply moral. While *The Hobbit* is often seen as a children's book, it contains many themes that would define Tolkien's later work: the importance of courage, the corrupting influence of greed, and the value of simple, unassuming virtues. Bilbo Baggins, the titular hobbit, is an unlikely hero. Bilbo is a small, comfort-loving creature drawn into an adventure that changes him forever. Through Bilbo's journey, Tolkien explores the idea that heroism is not limited to the mighty or the powerful but is often found in the most unexpected places. Bilbo's courage, resourcefulness, and humility ultimately make him instrumental in the success of the quest to reclaim the Lonely Mountain from the dragon Smaug.

Tolkien's magnum opus, *The Lord of the Rings*, took the mythic vision of *The Hobbit* to new heights. Published in three volumes between 1954 and 1955, *The Lord of the Rings* is an epic tale that weaves together multiple storylines, a vast cast of characters, and a deep moral struggle between the forces of good and evil. At the heart of the story is the One Ring, a powerful artifact created by the Dark Lord Sauron to dominate all life in Middle-earth. The Ring represents the corrupting influence of power and the temptation to use that power for one's own ends. Throughout *The Lord of the Rings*, characters are tested by their interactions with the Ring, and their responses reveal their true natures. Frodo Baggins, the Ring-bearer, is chosen not because of his strength or wisdom but because of his humility and resilience. Frodo's journey to destroy the Ring in the fires of Mount Doom is a journey of sacrifice, suffering, and ultimately redemption.

Tolkien's use of myth in *The Lord of the Rings* is subtle yet powerful. Unlike C. S. Lewis, who often employed direct allegory in works such as *The Chronicles of Narnia*, Tolkien preferred letting his stories' themes emerge naturally from the narrative. The struggle between good and evil in Middle-earth is not an abstract battle between allegorical figures but a deeply personal conflict that uniquely affects each character. The choices of characters such as Frodo, Sam, Aragorn, and Gollum ultimately determine the story's outcome. Tolkien's portrayal of evil is nuanced; Sauron may be a nearly omnipresent threat, but the true danger lies in the hearts of individuals and their susceptibility to temptation. The theme of free will is central to Tolkien's mythic vision and reflects his belief in the inherent dignity and responsibility of each person.

Tolkien's understanding of sub-creation and myth also extended to his treatment of beauty and nature in Middle-earth. The natural world is not merely a backdrop for the story but an integral part of the narrative, reflecting the goodness and creativity of the Creator. The forests of Lothlórien, the rolling hills of the Shire, the majestic peaks of the Misty Mountains—each of these landscapes is imbued with a sense of wonder and sacredness. Tolkien's portrayal of nature starkly contrasts the industrialization and mechanization that characterized the modern world. The devastation of Isengard by Saruman, who fell trees and pollutes the land in his quest for power, symbolizes the destructive consequences of modernity's disconnection from the natural world. In Tolkien's mythic vision, the beauty of creation is something to be cherished, protected, and celebrated.

Ultimately, Tolkien's concept of sub-creation and his mythic vision were an effort to restore meaning to a world that had lost its sense of wonder. By creating Middle-earth, Tolkien invited his readers into a world where good and evil were real, where beauty and courage mattered, and where even the smallest individuals could make a difference. His stories were not merely escapist fantasies but profound reflections on the human condition, offering hope, wisdom, and a vision of a reality that transcended the materialism and despair of the modern age. Tolkien's sub-creation was a response to the fragmentation and nihilism of his time, a reminder that beneath the surface of our world lies a much greater narrative. It is a story that stretches backward and forwards into an eternity of beauty, courage, and redemption. However, those are not the only themes found in Tolkien's sub-creation.

Power, Corruption, and the Nature of Evil

In Tolkien's legendarium, power, corruption, and the nature of evil are woven intricately into the narrative fabric of Middle-earth. These themes lie at the core of *The Lord of the Rings* and serve as a powerful counternarrative to the prevailing disillusionment of the twentieth century. Through his portrayal of the One Ring, the Dark Lords Sauron and Morgoth, and the choices faced by individual characters, Tolkien explores the corrupting influence of power and the subtle, pervasive nature of evil. His treatment of these themes reflects his deep understanding of human frailty and his belief in the possibility of redemption, even in the darkest of times.

The One Ring is the most potent symbol of power and corruption in Tolkien's work. Forged by Sauron in the fires of Mount Doom, the Ring embodies the desire for control and the temptation to dominate others. It grants immense power to its bearer but at a terrible cost by slowly corrupting the individual who wields it, bending their will to that of Sauron. The Ring's allure is so great that even the most virtuous characters are tempted by it. Gandalf, Galadriel, and Aragorn each face moments of temptation, and their refusal to take the Ring is a testament to their strength of character and wisdom. They recognize that, despite their good intentions, the power of the Ring would ultimately corrupt them and lead to the very evil they seek to oppose.

Tolkien's portrayal of the Ring's corrupting influence reflects his broader concerns about power and its potential for abuse. In *The Fellowship of the Ring*, Galadriel's moment of temptation is particularly significant. When Frodo offers her the Ring, she envisions herself as a powerful queen, beautiful and terrible, who would bring order to the world. Yet, she rejects the Ring, saying, "I pass the test. I will diminish, and go into the West, and remain Galadriel."[5] This moment is a powerful reminder that true wisdom lies not in seeking power but in recognizing its dangers and choosing humility instead. Galadriel's choice to "diminish" is an act of self-sacrifice that stands in stark contrast to the modern world's obsession with power, control, and self-aggrandizement.

The character of Boromir serves as another example of the corrupting influence of the Ring. Unlike Gandalf, Galadriel, and Aragorn, Boromir succumbs to the temptation of the Ring, believing it could be used to protect Gondor and defeat Sauron. His intentions are noble—he wants to save his people from the encroaching darkness—but his desire for the

---

5. Tolkien, *Fellowship of the Ring*, 476.

Ring ultimately leads him to betray Frodo and jeopardize the fellowship. Boromir's fall is a tragic reminder that the lure of power can twist even the noblest intentions. His redemption, however, comes in the form of his self-sacrificial defense of Merry and Pippin, demonstrating Tolkien's belief in the possibility of repentance and the power of redemption, even for those who have fallen.

Tolkien's exploration of power and corruption is not limited to the One Ring. The figure of Sauron, the primary antagonist of *The Lord of the Rings*, represents the embodiment of the desire for absolute power. Sauron is a being who has entirely given himself over to the pursuit of domination, seeking to bend all of Middle-earth to his will. He is a shadowy presence throughout the story, rarely seen but always felt. A symbol of the insidious nature of evil. Sauron's desire for control is mirrored in the actions of Saruman, who, though initially a force for good, is seduced by the promise of power and becomes an agent of Sauron's will. Saruman's fall is a cautionary tale about the dangers of pride and the belief that one can wield power without being corrupted by it.

The nature of evil in Tolkien's work is complex and multifaceted. Unlike many modern narratives that depict evil as an external force, Tolkien presents evil as something that exists within each individual. It is a potential that can be awakened by the desire for power, greed, or fear. This is perhaps most evident in the character of Gollum, who serves as a tragic illustration of the corrupting influence of the Ring. Once a simple hobbit-like creature named Sméagol, Gollum is utterly consumed by his desire for the Ring, which he calls his "precious." The Ring's hold on Gollum is so complete that it transforms him physically and spiritually, turning him into a creature of shadows and deceit. Yet, despite his fall, Gollum is not beyond pity. Bilbo and Frodo's compassion for Gollum is an important theme in both *The Hobbit* and *The Lord of the Rings*, highlighting Tolkien's belief in the inherent worth of every individual, no matter how far they have fallen.

The struggle between good and evil in Tolkien's work is not a simple binary conflict; it is a profoundly personal battle that takes place within the hearts of each character. Frodo's journey to destroy the Ring is as much spiritual as it is physical. It proves to be a test of his resilience, courage, and capacity for mercy. The burden of the Ring takes a tremendous toll on Frodo, and by the end of his journey, he is physically and emotionally scarred. In the climactic moment at Mount Doom, Frodo ultimately succumbs to the Ring's power, claiming it for himself. Only through Gollum's intervention—his desperate attempt to reclaim the Ring—is the quest fulfilled and the Ring destroyed. This ending is a powerful reminder that even the best of us are not immune to the corrupting influence of power and that the ultimate victory over evil often comes through unexpected means.

Tolkien's portrayal of the nature of evil is also evident in his depiction of Morgoth, the original Dark Lord and the primary antagonist of *The Silmarillion*. Morgoth's rebellion against Eru Ilúvatar, the Creator, is the catalyst for much of the suffering and strife that follows in the history of Middle-earth. Morgoth's desire to dominate and corrupt the world reflects his inability to create anything of his own; he can only pervert and destroy what has already been made. The idea that evil is ultimately a perversion of the good is a central theme in Tolkien's work and reflects his belief in the fundamental goodness of creation. Even in the face of great evil, Tolkien's world is one in which hope remains, and the possibility of redemption is never entirely lost.

The characters in *The Lord of the Rings* are constantly faced with choices that determine the course of their lives and the fate of Middle-earth. The power of the Ring lies in its ability to take away an individual's free will, bending them to its purposes. Therefore, the struggle to resist the Ring is a struggle to maintain one's autonomy and moral integrity. Samwise Gamgee, perhaps more than any other character, embodies the power of free will and the strength of the human (or hobbit) spirit. Sam's loyalty to Frodo, his refusal to give in to despair, and his unwavering determination to see the quest through to the end are what ultimately enable Frodo to reach Mount Doom. Sam's heroism is not the result of great power or strength but his steadfastness and love for his friend.

Tolkien's exploration of power, corruption, and the nature of evil serves as a powerful counternarrative to the nihilism and despair that characterized much of twentieth-century literature and culture. In a world that had witnessed the horrors of two world wars, the rise of totalitarian regimes, and the devastating consequences of unchecked power, Tolkien's work offered a different vision. A vision in which even the smallest individuals could make a difference, where hope could be found in the darkest of places, and where the struggle against evil was always worth fighting. His portrayal of the battle between good and evil was no mere fantasy but a profound reflection on the human condition, one that resonated deeply with readers who longed for a sense of meaning and purpose in a fragmented world.

In addition to *The Lord of the Rings*, Tolkien's shorter works, such as *Leaf by Niggle*, also explored the themes of power, creativity, and the nature of good and evil. *Leaf by Niggle* is a deeply allegorical tale about an artist named Niggle who is consumed with the desire to complete a grand painting of a tree. The story is a profound reflection on the nature of creativity, the tension between personal ambition and the demands of everyday life, and the ultimate purpose of human endeavor. Niggle's journey, which takes him from his earthly struggles to a place of healing and fulfillment, reflects Tolkien's belief in the redemptive power of creativity and the importance of selflessness and humility. The story is a reminder that true greatness lies not in the pursuit of power or recognition but in the quiet, often unnoticed acts of love and sacrifice that give life its fullest meaning.

Storytelling as Moral Instruction: The Fellowship and Community

Through his tales, particularly *The Lord of the Rings*, Tolkien sought to model how virtues such as courage, humility, sacrifice, and friendship are cultivated and how these values are essential to the flourishing of individuals and societies. At a time when modernity seemed to celebrate individualism and self-reliance to the detriment of communal ties, Tolkien offered a powerful reminder of the moral strength that can only be found in fellowship. The Fellowship of the Ring (as a concept and a group) lies at the heart of Tolkien's exploration of the power of community.

Formed as an alliance to take the One Ring to Mordor, the Fellowship brings together characters from diverse backgrounds: Frodo the Hobbit, Gandalf the Wizard, Aragorn the Ranger, Legolas the Elf, Gimli the Dwarf, Boromir of Gondor, and Frodo's Hobbit friends Sam, Merry, and Pippin. Each member represents a distinct culture with its own strengths, weaknesses, and worldview. Yet, despite their differences, they are united by a common purpose—the destruction of the Ring and the preservation of Middle-earth.

Tolkien's portrayal of the Fellowship is a powerful reflection of his belief in the necessity of unity and cooperation. The Fellowship members are not perfect; they each carry their own doubts, fears, and flaws. Boromir, for instance, is tempted by the Ring's power, leading to his eventual downfall. Yet, even in his failure, Boromir demonstrates courage and loyalty, sacrificing himself to protect Merry and Pippin from the orcs.

His story serves as a reminder that even flawed individuals can act heroically and that redemption is possible through sacrifice. The Fellowship's strength lies not in the individual heroics of its members but in their ability to support one another, bear each other's burdens, and remain committed to their shared mission.

Tolkien's emphasis on fellowship as a source of moral strength starkly contrasts with the individualistic ethos of modernity. The world of Middle-earth is a place where individual glory is subordinated to the greater good and where the bonds of friendship and loyalty are more potent than the pursuit of personal power. This is perhaps best exemplified in the relationship between Frodo and Sam. Frodo may be the Ring-bearer, tasked with the monumental burden of carrying the One Ring to Mount Doom, but it is Sam who ensures that Frodo can complete his quest. Sam's loyalty, perseverance, and selflessness are the qualities that ultimately make Frodo's success possible. Through Sam, Tolkien illustrates the profound moral value of humility and service to others, qualities that starkly oppose the pride and ambition that drive characters like Sauron and Saruman.

The Fellowship also highlights the theme of interdependence. Each member brings unique abilities and perspectives to the group, and it is only through their collective efforts that they are able to overcome the many obstacles they face. Legolas and Gimli initially view each other with suspicion due to the long-standing enmity between elves and dwarves but gradually develop a deep friendship based on mutual respect and shared experiences. Their relationship is a testament to Tolkien's belief in the possibility of reconciliation and the breaking down of barriers between different cultures. In a world where divisions between peoples often lead to conflict and hatred, Tolkien's depiction of Legolas and Gimli offers a hopeful vision of what can be achieved through understanding and solidarity.

The theme of fellowship is not limited to the Fellowship of the Ring itself but extends to the broader community of Middle-earth. Throughout *The Lord of the Rings*, Tolkien emphasizes the importance of alliances and the coming together of different peoples to resist the forces of darkness. The Ents, the Riders of Rohan, the people of Gondor, and the hobbits of the Shire all play crucial roles in the fight against Sauron. No one individual or group achieves victory over evil but through the combined efforts of many, each contributing in their own way. This emphasis on collective action is a powerful moral lesson about the importance of community and the need to work together for the common good.

Tolkien's portrayal of the Shire and its inhabitants also serves as a moral counterpoint to the darkness and corruption of Mordor. The hobbits are not great warriors or influential leaders; they are simple folk who value peace, friendship, and the joys of everyday life. Yet, it is precisely these qualities that make them resilient in the face of adversity. The Shire represents an ideal of community where individuals care for one another, where life is rooted in simple pleasures, and where the bonds of family and friendship are paramount. In contrast to the mechanized, oppressive power of Sauron's forces, the Shire embodies a vision of life in harmony with nature and grounded in genuine human connection.

Tolkien's use of storytelling to convey moral lessons is further evident in his depiction of leadership. Characters like Aragorn, Théoden, and Faramir exemplify the qualities of authentic leadership: humility, wisdom, and a willingness to serve others. Aragorn, destined to be king, does not seek power for its own sake. Instead, he accepts his role as a leader out of a sense of duty and responsibility to his people. His journey is one of self-discovery and growth as he learns to embrace his identity and the burden of leadership. Théoden, similarly, undergoes a transformation from a ruler who is manipulated and weakened by the influence of Wormtongue to a king who leads his people with courage and honor. Through these characters, Tolkien emphasizes that true leadership is not about domination or the pursuit of personal glory but about serving others and protecting what is good and just.

The moral instruction embedded in Tolkien's storytelling is not didactic or heavy-handed; instead, it is woven seamlessly into the fabric of his narrative. The characters' choices, their relationships, and their actions all serve to illustrate the virtues that Tolkien held dear. In a world increasingly marked by cynicism and the breakdown of communal ties, Tolkien's emphasis on fellowship and community offers a powerful reminder of the importance of these values. His stories invite readers to reflect on their own lives, to consider how they can contribute to the well-being of others, and to recognize the strength that comes from standing together in the face of adversity.

Ultimately, Tolkien's exploration of fellowship and community profoundly responded to the alienation and fragmentation of the modern world. By depicting characters who find strength, purpose, and hope through their connections with others, Tolkien offers a profoundly countercultural vision of life. His stories remind us that we are not meant to face life's challenges alone and that our most outstanding achievements are often the result of collective effort. That true fulfillment is found not in the pursuit of power or self-interest but in the bonds of friendship and the service of others. Through the lens of Middle-earth, Tolkien invites us to see the world anew, to recognize the beauty of fellowship and the moral imperative of community, and to understand that, even in the darkest of times, hope can be found when we stand together.

A Hope That Cannot Be Extinguished

Tolkien took up his pen to remind humanity of a reality beyond the material in a world that had grown increasingly disenchanted, bereft of transcendent purpose and hope. He understood that modernity, with its focus on industrial progress, reason, and individual autonomy, had torn down many of the narratives that once provided the foundation for community, beauty, and a sense of cosmic meaning. In response, Tolkien rebuilt these narratives, drawing on myth, legend, and, above all, the timeless values that connect humanity to its Creator.

Through the pages of *The Lord of the Rings*, Tolkien presented a world that echoed the familiar struggles of modern existence (conflict, disillusionment, temptation, and despair) but also provided a vision of hope, courage, and redemption. The characters of Middle-earth, notably the Fellowship of the Ring, were not just companions on an adventure; they were a fellowship of resilience, loyalty, and goodness in the face of overwhelming darkness. By focusing on the bonds that hold individuals together and the sacrifices they make for one another, Tolkien presented a vision of life that contrasted sharply with the fragmented and alienated existence of the modern world. He showed that the power of fellowship, forged through shared purpose and selfless acts, could counteract the forces of greed and power that threatened to dominate human life.

One of Tolkien's most enduring messages is that true meaning and beauty are found not in power or domination but in the humble and the ordinary. He conveyed this in his depiction of the Hobbits, who represented the world's small, seemingly insignificant people, those who were largely overlooked by the powerful. Yet, in the grand struggle for the fate of Middle-earth, it was Frodo, a simple hobbit, who carried the burden of the One Ring, and it was Samwise Gamgee who exemplified loyalty, courage, and love. Their journey was a testament to the truth that true heroism lies not in seeking glory but in persevering through suffering, showing kindness, and standing against evil, even when the odds are seemingly insurmountable. Tolkien writes in *The Fellowship*, "Yet such is oft the course of deeds that move the wheels of the world: small hands do them because they must, while the eyes of the great are elsewhere."[6]

Throughout his epic, Tolkien wove in powerful symbols that point to the deeper truths of existence. Consider the moment in *The Return of the King* when all seemed lost. The forces of darkness had gathered, and hope had all but vanished. But at the darkest hour, the Riders of Rohan appeared over the ridge, and the battle horn of Rohan echoed across the battlefield. This image of light breaking through when all seemed to be swallowed by shadow encapsulated Tolkien's fundamental belief that hope could not be extinguished, no matter how dark the times may seem. There was always a reason to stand, fight, and believe in the triumph of good over evil.

Tolkien portrayed such hope in a beautiful scene from *Return of the King*. He writes:

> There, peeping among the cloud-wrack above a dark tor high up in the mountains, Sam saw a white star twinkle for a while. The beauty of it smote his heart as he looked up out of the forsaken land, and hope returned to him. For like a shaft, clear and cold, the thought pierced him that in the end, the Shadow was only a small and passing thing: there was light and high beauty forever beyond its reach.[7]

This epitomizes Tolkien's defiance of the nihilism and devastation produced by the mechanistic worldview of modernity. His work insisted that there was "light and high beauty" beyond the reach of the darkness.

The culmination of Tolkien's work is a re-enchantment of the world, a reminder that there is a more incredible story unfolding, one filled with beauty, purpose, and deep meaning—realities that modernity had obscured but could never truly extinguish. Though filled with peril and darkness, the realm of Middle-earth was a place where courage, fellowship, and sacrifice triumphed. It provided readers with a vision of a moral universe where good and evil were real, where individual actions mattered, and where there was a higher order.

6. Tolkien, *Fellowship of the Ring*, 351.
7. Tolkien, *Return of the King*, 901.

Tolkien's response to modernity's meaning crisis was not merely a critique but a beacon of hope. He showed that the story of humanity is ultimately about redemption and restoration. It is about the return of the king, the rightful ruler who brings healing to the world. This imagery is not accidental, for it points beyond the pages of his books to the Christian hope that Tolkien himself cherished. The return of the king is not just the return of Aragorn to Gondor; it is a symbolic foreshadowing of the return of the true king, who will set all things right.

In many ways, Tolkien's work was like the Riders of Rohan cresting the hill at Helm's Deep: it brought hope to those left disillusioned and weary by the forces of modernity. His stories offered a vision of the world as immensely meaningful and infused with profound purpose. But more than that, they offered a call to action: to gather in fellowship, to resist the forces that sought to rob humanity of its meaning, and to stand for the beauty and goodness that flow from the Creator himself.

The Gift of Re-enchantment

J. R. R. Tolkien's mythic vision stands as a luminous testament to the enduring power of storytelling, beauty, and hope in a disenchanted world. Through his concept of sub-creation, he reclaimed the ancient purpose of myth: to reflect the eternal truths that underpin the human condition. Middle-earth, with its breathtaking landscapes, richly drawn characters, and profound moral depth, serves as a mirror for our own world, reminding us of the stakes in the battle between good and evil, the fragility of beauty, and the unyielding hope that shines even in the darkest moments.

Tolkien's work calls us to remember that the stories we tell are not mere entertainment but reflections of a deeper reality. A reality where eucatastrophe, the "good catastrophe," reminds us that redemption is always possible, even when all seems lost. His tales of courage, sacrifice, and renewal invite us to see ourselves as participants in a greater narrative, one that stretches beyond time and space to the eternal. In a world marked by fragmentation and despair, Tolkien offers the gift of re-enchantment, challenging us to see the world not as a series of isolated events but as a place filled with meaning, wonder, and divine purpose.

As we transition to the next chapter, the focus shifts from Tolkien's mythic vision to the imaginative and theological brilliance of his close friend and contemporary C. S. Lewis. While Tolkien used myth to awaken the heart's longing for transcendence, Lewis explored that longing directly, framing it as evidence of humanity's yearning for union with the divine. Together, these two thinkers—one the master craftsman of myth, the other the theologian of joy—present a complementary vision for addressing the modern crisis of meaning. Where Tolkien enchants us with the beauty of sub-creation, Lewis leads us into the deeper desire that those myths awaken, pointing us to the ultimate source of truth and fulfillment.

Tolkien's stories bring us to the threshold of wonder, and Lewis invites us to step through the door. In Tolkien's Middle-earth, we encounter the splendor of creation and the hope of redemption; in Lewis's works, we are guided toward the One who fulfills the longings that Tolkien's stories so powerfully stir. Together, their legacies remind us that meaning is not something we must construct but something we discover. It is a treasure buried in the stories, beauty, and desires that point us to the divine. As we leave Tolkien's world and enter Lewis's, the journey toward re-enchantment continues, drawing us ever closer to the source of all truth, beauty, and joy.

12

C. S. Lewis

Faith, Imagination, and the Argument from Desire

"If I find in myself a desire which no experience in this world can satisfy, the most probable explanation is that I was made for another world."

—C. S. Lewis[1]

PERHAPS, NO SINGLE WRITER did more to offer a profound response to humanity's restless search for meaning than C. S. Lewis. His life and works are a testament to the belief that the deepest desires of the human heart point beyond this world to something eternal. For Lewis, the aching longing for joy, or *Sehnsucht*, was not a source of despair but a clue. A beacon lighting the way toward ultimate truth.

Lewis's own journey from atheism to Christianity exemplified the power of this longing. Raised in a world shaped by skepticism and modernist ideals, Lewis found himself deeply dissatisfied with the answers offered by materialism. His early years were marked by a passionate love for literature, mythology, and beauty, which stirred in him an intense yearning for something more. This longing, which he later called joy, became the central thread of his intellectual and spiritual life. It was not mere happiness or pleasure but a piercing awareness of something

---

1. Lewis, *Mere Christianity*. 75.

just out of reach, something that awakened his soul to the possibility of transcendence.

"All joy reminds. It is never a possession, always a desire for something longer ago or further away or still 'about to be.'"[2] These words from *Surprised by Joy* capture the essence of Lewis's realization: the beauty and wonder we encounter in this world are not ends in themselves but signposts pointing to a greater reality. The books, landscapes, and friendships that stirred his heart were not the source of joy but the means by which it spoke to him, calling him toward the divine.

For Lewis, Christianity provided the answer to this longing. He came to see that the God who created the world also placed within humanity a desire for him, a desire that could only be fulfilled in his presence. This realization transformed Lewis's understanding of faith, imagination, and the human condition. He saw Christianity not as a cold system of dogma but as a story— *"the true myth"*—that fulfilled the deepest yearnings of the heart while satisfying the rigorous demands of reason.

Through his writings, Lewis sought to bridge the gap between the rational and the transcendent, the material and the spiritual. His works, from *Mere Christianity* to *The Chronicles of Narnia*, were aimed at reawakening a sense of wonder in a world that had become disenchanted. He offered not only arguments for the existence of God but also stories that touched the heart and rekindled a sense of childlike awe. In doing so, Lewis challenged the modern assumption that faith and reason were inherently at odds, presenting instead a vision of Christianity as the fulfillment of both our intellectual and imaginative needs.

In this chapter, we will explore how Lewis addressed the crisis of meaning in the modern world, not by rejecting reason but by expanding it to include the spiritual and the transcendent. We will see how his apologetic works provided rational arguments for faith while his imaginative stories re-enchanted the world, inviting readers to see reality through new eyes. Ultimately, this chapter will demonstrate how Lewis offered a compelling alternative to the disillusionment of modernity: a vision of a world infused with divine purpose, where the longing for joy points us beyond ourselves to the Creator, who alone can satisfy the deepest desires of the human heart.

Lewis's role as an apologist and storyteller was not only to defend Christianity but to invite people to experience it. To see that the world

---

2. Lewis, *Surprised by Joy*, 74.

is far richer, more mysterious, and more beautiful than the materialist narrative allows. C. S. Lewis became one of the most significant voices of hope in a century marked by despair. He provided a roadmap for re-enchanting the world, for recovering the sense of wonder and meaning lost in the disillusionment of modernity. In doing so, he set the stage for a broader movement that would continue to challenge the reductionist view of reality and call people back to faith, imagination, and the ultimate truth revealed in the Christian story.

Surprised by Joy

C. S. Lewis's journey to faith was anything but straightforward; it was a long, winding path marked by intense intellectual wrestling, deep personal struggles, and moments of profound insight. Understanding Lewis' early life and conversion is crucial to grasping how he would later address the modern crisis of disenchantment. His journey from atheism to Christianity mirrored the spiritual struggle of many in his generation who, in the wake of the world wars and the collapse of traditional certainties, were seeking something beyond the emptiness of materialism.

Born in Belfast, Ireland, in 1898, Lewis was raised in a Protestant household, but his early religious upbringing was not particularly deep or personal. He experienced a significant loss at the age of nine when his mother, Flora, died of cancer. This loss profoundly affected young Lewis, creating a void that he struggled to fill throughout his adolescence. His father, Albert, found it challenging to provide the emotional support Lewis needed. As a result, Lewis began to withdraw into himself, finding solace in books and his own imagination. This early encounter with suffering planted the seeds of doubt in Lewis's mind and influenced his eventual rejection of Christianity.

As a teenager, Lewis became an avowed atheist. He was deeply influenced by his readings of classical literature and the works of prominent atheistic philosophers. His intellectual pursuits led him to embrace a materialistic worldview that saw the universe as cold, indifferent, and devoid of inherent meaning. Influenced by the rationalist thinkers of his time, Lewis began to believe that all phenomena could be explained by natural processes. He was drawn to the scientific materialism that had become so pervasive in the late nineteenth and early twentieth centuries, and he saw Christianity as an outdated myth that could no longer stand up to the scrutiny of reason and science.

Lewis's education played a significant role in shaping this worldview. At the age of 15, he came under the influence of his tutor, W. T. Kirkpatrick, whom he affectionately referred to as "The Great Knock."[3] Kirkpatrick was a fierce rationalist who instilled in Lewis a rigorous commitment to logical thinking and a deep skepticism of anything that could not be empirically verified. Under Kirkpatrick's guidance, Lewis honed his skills in debate and argumentation, and his atheism became more firmly entrenched.

However, Lewis's journey to atheism was not without moments of tension. Despite his intellectual commitment to a materialistic worldview, he continued to feel a sense of longing (what he would later describe as "joy") that seemed to point beyond the natural world. This longing was often sparked by encounters with beauty, whether in nature, literature, or music. It was an experience that he could not easily explain or dismiss, and it created a tension within him that would ultimately lead him to question the adequacy of his atheism.

Lewis's experiences during World War I further deepened his sense of disillusionment. He served as a second lieutenant in the British Army and was sent to the front lines in France, where he witnessed the horrors of trench warfare. The brutality of the war, the senseless loss of life, and the stark reality of human suffering left a lasting impact on Lewis. The experience undergirded his belief in the emptiness of the universe and seemed to reinforce his atheistic convictions. Yet, paradoxically, it also deepened his longing for something more. For something that could make sense of the chaos and provide a foundation for hope.

After the war, Lewis returned to Oxford, where he pursued his studies in literature and philosophy. During this time, Lewis began to experience a series of intellectual and spiritual awakenings that would eventually lead him to embrace Christianity. One of the key influences in this process was his friendship with J. R. R. Tolkien, a devout Catholic and fellow professor at Oxford. Tolkien, along with other members of the Inklings (a literary group that included writers such as Charles Williams and Owen Barfield) challenged Lewis's atheistic assumptions and encouraged him to consider the possibility that his longings for joy were pointing him toward the greatest truth.

---

3. Lewis, *Surprised by Joy*, 128.

Tolkien, in particular, played a crucial role in helping Lewis understand the power of myth and the possibility that Christianity could be the "true myth"—a story that not only captured the most profound human longings but was also grounded in historical reality. During one memorable conversation in 1931, Tolkien and another friend, Hugo Dyson, walked with Lewis along the River Cherwell, discussing the nature of myth and the Christian story. Tolkien argued that the Christian narrative of a God who enters into human history to redeem humanity was not just another myth but the fulfillment of all myths. It was a story that was both profoundly meaningful and objectively true.

This conversation had a profound impact on Lewis. It helped him see that his longing for joy, what he described as an "unsatisfied desire which is itself more desirable than any other satisfaction," was not a mere illusion but a signpost pointing him to the divine.[4] It was a breakthrough moment that allowed him to reconcile his love for myth and imagination with his commitment to reason and truth.

Shortly after this conversation, Lewis had what he described as the "most dejected and reluctant convert in all England."[5] He moved from atheism to a belief in God, and eventually, in 1931, he embraced Christianity. This conversion was not a sudden, emotional experience but the culmination of a long intellectual and spiritual journey. Lewis described his experience of coming to faith as being "surprised by joy." He came to the realization that the very thing he had been seeking all his life, the source of his deepest longings, was found in the person of Jesus Christ.

Lewis's conversion marked a turning point not only in his personal life but also in his intellectual pursuits. He became one of the most influential Christian apologists of the twentieth century, using his formidable intellect and literary talent to defend the Christian faith and to address the deep spiritual hunger of his time. His journey from atheism to Christianity gave him a unique perspective on the challenges faced by those who, like himself, had struggled with doubt and disillusionment. It allowed him to speak with empathy and insight to a generation that had experienced the collapse of traditional certainties and was searching for something that could restore meaning and hope.

In the years following his conversion, Lewis began to write prolifically, producing works that addressed both the intellectual and

---

4. Lewis, *Surprised by Joy*, 15.
5. Lewis, *Surprised by Joy*, 221.

imaginative dimensions of faith. He believed Christianity was not only true but also deeply beautiful, capable of satisfying both the mind and the heart. His writings, which ranged from theological treatises to children's stories, were aimed at helping others see the world through the lens of faith, creating enchanted worlds where every aspect of reality was infused with divine meaning.

An Apologetic for the Intellect

C. S. Lewis was not content merely with presenting Christianity as a comforting narrative or a nostalgic return to past beliefs. He recognized that the modern world was full of intellectual challenges that demanded robust, reasoned responses. Lewis's apologetic works were his answer to these challenges, his attempt to engage with the skepticism and rationalism that characterized much of modern thought. By addressing the doubts and questions of both believers and non-believers, Lewis sought to demonstrate that Christianity was not only reasonable but also provided the most satisfying answers to the fundamental questions of human existence.

One of Lewis's most influential apologetic works is *Mere Christianity*. Originally delivered as a series of radio broadcasts during World War II, *Mere Christianity* aimed to present the core beliefs of Christianity in a way that was accessible to a broad audience. Lewis's approach in this work was to build a rational case for Christianity from the ground up, starting with the shared human experience of morality. He argued that the existence of a universal moral law (a sense of right and wrong shared by all people) pointed to the existence of a moral lawgiver, namely, God.

Lewis recognized that modernity had largely dismissed the idea of objective morality, favoring a relativistic view of ethics instead. However, Lewis contended that the very fact that humans make moral judgments and feel the weight of moral obligation suggested that there was something more than mere social convention at play. In *Mere Christianity*, he wrote, "If no set of moral ideas were truer or better than any other, there would be no sense in preferring civilized morality to savage morality, or Christian morality to Nazi morality."[6] By appealing to the shared human experience of moral truth, Lewis sought to demonstrate that belief

---

6. Lewis, *Mere Christianity*, 13.

in God was not only rational but also necessary to make sense of our deepest moral intuitions.

Another significant apologetic work by Lewis is *The Problem of Pain*. In this book, Lewis tackled one of the most challenging questions for believers and skeptics alike: How can a loving, all-powerful God allow suffering and evil to exist? This question became particularly urgent in the aftermath of two world wars as the world grappled with the reality of immense suffering and loss. Lewis acknowledged the emotional weight of this question but sought to provide a rational framework for understanding it.

In *The Problem of Pain*, Lewis argued that the existence of pain and suffering was not incompatible with the existence of a good God. He suggested that suffering, while challenging and often incomprehensible, could serve a greater purpose in the context of a fallen world. Lewis wrote, "God whispers to us in our pleasures, speaks in our conscience, but shouts in our pains: it is His megaphone to rouse a deaf world."[7] For Lewis, pain was a means by which God could draw human beings closer to himself, breaking through the illusions of self-sufficiency and reminding them of their dependence on the Creator. While this answer did not eliminate the emotional difficulty of suffering, it provided a way to understand it within the larger narrative of God's redemptive work.

Miracles is yet another of Lewis's apologetic works that directly engaged with the skepticism of his time. In this book, Lewis addressed the modern assumption that miracles were impossible due to the inviolability of natural laws. He challenged the materialist worldview underpinning this skepticism, arguing that the belief in natural laws did not preclude the possibility of supernatural intervention. Instead, Lewis suggested that the natural world was open to the influence of a higher, transcendent reality. He famously argued that if a Creator established the natural order, then that same Creator could choose to act within or outside that order.

Lewis approached the question of miracles not merely from the standpoint of faith but from the standpoint of reason. He contended that the modern dismissal of miracles was based on a philosophical presupposition of naturalistic materialism that could not account for the richness of human experience, including our encounters with beauty, love, and meaning. In *Miracles*, Lewis invited his readers to consider the possibility that the natural world was not a closed system but rather part of

---

7. Lewis, *Problem of Pain*, 81.

a larger, divinely orchestrated reality. By doing so, he sought to open the minds of skeptics to the possibility of the supernatural and to challenge the reductionist tendencies of modern thought.

Lewis also addressed the challenges posed by modern psychology and the reduction of human beings to mere biological or psychological mechanisms. In *The Abolition of Man*, Lewis critiqued the trend toward moral relativism and the rejection of objective values, which he saw as a consequence of modern educational practices and the influence of scientism. He argued that if humanity continued down this path of denying the existence of objective moral truths and reducing human beings to mere products of biology and conditioning, then the result would be the "abolition of man." In other words, we would lose what made us truly human: our capacity for moral judgment, our sense of wonder, and our ability to recognize and respond to the transcendent.

In *The Abolition of Man*, Lewis defended the concept of the "Tao," which was a term he used to describe the universal moral law that underlies all human cultures. He argued that this moral law was not a human invention but a reflection of the divine order and that to reject it was to undermine the very foundation of civilization. Lewis's critique of modern education and his defense of objective values were deeply relevant to the intellectual challenges of his time, as he sought to show that the rejection of moral absolutes would ultimately lead to a dehumanized and disenchanted world. He would write in this work, "Each new power won by man is a power over man as well. Each advance leaves him weaker as well as stronger."[8]

Through his apologetic works, Lewis provided a comprehensive response to the intellectual challenges of modernity. He engaged with questions of morality, suffering, miracles, and the nature of humanity in a way that was both intellectually rigorous and deeply personal. Lewis understood that the modern world needed more than abstract arguments: it needed a vision of faith that could speak to the heart as well as the mind. His apologetics were not just about proving the truth of Christianity; they were about showing that Christianity offered the most compelling answers. Yet, his apologetic method would not be solely aimed at the intellect, but in his works of fiction, he would direct it towards the imagination.

---

8. Lewis, *Abolition of Man*, 37.

An Apologetic for the Imagination

Lewis's imaginative fiction sought to touch the heart and soul, rekindling a sense of wonder in a world that had grown weary and cynical. C. S. Lewis's fiction was not merely an escape from reality; it was a means of illuminating reality, revealing deeper truths through story and symbol. The imaginative worlds that Lewis created in his novels were designed to bypass the defenses of the skeptical mind and speak directly to the imagination, awakening a sense of transcendence and pointing readers toward a greater reality.

One of the most enduring examples of Lewis's imaginative fiction is *The Chronicles of Narnia*. These beloved stories, which have captivated readers of all ages for generations, are filled with rich symbolism that speaks to the truths of the Christian faith. Through the land of Narnia, Lewis sought to create a world that would convey profound spiritual realities in a way that was accessible and compelling, particularly to those who might be resistant to more direct expressions of faith. The character of Aslan, the great lion who serves as the central figure of the series, is perhaps the most potent symbol in Lewis's fiction. Aslan embodies Christ's grand qualities—fierce and gentle, powerful and loving, just and merciful. Through Aslan's sacrificial death and resurrection in *The Lion, the Witch, and the Wardrobe*, Lewis presents a powerful allegory of the gospel, one that invites readers to see the beauty and wonder of the Christian story in a new light.

The symbolism of Aslan is not merely a didactic device; it invites readers into an experience of the divine. In Narnia, the reader encounters a world where the laws of nature are infused with magic, ordinary children are called to be heroes, and the presence of Aslan brings hope and transformation. This re-enchanted world starkly contrasts the disenchanted worldview of modernity, where everything is reduced to mere matter and mechanism.

In addition to *The Chronicles of Narnia*, Lewis's science fiction trilogy (*Out of the Silent Planet*, *Perelandra*, and *That Hideous Strength*) offers another powerful example of how he used the art of story to challenge the assumptions of modernity. These novels explore themes of spiritual warfare, the nature of evil, and the cosmic significance of human choices. In *Out of the Silent Planet*, Lewis introduces readers to a vision of the universe that is alive with spiritual meaning, in stark contrast to the cold, mechanistic view of the cosmos that had come to dominate modern thought. The protagonist, Dr. Ransom, embarks on a journey to Mars (or Malacandra, as it is known to its inhabitants), where he discovers a world that has not been tainted by the fall. Through his interactions with the alien races of Malacandra, Ransom comes to see the beauty of a creation that is in harmony with its Creator, offering a vision of what humanity has lost and what might be restored.

Perelandra, the second book in the trilogy, takes the reader to Venus, where Ransom participates in a cosmic struggle between good and evil. The story serves as a retelling of the Eden narrative, with Ransom fighting to prevent the "unmaking" of a new world. Through the vivid descriptions of the unfallen world of Perelandra, Lewis invites readers to imagine what might have been: a world without sin, filled with beauty, innocence, and the presence of God. The novel explores profound questions about freedom, temptation, and the nature of obedience, ultimately pointing readers to the hope of redemption and the possibility of restoration.

The final book in the trilogy, *That Hideous Strength*, is perhaps the most explicitly critical of modernity. It presents a dystopian vision of a world where the pursuit of power and control has led to the dehumanization of society. The story's villains, the National Institute for Coordinated Experiments (N.I.C.E.), embody the dangers of scientism. As explained in previous chapters, this is the belief that science and technology alone can solve all of humanity's problems. Through this chilling portrayal of a technocratic society, Lewis warns of the dangers of reducing human beings to mere objects to be manipulated and controlled. Yet even amid this dark vision, Lewis offers hope by providing a reminder that true power lies not in domination but in love, humility, and the recognition of the sacredness of creation.

In *The Great Divorce*, an allegorical tale exploring the nature of heaven and hell, choice, and the human condition, Lewis presents a group of souls from hell who can visit heaven's outskirts and choose whether to stay. The story is a powerful exploration of the nature of free will, the consequences of our choices, and how people can become so attached to their own sins and desires that they refuse the joy offered. Through vivid imagery and compelling characterizations, Lewis illustrates the idea that heaven and hell are, in a sense, the natural outworking of the choices we make in life. Those who choose to reject God ultimately create their own hell, while those who choose to surrender to his love find eternal joy. Lewis writes:

There are only two kinds of people in the end: those who say to God, "Thy will be done," and those to whom God says, in the end, "Thy will be done." All that are in Hell, choose it. Without that self-choice there could be no Hell. No soul that seriously and constantly desires joy will ever miss it. Those who seek find. Those who knock it is opened.[9]

The Great Divorce is also notable for its portrayal of heaven's overwhelming beauty and reality. The souls from hell, who are described as ghost-like and insubstantial, find themselves unable to fully experience the solid, vibrant reality of heaven. The grass is too sharp for their feet, the light too bright for their eyes. This imagery powerfully conveys the idea that heaven is not merely a continuation of earthly life but a deeper, more substantial reality. A reality that requires transformation and surrender to fully enter. Through this story, Lewis challenges the modern tendency to view heaven as a vague, ethereal concept, instead presenting it as the ultimate fulfillment of all that is true, good, and beautiful.

Though not a work of fiction in the same sense as Narnia or the space trilogy, *The Screwtape Letters* is another masterful example of how Lewis used storytelling to convey profound spiritual truths. The book takes the form of a series of letters from a senior demon, Screwtape, to his nephew, Wormwood, offering advice on how to tempt and corrupt a human soul. Through this satirical and often darkly humorous narrative, Lewis provides deep insights into the nature of temptation, the subtleties of spiritual warfare, and how human beings can be led away from God.

The Screwtape Letters is particularly effective in exposing the lies and deceptions that can lead to a disenchanted view of the world. Screwtape's advice to Wormwood often involves encouraging the "patient" to focus solely on the material aspects of life, to see faith as irrational, and to view the world through a lens of cynicism and despair.[10] By presenting these strategies from the enemy's perspective, Lewis not only reveals the spiritual battle in the hearts and minds of individuals but also challenges readers to recognize and resist the forces that seek to strip life of its meaning and wonder.

Through these imaginative works, Lewis sought to do more than entertain; he aimed to reawaken a sense of enchantment to help readers see the world as infused with eternal significance. The stories he told were not just allegories or didactic tools; they were invitations to experience a

---

9. Lewis, *Great Divorce*, 64.
10. Lewis, *Screwtape Letters*, 12.

deeper reality, to see the world through the lens of faith, and to recognize the presence of the divine in the ordinary. In a time when the modern worldview had stripped life of its mystery and meaning, Lewis's fiction offered a powerful reminder that the universe is far richer, more beautiful, and more meaningful than we often realize.

The symbolism in Lewis's fictional works bridges the seen and the unseen, the material and the spiritual. In Narnia, the figure of Aslan embodies the mystery of divine love and sacrifice; in the space trilogy, the vastness of the cosmos points to the grandeur of the Creator and the cosmic significance of human choices; and in *The Screwtape Letters*, the cunning deceptions of Screwtape reveal the reality of spiritual warfare and the importance of vigilance in the life of faith. Through these symbols and stories, Lewis sought to restore a sense of wonder and hope to a world that had grown cynical and disillusioned.

Lewis understood that the human heart longs for more than what the material world can offer. We long for meaning, beauty, and a sense of belonging in a universe that is more than just a collection of atoms and molecules. His fiction speaks to this longing, inviting readers to journey to other worlds, to encounter the divine, and to see their own world in a new light. By re-enchanting the imagination, Lewis provided a powerful antidote to the disenchantment of modernity, offering a vision of reality filled with hope, purpose, and the presence of a loving Creator.

Ultimately, Lewis's imaginative fiction was an invitation to see the world as it truly is: a creation that is deeply loved by its Creator, a place where every moment is charged with divine significance, and where the longing for joy points us beyond ourselves to the One who alone can satisfy the deepest desires of the human heart. In a disenchanted age, Lewis's stories continue to speak, reminding us that the world is far more mysterious and wonderful than we could ever imagine and that our lives are part of a much larger, much more beautiful story—the story of God's love for his creation.

Modernity's Nihilism Crushed by the Weight of Glory

C. S. Lewis's works responded robustly to the nihilism and despair that had taken hold of the modern world. At a time when many were questioning whether life had any meaning at all, Lewis offered a vision of hope, joy, and moral order that stood in stark contrast to the bleak outlook of modernity. His writings spoke and continue to speak to the deepest human longings for purpose and transcendence, offering a compelling case for why the Christian faith is not only intellectually credible but also profoundly satisfying to the human heart.

In his book *The Weight of Glory*, Lewis addresses the human longing for something beyond the material world—a longing that he believed pointed to our true home in the presence of God. He argued that the desire for beauty, joy, and transcendence was not something to be dismissed as mere wishful thinking but was evidence of our divine origin and destiny. He wrote:

> The books or the music in which we thought the beauty was located will betray us if we trust to them; it was not in them, it only came through them, and what came through them was longing. These things—the beauty, the memory of our own past—are good images of what we really desire, but if they are mistaken for the thing itself, they turn into dumb idols, breaking the hearts of their worshippers. For they are not the thing itself; they are only the scent of a flower we have not found, the echo of a tune we have not heard, news from a country we have never yet visited.[11]

For Lewis, the longing for beauty and joy was a signpost pointing to the ultimate reality of God, the source of all that is good and beautiful.

The Weight of Glory is a reflection of beauty and longing and a powerful critique of the nihilism that had taken root in the modern world. Lewis believed that the modern tendency to dismiss spiritual longing as mere emotionalism or escapism was a tragic mistake. He argued that our desire for something beyond the material world was not a weakness but a reflection of our true nature as beings created in the image of God. He states, "Indeed if we consider the unblushing promises of reward and the staggering nature of the rewards promised in the Gospels, it would seem that Our Lord finds our desires not too strong, but too weak."[12] The problem is not that people desire too much but that they settle for too little. They seek fulfillment in the transient pleasures of this world rather than in the eternal joy that can only be found in God.

Through his writings, Lewis sought to show that the Christian faith offered a coherent and satisfying answer to modernity's existential challenges. He believed that the modern rejection of God had led to a loss

---

11. Lewis, *Weight of Glory*, 30–31.
12. Lewis, *Weight of Glory*, 1–2.

of meaning and purpose and that people could only find the hope and joy they longed for by returning to faith. In *Mere Christianity*, Lewis presents the Christian faith as the answer to the problem of human sin and brokenness, offering a vision of redemption and transformation that is both intellectually compelling and emotionally satisfying. He writes, "God cannot give us a happiness and peace apart from Himself, because it is not there. There is no such thing."[13] For Lewis, true happiness and peace could only be found in a relationship with God, the source of all that is good and true.

Lewis also addressed the modern crisis of morality, arguing that the rejection of God had led to a loss of moral order and a descent into relativism and nihilism. He argues that without a belief in an objective moral law, society is left without any foundation for distinguishing between right and wrong, and the result is a loss of human dignity and a descent into chaos. Moral law was not something imposed on us from the outside but was an expression of our true nature as beings created in the image of God. Lewis writes, "A man does not call a line crooked unless he has some idea of a straight line."[14] In other words, the fact that we recognize injustice and evil is evidence of an objective moral standard that transcends human society, a standard that ultimately points to God.

Lewis also explored the themes of hope, joy, and moral order in his fiction, using storytelling to convey spiritual truths. In *The Chronicles of Narnia*, the characters experience moments of profound joy and wonder, often in the presence of Aslan, the great lion who represents Christ. These moments of joy are not just emotional highs; they are glimpses of a deeper reality, a foretaste of the ultimate joy that awaits those who belong to God. In *The Last Battle*, the final book of the series, Lewis presents a vision of the end of the world and the beginning of a new, eternal reality. This reality is more vivid, real, and beautiful than the characters have ever experienced. Through these stories, Lewis invites readers to see that Christian hope is not just wishful thinking but is grounded in the reality of God's love and the promise of eternal life.

Lewis's response to the nihilism of modernity was an invitation to experience the joy and hope of knowing God. He believed that the Christian faith offered a vision of reality far richer and more meaningful than the disenchanted, materialistic view of the modern age. Through his

---

13. Lewis, *Mere Christianity*, 31.
14. Lewis, *Mere Christianity*, 25.

apologetic writings, imaginative fiction, and personal testimony, Lewis sought to show that the world is not a cold, indifferent place but one infused with divine purpose and love. He offered a vision of a world where good and evil are real, where beauty and truth are intertwined, and where the longing for joy points us beyond ourselves to the Creator, who alone can satisfy the deepest desires of the human heart.

In a century marked by despair and disillusionment, C. S. Lewis emerged as a powerful voice of hope, joy, and moral clarity. He provided a roadmap for re-enchanting the world, for recovering the sense of wonder and meaning lost in the disillusionment of modernity. Through his writings, Lewis invited his readers to see the world through new eyes. To recognize that there is more to reality than what can be measured and quantified and that the greatest truths of our existence are found not in the material world but in the presence of God.

A Remarkable Legacy

Lewis's legacy as one of the most significant voices of the twentieth century cannot be overstated. At a time when the modern world was grappling with profound disillusionment and a pervasive sense of meaninglessness, Lewis emerged as a beacon of hope, offering an intellectually robust and imaginatively compelling vision of Christianity. His works have had an enduring impact, not only for their theological insight but also for their ability to rekindle a sense of wonder and enchantment in a world that had grown increasingly skeptical of faith.

Lewis's impact extended far beyond the realm of traditional Christian apologetics. His works reach a broad and diverse audience: those who are intellectually curious, those who are spiritually seeking, and even those who are doubtful or hostile towards religion. By addressing the rational and imaginative aspects of human experience, Lewis provided a holistic defense of the faith that appeals to the whole person. His works remind readers that Christianity is not merely a set of doctrines but a transformative story that speaks to the deepest longings of the human heart.

Through *Mere Christianity*, Lewis articulated the rational foundation of the Christian faith in a way that resonated with both believers and skeptics. His ability to communicate complex theological concepts in clear, relatable language helped bridge the gap between faith and reason, making Christianity accessible to those who had been alienated by the intellectual climate of modernity. Meanwhile, works like *The Problem of Pain* and *The Weight of Glory* demonstrated Lewis's sensitivity to the existential struggles of his time, offering both a defense of God's goodness and an invitation to embrace the beauty of divine grace.

But it was through his imaginative fiction that Lewis left his most profound mark. *The Chronicles of Narnia*, *The Great Divorce*, and *The Screwtape Letters* continue to inspire readers of all ages, inviting them to see the world through a lens of wonder, courage, and hope. Lewis understood that stories have a unique power to convey truth in a way that mere arguments cannot. By creating richly imagined worlds and compelling characters, he was able to communicate the beauty and depth of the Christian story in a way that spoke directly to the heart. His fiction has entertained and transformed lives, inviting readers to consider the deeper realities of good and evil, sacrifice, redemption, and the eternal significance of their choices.

His influence extends far beyond his own writings. He played a crucial role in reawakening an appreciation for myth, imagination, and the transcendent in an age that had largely dismissed such things as relics of a pre-scientific past. His works continue to inspire theologians, writers, artists, and ordinary believers, reminding them that faith is both profoundly reasonable and immensely beautiful. By refusing to separate reason from imagination, Lewis helped restore a profound understanding of what it means to be human. One that recognizes the importance of both intellect and wonder in the search for truth.

C. S. Lewis stood as a voice of hope in a century marked by growing cynicism and despair. He dared to suggest that the longing for meaning, beauty, and joy was not an illusion but a signpost pointing to the ultimate reality of God. He invited his readers to see that the world, far from being a cold, indifferent machine, was infused with divine purpose and love. His works continue to offer hope to those who find themselves disenchanted by the materialism and nihilism of modernity, pointing them to the incomprehensible joy that can only be found in Christ.

Yet, Lewis's voice is not the final word in our journey. While his emphasis on longing and imagination is essential, it must be complemented by a sober critique of the forces that have shaped the modern world and continue to challenge our ability to perceive the transcendent. This is where Jacques Ellul, the next figure in our exploration, enters the conversation. While Lewis invites us to rediscover joy and beauty, Ellul confronts us with the pervasive influence of technology and the modern systems that often obscure or distort that joy. Together, their insights form a complementary vision: Lewis helps us rekindle our longing for God, and Ellul equips us to navigate the technological and cultural challenges that threaten to suppress it.

13

Jacques Ellul
Technology, Personhood, and Authentic Living

"...we can be confident that the final result will be that technique will assimilate everything to the machine; the ideal for which technique strives is the mechanization of everything it encounters."

—Jacques Ellul[1]

IN THE MID-TWENTIETH CENTURY, when many celebrated the promise of technology to solve humanity's greatest problems, Jacques Ellul stood out as a profound prophetic voice warning of its unchecked power. A French sociologist, theologian, and philosopher, Ellul devoted his life to understanding the profound transformation wrought by the rise of the technological society. He was neither a Luddite nor a pessimist but a realist with a deeply Christian perspective who saw in technology a force that threatened to reshape human life, often at the cost of personhood, freedom, and spiritual depth.

Ellul's central insight was both radical and unsettling: technology, or what he termed *technique*, was no longer a tool under human control. Instead, it had become an autonomous system driven by its own internal logic of efficiency and progress. In his landmark work *The Technological*

---

1. Ellul, *Technological Society*, 12.

Society, Ellul captures a vision of the relentless momentum of technological advancement which basically says that what can be done will be done. This was not a celebration but a warning. For Ellul, the technological society represented a totalizing system that absorbed all other aspects of life: politics, culture, education, and even faith (AI much?), reducing them to mere functions of technical efficiency.

The consequences of this shift, Ellul argued, were profound. By prioritizing progress over purpose and efficiency over ethics, the technological society eroded the very foundations of human dignity and meaning. Individuals were no longer seen as ends in themselves but as resources to be optimized or problems to be solved. Community and connection gave way to isolation, as relationships were increasingly mediated by machines rather than forged through genuine encounters. The result was a world in which humanity would become alienated, not only from nature and each other but from our own spiritual essence.

What made Ellul's critique particularly compelling was his theological lens. As a Christian, he saw the technological society as both a cultural or philosophical issue and a spiritual crisis. He believed that the relentless pursuit of technological advancement had become a form of idolatry, displacing God as the ultimate source of meaning and purpose. Ellul writes, "The power of technique, mysterious though scientific, which covers the whole earth with its networks of waves, wires, and paper, is to the technician an abstract idol which gives him a reason for living and even for joy."[2] The answer, Ellul would argue, lay not in rejecting technology outright but in reclaiming personhood, community, and authentic living through faith.

As we delve into Ellul's thought, we will see how his prophetic voice calls us not to despair but to discern—to recognize the ways technology shapes our lives and to reclaim our identity as persons created in the image of God. In an age that often values machines over people and progress over purpose, Ellul challenges us to live authentically, to foster genuine community, and to seek meaning not in what we can produce but in who we are and to whom we belong. Ellul reminds us that the modern world, for all its advancements, cannot satisfy the deepest longings of the human heart. His vision is not a call to retreat but to resist, to live faithfully and fully in a world where technology must serve humanity, not enslave it.

---

2. Ellul, *Technological Society*, 144–45.

The Rise of the Technological Society

Jacques Ellul's analysis of technology begins with his stark observation that the modern world is no longer defined by humanity's relationship to tools but by the overwhelming presence of *technique*. By this, Ellul does not mean technology in the narrow sense of machines or inventions but rather a way of thinking and acting that prioritizes efficiency, optimization, and progress above all else. For Ellul, technique is the driving force of the modern world, shaping how we work and how we think, live, and relate to one another. He declared, "Technique has become autonomous; it has fashioned an omnivorous world which obeys its own laws and has renounced all tradition."[3]

Ellul's insight that technology as self-perpetuating and autonomous is critical to understanding his critique. Unlike tools of the past, which were created to serve specific human needs, modern technological systems evolve independently of those needs. Once a new technique or invention is discovered, it inevitably seeks implementation, not because it fulfills a moral or societal good but because it can be done. Herein lies the great danger—just because something can be done does not mean it should.

To illustrate this autonomy, consider the rapid proliferation of digital surveillance technologies in the twenty-first century. These systems, often justified as necessary for security, expand relentlessly, creating a world where privacy is increasingly rare. The driving force is not merely human intent but the internal momentum of the technological system itself—each advancement demanding the next, each efficiency building upon another, until the system seems to operate beyond human control. As Ellul noted, "When technique enters into every area of life, including the human, it ceases to be external to man and becomes his very substance. It is no longer face to face with man but is integrated with him, and it progressively absorbs him."[4]

This relentless drive toward efficiency, Ellul argued, comes at a profound cost: the erosion of ethical, spiritual, and cultural values. In a society dominated by technique, moral considerations are often subordinated to technical feasibility. The question shifts from "Should we do this?" to "Can we do this?" Wendell Berry, another sharp critic of modernity, observed, "Technology joins us to energy, to life. It is not, as many technologists would have us believe, a simple connection. Our

---

3. Ellul, *Technological Society*, 14.
4. Ellul, *Technological Society*, 6.

technology is the practical aspect of our culture. By it, we enact our religion, or our lack of it."[5]

One of Ellul's most urgent concerns was how technological society erases human connection with the transcendent. He believed that the prioritization of technique led to a world increasingly detached from its ultimate source of meaning and easily given to any ideologies driven by the system. Regarding this, he writes, "Technique also encourages and develops mystical phenomena. It promotes the indispensable alienation from the self-necessary, for example, for the identification of the individual with an ideology."[6]

The rise of the technological society was not merely a historical development but a paradigm shift. As technology expanded its reach, it began to absorb and transform every other sphere of life. What once existed as distinct realms of human activity became subsumed into the logic of technique, reshaped to maximize efficiency and output. Ellul noted, "Technique must reduce man to a technical animal, the king of the slaves of technique. Human caprice crumbles before this necessity; there can be no human autonomy in the face of technical autonomy."[7] For example, in education, technological systems often emphasize measurable outcomes over the development of wisdom or moral character. Standardized testing, digital learning platforms, and algorithm-driven curriculums may increase efficiency, but they can also reduce the richness of education to a series of data points, stripping away the relational and transformative aspects of learning.

Ellul's critique finds resonance in the work of cultural historian Lewis Mumford, who described the rise of what he called the "megamachine," which referred to a system of technological and bureaucratic control that increasingly dominates human life. Mumford writes, "Individual initiative and responsibility had no place in the megamachine; for such freedom might mean countermanding faulty orders or disobeying immoral ones."[8] Ellul's insights extend this critique, showing how the worship of efficiency replaces the pursuit of the good life with a relentless drive for more: more speed, more productivity, more control. To be anything else is to be "out of step."

---

5. Berry, *Art of the Commonplace*, 280.
6. Ellul, *Technological Society*, 423.
7. Ellul, *Technological Society*, 138.
8. Mumford, *Myth of the Machine*, 183.

In understanding the rise of the technological society, Ellul forces us to confront an uncomfortable truth: technology is not neutral. It shapes the way we see the world, the values we prioritize, and the relationships we form. It embeds itself into the very fabric of our existence, subtly redefining what it means to be human. Technology often provides us with a sense of mastery, but it can also blind us to the reality that we are creatures, not gods.

Ellul's analysis of the technological society is not a condemnation of all technology but a call to discernment. By exposing the autonomy and power of technique, he challenges us to ask deeper questions: What kind of world are we building? What values are we sacrificing for the sake of progress? And how can we reclaim our humanity in the face of a system that so often seeks to suppress it?

As we move forward, these questions will guide our exploration of Ellul's warnings about the dehumanizing effects of technology and his vision for a life that resists its pressures. Ellul's critique does not leave us without hope, but it begins with a clear-eyed recognition of the challenges we face. His prophetic voice calls us to confront the reality of the technological society, not with despair but with courage and a commitment to rediscover what it means to live as fully human beings.

The Crisis of Personhood

Ellul saw the technological society as one that diminishes personhood, turning people into objects to be manipulated or data points to be processed. This dehumanization manifests in countless ways, from the commodification of personal relationships through dating apps to the reduction of human labor to economic efficiency metrics. The result, Ellul argued, is a world in which individuals are valued not for who they are but for what they can produce. Man becomes a stranger to himself, a tool among tools, his identity lost in the collective logic of technique.

This loss of identity contributes directly to the crisis of meaning. Human beings, Ellul observed, are not merely functional entities; they are spiritual creatures, created for relationship, creativity, and reflection. When these dimensions of life are subordinated to the demands of efficiency, people experience a profound sense of alienation—from themselves, from others, and from the divine. In its pursuit of progress, the technological society often leaves individuals feeling purposeless, trapped in a system that cares little for their deepest longings.

Ellul also identified alienation as a central feature of the technological society. In a world dominated by systems, individuals are increasingly isolated from one another, their relationships mediated by screens and algorithms. This alienation is not merely physical but existential: the technological society fosters a sense of detachment as individuals struggle to find connection and purpose in a world that prioritizes efficiency over relationships.

The rise of digital communication technologies provides a stark example. While these tools promise to bring people closer together, they often have the opposite effect, replacing deep, meaningful interactions with shallow, transactional exchanges. As philosopher Albert Borgmann observed, "Indifference and disengagement are the ways in which technology has invaded and subverted public life and left us with a semblance of the public."[9] Such trends erode the bonds of community, leaving individuals feeling isolated and disconnected in a world that increasingly resembles a machine. This loss of community further deepens the crisis of meaning. Human beings, Ellul argued, are created for relationship, both with one another and with God. When these relationships are undermined, individuals lose a vital source of purpose and identity.

One of Ellul's most striking insights was his rejection of the idea that technology is neutral. Many assume that technology is a tool shaped entirely by how humans choose to use it. Ellul, however, argued that technology is not passive but active. It shapes human values, behaviors, and perceptions in ways that often go unnoticed. Technique does not simply answer a need; it creates new needs, new desires, and new dependencies.

In a technological society, value is increasingly measured in terms of utility and productivity, sidelining questions of moral or spiritual significance. This shift has profound implications for how people understand themselves and their purpose. When everything is reduced to what can be measured and optimized, the deeper questions of existence—Why am I here? What is my purpose?—are left unanswered, fostering a sense of emptiness and despair.

Ellul's critique resonates with the insights of other thinkers, such as Václav Havel, who observed that the modern obsession with technology and progress often masks a deeper existential emptiness and pushes us further into one. Havel writes:

9. Borgmann, *Power Failure*, 50.

> Technology—that child of modern science, which in turn is a child of modern metaphysics—is out of humanity's control, has ceased to serve us, has enslaved us and compelled us to participate in the preparation of our own destruction. And humanity can find no way out: we have no idea and no faith, and even less do we have a political conception to help us bring things back under human control. We look on helplessly as that coldly functioning machine we have created inevitably engulfs us, tearing us away from our natural affiliations.[10]

The dehumanizing effects of technology are not limited to individuals; they ripple outward, shaping entire cultures and societies. Ellul warned that the technological society fosters a cycle of dehumanization, where individuals and communities become increasingly alienated from their own humanity. This spiral, he argued, deepens the crisis of meaning, as people struggle to find their place in a world that seems to value machines over human beings.

The voices of thinkers like Borgmann, Havel, and Ellul call us to confront this reality with courage and clarity. They challenge us to recognize the ways in which technology shapes not only our actions but also our values, perceptions, and relationships. Their critique is not a rejection of technology but a call to reclaim our humanity in the face of its dehumanizing tendencies.

Faith in a Technological World

At the heart of Ellul's response to the technological society lies his unwavering conviction that faith in God offers a counternarrative to the forces of dehumanization and alienation. Ellul believed that the modern obsession with technology is, at its core, a spiritual crisis. It is a displacement of God with a false hope in human ingenuity. Modern man believes in technology the way his ancestors believed in God. For Ellul, this misplacement of faith not only compound the crisis of meaning but also require a radical reorientation toward the transcendent.

This framework begins with the recognition of two competing realities: the kingdom of God and the kingdom of technique. The kingdom of God, as Ellul understood it, is characterized by love, grace, humility, and community. It calls individuals into a relationship with the Creator

---

10. Havel, *Living in Truth*, 114.

and with one another, affirming human value and purpose as beings made in God's image. In contrast, the kingdom of technique is marked by efficiency, control, and the prioritization of systems over people. It reduces individuals to means rather than ends, fostering alienation and disconnection. Ellul details the danger of the materialist embrace of the technique as man's telos when he writes:

> Action which is entirely directed towards the material world, by eliminating its spiritual elements, in the last resort necessarily destroys this spiritual reality which lies at the heart of intelligence. The latter has become more and more the slave of its method, and can no longer find a way of escape. That which ought to be the liberation of the intelligence is the worst slavery that it has ever known—set free from dogmas it is the slave of means.[11]

For Ellul, the tension between these two kingdoms is unavoidable. To live as a Christian is to live in contradiction to the values of the technological society. This contradiction does not mean rejecting technology outright but approaching it with discernment, ensuring that it serves humanity rather than enslaving it. Ellul believed that Christians are called to resist the dehumanizing tendencies of technique by embodying the values of God's kingdom: values that prioritize relationship, humility, and the sacredness of life.

Ellul viewed the Christian's role in the technological society as inherently prophetic. Like the prophets of the Old Testament who called Israel back to faithfulness in the face of idolatry, Ellul believed that Christians are called to challenge the idolatry of technology. This prophetic role involves exposing the lies of the technological society: its false promises of salvation through progress, its dehumanizing effects, and its tendency to obscure the transcendent.

This critique must be grounded in the gospel, which offers an alternative vision of life rooted in love, grace, and hope. He argued that Christians must serve as a countercultural witness, demonstrating that meaning and purpose are found not in what we produce or achieve but in our relationship with God and others. Ellul writes:

> This dissociation of our life into two spheres: the one 'spiritual,' where we can be 'perfect,' and the other material and unimportant: where we behave like other people, is one of the reasons why the Churches have so little influence on the world...All we

---

11. Ellul, *Presence of the Kingdom*, 112.

can say is: that this is the exact opposite of what Jesus Christ wills for us, and of that which He came to do.[12]

This emphasizes the importance of discernment in navigating the challenges of the technological society. Ellul warned that Christians must not passively accept every technological innovation as inherently good or neutral. Instead, they must critically evaluate its impact on human life, community, and faith. The question is not whether we can use technology but whether its use aligns with the values of the kingdom of God.

This discernment requires wisdom and humility, recognizing that not all progress is beneficial and that some innovations may come at the cost of our humanity. For example, the rise of automation and artificial intelligence are developments that, while increasing efficiency, risk devaluing human labor and creativity. Ellul urges Christians to ask difficult questions: Does this technology enhance our ability to love and serve one another? Does it draw us closer to God, or does it distract us from the eternal?

Ellul emphasized the importance of community in resisting the pressures of the technological society. The church has a vital role to play as a countercultural community, offering a space where individuals can rediscover their personhood and find meaning beyond the logic of efficiency. The church, he believed, should model a way of life that prioritizes love, generosity, and humility over productivity and control.

Preserving Human Dignity in an Era of AI

Jacques Ellul's vision for authentic living stands as both a critique of and a roadmap through the challenges posed by the technological society. In an age where artificial intelligence, automation, and rapid technological advancement threaten to reshape every aspect of our existence, Ellul's insights remain profoundly relevant. His work compels us to consider not only how we use technology but how it uses us: how it shapes our values, our relationships, and our understanding of what it means to be human. As AI increasingly encroaches on domains once thought to be exclusively human—art, writing, decision-making, ethics—Ellul's ideas offer both a warning and a foundation for hope. Ellul believed that the key to resisting the dehumanizing effects of the technological society lies in reclaiming what he called *authentic living*. This concept is not simply about rejecting

---

12. Ellul, *Presence of the Kingdom*, 14.

technology; it is about living intentionally, with an awareness of how our tools shape us and a commitment to protecting the intrinsic value of human life.

The rapid development of artificial intelligence has amplified many of the concerns Ellul raised decades ago. From the rise of autonomous systems in warfare to algorithms that determine what we see, buy, and even believe, AI exemplifies the autonomy of technology Ellul warned against. While these tools offer incredible potential, they also risk reducing human beings to data points and resources to be optimized.

As AI systems take over increasingly complex tasks, they risk undermining the uniqueness of human creativity, judgment, and relationality. Philosopher Martin Heidegger echoed this concern when he warned that technology's ultimate danger lies in its capacity to reduce human beings to mere "standing-reserve"—resources to be managed rather than persons with intrinsic worth.[13]

Ellul challenges us to resist this trend by reaffirming human dignity as rooted not in productivity but in being created in the image of God. This theological insight is a vital counterpoint to a society increasingly tempted to measure worth in terms of output and efficiency. In a world of intelligent machines, Ellul reminds us that humans are not simply programmable entities but relational beings whose value transcends material utility.

We must be aware of the subtle ways technology reshapes our desires and perceptions. AI-driven personalization, whether through social media algorithms, targeted advertisements, or recommendation engines, risks narrowing our view of the world, trapping us in echo chambers that reinforce biases and limit genuine discovery. These systems, while efficient, often prioritize engagement over truth, fostering a society more fragmented and polarized than ever before.

Ellul's call for authentic living is a direct response to this danger. He believed that living authentically requires a commitment to truth, community, and transcendence, values that resist the commodification of human life. Authentic living demands that we critically engage with technology, asking not only what it can do but what it does to us. It calls us to slow down, cultivate relationships, and seek meaning in what is eternal rather than ephemeral.

Ellul's emphasis on discernment and resistance is particularly relevant in an era where AI's influence extends into ethics, governance, and

---

13. Heidegger, *Question Concerning Technology and Other Essays*, 20.

creativity. Systems like ChatGPT, autonomous vehicles, and predictive policing illustrate how technology increasingly makes decisions that affect human lives. Ellul would urge us to remember that these systems, while powerful, are not neutral. They carry the values and biases of their creators, and their widespread adoption can have unintended consequences.

Ellul's work provides not only a foundation but a starting point for addressing the challenges of the technological society. His insights must be expanded and adapted to meet the unique demands of an AI-driven world. This involves not only critiquing technology but also constructing practices and systems that prioritize human flourishing.

Ellul's prophetic voice calls us to remember that technology, for all its power and promise, must remain a servant, not a master. The path forward lies in balancing the incredible advancements of the modern age with the timeless truths that ground us as human beings created in the image of God. We must resist the temptation to define ourselves by efficiency or productivity and instead reclaim the sacredness of personhood, the richness of community, and the depth of spiritual life.

As we continue the journey into a world shaped by AI and ever-accelerating technological change, Ellul's legacy offers a compass and a reminder that progress must serve humanity and not the other way around. By grounding our lives in faith, fostering authentic relationships, and embracing the mystery of existence, we can ensure that the path of discovery does not lead us to lose ourselves but instead brings us closer to the truth of who we are and who we are called to be.

The Path to Meaning

Jacques Ellul provided a roadmap for reclaiming meaning and authenticity in a world increasingly dominated by systems and efficiency. For Ellul, the antidote to the dehumanizing effects of technology lay in a deliberate choice to live differently. Humanity must resist the pressures of conformity and embrace a way of life rooted in faith, personhood, and community. This resistance, however, requires a profound awareness of how modern systems, including technology and propaganda, shape not only our actions but also our thoughts, values, and desires.

In his seminal work *Propaganda: The Formation of Men's Attitudes*, Ellul demonstrated how propaganda operates as a subtle and pervasive force in modern society, shaping public opinion and individual behavior. Unlike traditional forms of coercion, propaganda infiltrates the very fabric of culture, influencing how people perceive reality and make decisions. Ellul argued that propaganda is inseparable from the technological society, as it leverages the tools of mass communication to normalize the values of efficiency, progress, and control. He writes:

> "To draw the individual into the net of propaganda, each technique must be utilized in its own specific way, directed toward producing the effect it can best produce, and fused with all the other media, each of them reaching the individual in a specific fashion and making him react anew to the same theme—in the same direction, but differently."[14]

Ellul's analysis of propaganda reveals its role in deepening the crisis of meaning. By inundating individuals with messages designed to elicit conformity, propaganda erodes personal autonomy and critical thinking, reducing people to passive recipients of information. This dynamic aligns with Ellul's broader critique of technology as a system that prioritizes utility over authenticity. In a society dominated by propaganda, individuals lose their ability to ask fundamental questions about purpose and truth, instead accepting the narratives imposed by the system.

Ellul also emphasized the importance of community in resisting the dehumanizing effects of technology and propaganda. He believed that authentic relationships are essential for finding meaning and purpose, as they provide a context for love, accountability, and mutual support. In a world where technology often isolates individuals, the church has a unique role to play as a countercultural community—a place where people can reconnect with their true selves and with God.

Community, for Ellul, was not merely a social construct but a spiritual necessity. He saw the church as a prophetic voice, calling individuals to reject the idols of efficiency and progress and to embrace a life centered on grace, humility, and love. This vision challenges modern Christians to live in a way that contrasts sharply with the values of the technological society, demonstrating that meaning is found not in accumulation or control but in connection and faithfulness.

Ellul's vision for authentic living is a call to resistance—not a rejection of technology but a refusal to let it define us. It is a call to rediscover what it means to be human, to prioritize relationships over efficiency,

---

14. Ellul, *Propaganda*, 10.

and to seek meaning in the eternal rather than the ephemeral. In a world dominated by systems, Ellul challenges us to live faithfully, to embody the values of the kingdom of God, and to offer hope to those who feel lost in the machinery of modern life.

As we turn to the next chapter on Francis Schaeffer, we will see how Ellul's critique of the technological society complements Schaeffer's deep concern for the collapse of absolute truth in modern thought. While Ellul exposes how technology and propaganda shape human behavior and erode personhood, Schaeffer traces the intellectual roots of this crisis, showing how the abandonment of objective truth has led to moral relativism, existential despair, and cultural fragmentation. Schaeffer's work offers a compelling response, calling for a return to a coherent Christian worldview that speaks both to the mind and to the heart. Together, their insights challenge us to resist the forces that strip life of meaning while equipping us with a firm intellectual and spiritual foundation to reclaim the God who is there.

14

Francis Schaeffer

Reclaiming the God Who Is There

"Nihilism is the product of a simple equation: God Is Dead; therefore, Man is Dead; therefore, Meaning is Dead."

—Francis Schaeffer[1]

From his small yet influential retreat in the Swiss Alps (L'Abri), Francis Schaeffer welcomed seekers, skeptics, and students, engaging in deep conversations about philosophy, art, theology, and the meaning of life. His work was not merely academic but intensely personal, born from a deep concern that modern humanity, having severed itself from God, was plunging headlong into existential despair. Schaeffer emerged as a prophet-like figure, standing at the crossroads of faith and culture, warning of the consequences of a world that had abandoned absolute truth.

Few thinkers in the modern era have been as effective at diagnosing the intellectual, moral, and cultural crisis of the West as Schaeffer. He saw, with remarkable clarity, how the philosophical shifts of previous centuries had created a world that no longer believed in truth, where relativism, nihilism, and fragmented thinking had left individuals disconnected from meaning. For Schaeffer, these were not abstract academic concerns;

---

1. Schaeffer, *God Who Is There*, 80.

they were the root causes of personal and societal collapse. His urgent message was simple yet profound: if we lose belief in the God who is there, we lose all rational basis for meaning, morality, and human dignity.

At a time when many Christians were retreating into either anti-intellectualism or cultural accommodation, Schaeffer refused both extremes. He championed a robust Christian worldview that could stand up to the most rigorous philosophical scrutiny while remaining deeply transformative in practice. His approach blended apologetics, cultural critique, and relational engagement, inviting people not just to believe in Christianity but to see it as the only livable foundation for reality itself.

This chapter will explore Schaeffer's critique of modernity, his defense of absolute truth, and his vision for a holistic, intellectually credible, and existentially fulfilling Christianity. As we delve into his work, we will see that Schaeffer was not just a critic of secular thought but a builder of bridges, helping people find their way back to a faith that is both intellectually satisfying and spiritually nourishing. His insights remain as urgent today as they were in his own time, as the world continues to wrestle with the consequences of relativism, cultural fragmentation, and the longing for a truth that can truly set us free.

The Collapse of Truth

Francis Schaeffer's great strength as a thinker and cultural critic was his ability to trace the genealogy of ideas. He was able to see not only what the modern world had become but how it had arrived there. He was not content merely to observe cultural trends: he sought to uncover the intellectual and spiritual assumptions that shaped them. For Schaeffer, the great tragedy of the modern age was its loss of truth—not merely religious truth but the very foundation of knowledge, ethics, and reality itself.

In his work *How Should We Then Live*, Schaeffer writes:

> No totalitarian authority nor authoritarian state can tolerate those who have an absolute by which to judge that state and its actions. The Christians had that absolute in God's revelation. Because the Christians had an absolute, universal standard by which to judge not only personal morals but the state, they were 'counted as enemies...'[2]

---

2. Schaeffer, *How Should We Then Live*, 26.

Modernity's rejection of objective truth led to more than moral ambiguity. It created a void in which power and pragmatism replaced principle. Without a transcendent standard, what remained was an age defined by confusion, manipulation, and, ultimately, despair.

Schaeffer traced the roots of this crisis back to the Enlightenment, where the West shifted its foundation from a God-centered understanding of reality to a purely human-centered one. At first, this shift did not seem catastrophic; many Enlightenment thinkers still assumed a stable moral order, even as they rejected divine revelation. But, as Schaeffer pointed out, when one starts with man alone, inevitably, one has no basis for meaning, morals, or beauty. The Enlightenment's confidence in reason apart from God gradually eroded into skepticism, relativism, and, ultimately, nihilism.

Schaeffer saw this progression clearly: as the nineteenth and twentieth centuries unfolded, thinkers such as Hegel, Nietzsche, and Sartre carried Enlightenment humanism to its logical conclusion—the denial of any objective meaning in the universe. The consequences were devastating. What began as a philosophical shift among elites filtered down into art, literature, education, and eventually everyday life. Schaeffer lamented that modern man "has both feet firmly planted in mid-air," adrift, without foundation, trying to construct meaning in a universe that no longer provided it.[3]

This collapse was evident in the two-story divide, one of Schaeffer's most insightful contributions to understanding modern thought. He argued that Western civilization had split reality into two separate levels. The lower story consisted of science, reason, and empirical facts—the realm of what was deemed "objectively real." The upper story included ethics, beauty, religion, and human meaning—the realm of subjective values.[4] By making this distinction, modernity exiled meaning to the upper story, rendering it private, personal, and ultimately irrelevant to public life. Schaeffer warned that this division had disastrous consequences, mainly the loss of any hope regarding a unified field of knowledge.

This fragmentation left modern people deeply conflicted. Modern man longed for beauty, purpose, and moral order, but their intellectual framework provided no reason to believe in them. Schaeffer's diagnosis was stark: modern thought had committed intellectual suicide, cutting

---

3. Quoted in Beckwith and Koukl, *Relativism*, 5.
4. For his full analysis of this, see Schaeffer's *Escape from Reason*.

itself off from the only foundation that could sustain truth—the existence of a personal, knowable God.

Schaeffer, however, was not content to leave his critique in the realm of abstract ideas; he vividly demonstrated how the loss of truth reshaped every sphere of life, from politics to art to personal identity. In the realm of ethics, Schaeffer observed that relativism had destroyed the moral clarity of the West. If there were no absolute truths, then morality was reduced to social consensus or individual preference. In *How Should We Then Live*, he notably warned that, in such a world, morality would inevitably be determined by those with the most power. He writes, "If there is no absolute beyond man's ideas, then there is no final appeal to judge between individuals and groups whose moral judgments conflict. We are merely left with conflicting opinions."[5] This was not mere speculation: Schaeffer saw in history the devastating results of this shift, particularly in the totalitarian ideologies of the twentieth century.

In art and culture, Schaeffer pointed to the increasing alienation and fragmentation evident in modern literature, painting, and music. He saw the shift from classical beauty to abstract despair as a symptom of deeper philosophical currents. He argued that modern art no longer sought to reflect reality but to mirror the meaninglessness that its creators had come to accept. He saw modern art as an expression of the same despair that permeates modern philosophy and modern life. From the chaotic works of Jackson Pollock to the existential absurdity of Samuel Beckett, Schaeffer saw a civilization that had lost its vision of order and coherence.

On a deeply personal level, Schaeffer recognized that the abandonment of truth left people spiritually disoriented. Without a transcendent reference point, individuals were left to construct their own meaning, a burden too great for the human soul to bear. This, for Schaeffer, was the ultimate tragedy of secularism: not just that it was intellectually false but that it was existentially unbearable.

By the late twentieth century, Schaeffer described a Western culture in free fall, accelerating toward moral chaos, spiritual emptiness, and societal collapse. Yet he did not despair: he believed that Christianity offered the only real alternative to the crisis. Schaeffer's work was not merely about critiquing modernity; it was about calling people back to a coherent, livable worldview.[6] He issued a clarion call to Christians to

---

5. Schaeffer, *How Should We Then Live*, 145.
6. See Schaeffer's *God Who Is There* and *He Is There and He Is Not Silent*.

reclaim the foundation of absolute truth, not only through apologetics but through a renewed way of living. Schaeffer believed that Christianity was not just a set of propositional truths but a holistic vision of reality that had to be both defended and embodied.

Schaeffer's Answer to the Crisis

If human beings were no longer anchored in a transcendent reality, if all meaning was self-constructed, then everything—ethics, purpose, and even identity—became negotiable, vulnerable to the whims of culture and power. But Schaeffer did not simply lament this decline; he insisted that Christianity, rightly understood, provided the only intellectually credible and existentially satisfying answer to the meaning crisis.

The God Who Is There was written to reintroduce modern people to a God who is not an abstraction or an impersonal force but a real, personal being—a being who is both transcendent and immanent, absolute and relational. Schaeffer's conviction was that Christianity is not merely a system of religious sentiments or ethical principles but the true and total reality that explains all of existence.

Schaeffer titled one of his books *He is There and He is Not Silent*. With these words, and throughout the book, he boldly proclaimed that God is not only real but that he has spoken, revealing himself in history, in Scripture, and ultimately in the person of Jesus Christ. This, for Schaeffer, was the central issue: in a world that had abandoned the possibility of knowing objective truth, Christianity alone offered truth that was both rational and relational, both propositional and personal. He writes:

> We can say it in another way, however, and that is that the infinite-personal God, the God who is Trinity, has spoken. He is there, and he is not silent. There is no use having a silent God. We would not know anything about him. He has spoken and told us what he is and that he existed before all else, and so we have the answer to the existence of what is.[7]

One of Schaeffer's most enduring contributions was his insistence that Christianity is a unified, comprehensive worldview that provides a foundation for every area of life. This included not just private religious experience but also philosophy, ethics, art, science, and politics. In contrast to the compartmentalized thinking of modernity, which had

---

7. Schaeffer, *He Is There and He Is Not Silent*, 18.

separated faith from reason, Schaeffer presented a vision of Christianity as the only fully integrated perspective on reality.

This meant that Christianity was not simply a belief system for personal devotion; it was a claim about the way the world actually is. Schaeffer argued that many Christians had unwittingly accepted modernity's false division between sacred and secular, reducing their faith to a private experience rather than an all-encompassing reality. This, he believed, was why so many believers struggled to respond effectively to the challenges of their time. Christians had conceded too much, allowing Christianity to be treated as a mere matter of personal preference rather than the foundation of all knowledge and existence.

At the heart of Schaeffer's response to modernity's collapse was the necessity of recovering the authority and coherence of biblical revelation. He saw the abandonment of Scripture as the primary reason the West had lost its way, arguing that without divine revelation, humanity is left with nothing but speculation and self-invention. Unless our epistemology is right, everything else is going to be wrong.

Epistemology refers to our theory of knowledge, our ability to distinguish between truth and falsehood. Schaeffer saw modern skepticism as the inevitable result of rejecting God as the ultimate source of knowledge. If knowledge is purely subjective, then certainty is impossible, and all that remains is opinion and power. This, Schaeffer argued, was precisely what had happened in the twentieth century.

In contrast, Christianity provided a solid epistemological foundation—a way of knowing that was rooted in God's self-revelation. Schaeffer, in his major works, regularly pointed to three key pillars of this foundation:[8]

1. *The Existence of an Objective God*—A personal, infinite God who is the source of all reality and meaning.

2. *The Reality of Divine Revelation*—God has spoken, and his Word (both in nature and Scripture) provides real, knowable truth.

3. *The Historical Foundation of Christianity*—Unlike existentialist or mystical religious claims, Christianity is grounded in historical events—especially the incarnation, crucifixion, and resurrection of Jesus Christ.

---

8. See Schaeffer, *God Who Is There* and *He Is There and He Is Not Silent*.

By restoring confidence in biblical authority, Schaeffer sought to rescue modern people from their epistemological free fall and give them a firm foundation.

One of Schaeffer's most striking arguments was that modern secularists, despite their claims of rational superiority, had actually abandoned reason. Having rejected God, they had cut themselves off from the only foundation that made logic, science, and morality meaningful. He insisted that Christianity is not opposed to reason; it is the only worldview that fully sustains it. Not that reason inherently gives credence to faith but that reason and faith are both based upon the existence of the infinite-personal God who is there.

In other words, faith and reason were not opposites but deeply connected—Christianity did not ask people to abandon logic but to embrace a larger rationality that included both natural and supernatural realities. He lamented that many believers had accepted a narrow and defensive posture, retreating from intellectual engagement rather than showing the world that Christianity provides the most rationally satisfying framework for life and the only presuppositional basis by which such a rational framework can exist.

Schaeffer's work was particularly significant in showing that modern secularists were actually living in contradiction to their own worldview. They spoke of morality, justice, and human dignity, but their philosophical foundations provided no reason why such things should exist. Christianity, on the other hand, could account for these values, rooting them in the character and nature of a just and loving Creator.

Schaeffer's message was clear: Christianity is not a blind leap of faith, contra Kierkegaard, but instead, a comprehensive and coherent worldview that makes sense of both the mind and the soul. It is both true to reason and satisfying to the deepest human longings. It is a faith that invites both intellectual conviction and existential rest. It is a faith that "encapsulates reason, and is not a belief in the void."[9]

Schaeffer's apologetic was not merely philosophical; it was deeply relational. Unlike sterile systems of thought, Christianity was not just about an idea but a person—the living God who had entered human history to redeem broken people. Christianity is not a monolithic religion based on a collection of abstract ideas; rather, it is a personal relationship with the infinite-personal God.

---

9. Schaeffer, *God Who Is There*, 65.

This was Schaeffer's final, resounding answer to modernity's meaning crisis: the universe is not silent, and human beings are not alone. The aching emptiness of modern thought was the result of trying to find meaning without the presence of a personal God. But in Christ, Schaeffer argued, we encounter the fulfillment of our deepest intellectual and emotional needs. The answer to modern despair was not merely a more convincing argument; it was a return to the God who speaks, who loves, and who is there.

Schaeffer's response to modernity was not simply intellectual but deeply practical. His goal was not just to refute bad ideas but to restore a foundation for living and to reclaim truth in every sphere of life. Christianity, rightly understood, was not just a religion to be believed but a way of life to be lived, a vision of reality that made sense of everything from philosophy to family, from science to the arts.

True Spirituality

For all his intellectual rigor, Schaeffer was deeply concerned that many Christians had embraced a purely rational or doctrinal faith that, while perhaps sound in belief, was lifeless in practice. In his view, defending absolute truth was not enough—it had to be lived out in vibrant, personal, and transformative ways.

This conviction set Schaeffer apart from many of his contemporaries in the realm of Christian apologetics. Unlike figures who engaged primarily in literary and philosophical argument or those like Ellul, who critiqued the dangers of technological society, Schaeffer wove intellectual conviction together with deeply embodied Christian living. He believed that the greatest tragedy of modern Christianity was its failure to demonstrate a faith that was not only true but visibly different from the world around it.

Schaeffer's vision for Christianity was holistic, encompassing the mind, the heart, and the hands. It was not enough to have the correct theology if it did not produce real love, real transformation, and real community. He was particularly critical of what he called *"sterile orthodoxy"*—a form of Christianity that upheld correct doctrine while lacking spiritual vibrancy and relational authenticity.[10] He saw this as one of the greatest

---

10. Schaeffer, *True Spirituality*, 25.

failures of the modern church: it had become doctrinally defensive but spiritually anemic.

His book *True Spirituality* was an attempt to reclaim a fully realized Christian life, one in which faith was not merely believed intellectually but experienced relationally and lived out communally. He insisted that Christianity was not just a worldview to be argued for but a reality to be lived in. In this, his ideas bear a striking resemblance to the subject of our next chapter, Dallas Willard, who would later emphasize the importance of spiritual disciplines and the inner transformation of the soul. Both men recognized that modern evangelicalism had become preoccupied with external defenses while neglecting the inward formation of Christ-like character.

However, Schaeffer's concern went beyond personal spirituality, he was equally insistent that Christian faith must be embodied in the life of the church. He lamented that many Christian communities had become indistinguishable from the surrounding culture, either capitulating to secular ideologies or withdrawing into legalistic enclaves. Neither, he argued, was the answer. Instead, he envisioned a radically different kind of Christian community, one that would be both intellectually serious and deeply loving, a place where truth and beauty could flourish together. He writes, "There is to be true community, offering true spiritual and material help to each other."[11]

It was this vision that led Schaeffer and his wife, Edith, to establish L'Abri (French for "The Shelter"), a small Christian community in the Swiss Alps. L'Abri became more than just a retreat: Schaeffer envisioned it as a living experiment in Christian hospitality, intellectual engagement, and authentic faith. Schaeffer welcomed doubters, seekers, and scholars into his home, engaging them in conversations about philosophy, theology, and the struggles of modern life. But these discussions were never mere debates: they took place over shared meals, in the rhythms of communal living, and in an atmosphere of genuine care and hospitality.

This approach to Christian witness was radically countercultural. At a time when many apologetics ministries focused solely on debates, lectures, and formal arguments, Schaeffer modeled a different way, one that was deeply relational and built on love as well as truth. In this, he anticipated the kind of "relational apologetics" that would later be championed

---

11. Schaeffer, *True Spirituality*, 176.

by figures such as Timothy Keller, who emphasized the need to engage not only the mind but the affections and the imagination.

Yet Schaeffer was also profoundly aware of the cost of authentic Christianity. He did not promise an easy or comfortable faith; instead, he spoke of the "moment-by-moment reality of the Holy Spirit," insisting that true Christian living required a constant dying to self and surrender to Christ.[12] He saw the life of faith as a continuous struggle against complacency, hypocrisy, and self-sufficiency.

Schaeffer's insistence on authentic spirituality was provoked by the fact that he had grown deeply troubled by what he saw as the increasing worldliness of the church, particularly its tendency to adopt pragmatic methods rather than spiritual depth. He feared that much of American Christianity was becoming a political movement rather than a spiritual force, focused more on cultural power than on Christlike witness. His warnings were prescient. In the decades since his death, the evangelical movement has often struggled with precisely the issues he identified: an obsession with influence and cultural dominance at the expense of the transformative witness of the gospel.

Despite his critiques, Schaeffer never became a cynic. He believed deeply in the power of the gospel to restore, renew, and transform. He saw that even in a world that had lost its sense of truth, God was still there calling people back, breaking through the despair, and offering real hope. In this, he shared common ground with Viktor Frankl, whose reflections on suffering and meaning echoed Schaeffer's conviction that human beings cannot survive without a transcendent purpose. Yet unlike Frankl, who remained somewhat open-ended in his conclusions, Schaeffer was emphatic: only Christianity provided a foundation strong enough to sustain meaning, truth, and morality in the face of life's great tragedies and uncertainties.

Reclaiming Beauty, Culture, and the Christian Imagination

Francis Schaeffer was not content merely to analyze or critique the collapse of truth in the modern world, he also believed that Christians must actively work to restore what had been lost. He saw that the crisis of modernity was not only intellectual but also aesthetic and cultural. If

---

12. Schaeffer, *True Spirituality*, 18.

Christianity were true, it had to shape not just how people thought but how they created, built, and lived. Schaeffer believed that truth, goodness, and beauty were inseparably linked and that the loss of transcendent truth had led directly to the distortion of beauty in art, music, literature, and even daily life.

This placed Schaeffer in conversation with thinkers like Lewis and Tolkien, who had long championed the role of imagination in the recovery of meaning. Lewis in particular had argued that reason is the organ of truth, but imagination is the organ of meaning—a perspective that Schaeffer shared but sought to expand. Where Lewis and Tolkien focused primarily on storytelling as a vehicle for truth, Schaeffer took a broader approach, engaging with the entire realm of culture: visual art, philosophy, film, architecture, and beyond. He called for a distinctly Christian presence in these spheres, one that did not merely copy secular forms but sought to create with excellence, depth, and originality.

This belief set Schaeffer apart from many of his evangelical contemporaries. In the mid-to-late twentieth century, much of conservative Christianity (often referred to as the Moral Majority) had adopted a defensive posture toward culture, either retreating into fundamentalist separatism or engaging in superficial moral critiques of popular media. Schaeffer saw this approach as deeply inadequate. He argued that Christians should not simply condemn secular art and literature but seek to understand it, engage with it, and contribute to it. Instead of rejecting modern culture outright, he called believers to examine the underlying worldviews shaping it and respond with thoughtful, creative alternatives.

This approach had clear parallels with Jacques Ellul, who had likewise critiqued the way technology and media had reshaped human perception and behavior. However, while Ellul tended toward a more pessimistic assessment, warning of technology's creeping dehumanization, Schaeffer maintained a greater optimism that Christian engagement could reshape and redeem culture rather than simply resist it. Where Ellul warned of the dangers of propaganda and manipulation, Schaeffer urged Christians to actively cultivate beauty and depth as an antidote to cultural shallowness.

Schaeffer's vision for cultural engagement was rooted in history. He argued that the great works of Christian civilization—its cathedrals, paintings, literature, and music—testified to a faith that shaped entire cultures.[13] He lamented that by the modern era, Christianity had largely abandoned its commitment to artistic excellence, leaving culture to be dominated by secular voices and perspectives. He called for a recovery of the Christian imagination, one that would create art, literature, and architecture that reflected God's order, truth, and beauty.

In *How Should We Then Live*, he traced how shifts in theology and worldview had impacted creative expression over time, showing how the loss of a transcendent moral order had led to increasing fragmentation and abstraction in art. This was not merely an aesthetic shift; it was a sign of cultural despair. Schaeffer pointed to the shift from the harmonious compositions of the Renaissance to the disjointed, often chaotic works of modernism as evidence of a civilization losing its coherence. He saw the same pattern in literature, music, and film, where increasing nihilism and absurdity reflected a deep existential crisis.

As Schaeffer's life and ministry drew to a close, his concerns grew more urgent. He saw Western civilization drifting further from truth, further from coherence, and further from its Christian heritage. Yet he remained convinced that the church still had an opportunity to bear witness if it was willing to fully embrace the implications of its own message.

His final challenge to the church was this: if Christians truly believed that God was there, then their lives, their communities, and their creative works should reflect that reality. He warned against Christianity becoming just another ideological system, shaped by political expediency or cultural trends rather than genuine faith. He lamented that many believers had adopted pragmatic or power-driven approaches rather than modeling the radical love of Christ. Yet, his ultimate message was one of hope and responsibility. He believed that every Christian was called to be a signpost, a living argument for the reality of God. This was the essence of his apologetic, not just proving Christianity intellectually but demonstrating its truth through a way of life that was beautiful, sacrificial, and deeply human.

His vision paved the way for Dallas Willard, whose work would focus on the inward spiritual formation necessary to sustain such a witness. If Schaeffer emphasized truth as the foundation, Willard would emphasize transformation as its fulfillment. Together, their voices form a powerful call to reclaim both the intellectual and the spiritual life, to

---

13. Schaeffer, *How Should We Then Live*, 30.

recover a Christianity that is both deeply rooted in truth and radically embodied in practice.

Schaeffer's legacy is not merely that of a philosopher, a theologian, or an apologist. He was a man who sought to live out the reality of what he believed. He called the church to a deeper engagement with culture, a more vibrant spirituality, and a more courageous defense of truth. His life was a testimony to what it means to believe that God is truly there and that Christianity is not just a comforting tradition but the true and unshakeable foundation of reality.

As we transition to the next chapter, we turn to Dallas Willard, who will take up the task of addressing not only the crisis of truth but the crisis of spiritual formation. If Schaeffer showed why the world needed a coherent, rational, and culturally engaged Christianity, Willard demonstrates how such a faith must be cultivated in the soul through spiritual disciplines, practices, and an intentional pursuit of the presence of God. Together, their voices form a bridge from worldview to transformation, from the intellectual defense of faith to the daily experience of its power. Schaeffer's challenge remains with us today: if God is truly there, then our lives must reflect that reality.

15

Dallas Willard

Spiritual Disciplines and the Renewal of the Soul

"Today it is more likely to be said that it is contained in "the human quest for meaning or wholeness." Moral understanding can, allegedly, be established by careful human thought and experience apart from any historical tradition. But the centuries-long attempt to devise a morality from within merely human resources has now proven itself a failure."
—Dallas Willard[1]

DALLAS WILLARD, A PHILOSOPHER, theologian, and mentor to countless seekers, spent his life calling people back to the transformative power of the kingdom of God. His many literary works do not merely offer theories or abstract ideas. They are a roadmap for rediscovering meaning in a world that often feels cold and disenchanted. Willard's vision was simple yet profound: life in the kingdom of God, here and now, is available to all who are willing to become disciples of Jesus, intentionally shaping their souls through grace and spiritual discipline.

Willard's work speaks directly to the crisis of meaning explored throughout this book. Where modernity has left humanity fragmented, Willard offers a vision of integration—a way of aligning the heart, mind,

---

1. Willard, *Divine Conspiracy*, 131.

body, and soul with God's eternal purposes. Where technology and consumerism have dehumanized, Willard's call to spiritual formation restores dignity and purpose. Where the disappearance of moral knowledge has led to relativism and despair, Willard reclaims the moral and spiritual truths that anchor life in the transcendent reality of God's kingdom.

Willard's message is about personal and spiritual transformation. He does not leave his readers with a diagnosis of the modern soul's ailment; he offers a prescription for healing. He believed that true change was possible, not through superficial adjustments or quick fixes but through the slow, intentional work of discipleship. Through the act of discipleship, Willard taught that we are gradually becoming who we will forever be, one small choice at a time.

Willard's legacy is one of hope and renewal. In a time when the noise of modern life threatens to drown out the still, small voice of God, Willard invites us to listen, to slow down, and to embrace the life we were created to live. He reminds us that meaning is not found in what we achieve or acquire but in the persons we are becoming as we walk with God. As we delve into Willard's insights, we will discover a vision of life that not only addresses the crisis of meaning but also reclaims the joy and beauty of living in the reality of God's kingdom.

This chapter, the culmination of our exploration of the "Voices of Restoration," calls us to take seriously Willard's invitation to become students of Jesus, to live intentionally, and to find our deepest purpose in the presence of God. It is an invitation to move beyond the disillusionment of modernity and into the fullness of life. A life that is, as Jesus described, abundant.

The Crisis of Moral Knowledge and the Need for Renovation

Dallas Willard's response to the modern crisis of meaning begins with a clear diagnosis of its roots: the disappearance of moral knowledge. In his posthumously published work, *The Disappearance of Moral Knowledge*, Willard meticulously traced how Western thought had sidelined the notion of objective moral truth over centuries. What once served as a shared framework for understanding human purpose and guiding individual and societal behavior had been replaced by a fragmented, relativistic view of morality.

This loss of moral knowledge is not merely an intellectual problem but a spiritual and existential one. Without a shared moral framework, individuals and societies are left adrift, unable to anchor their lives in anything enduring or meaningful. The result, Willard argued, is a culture of profound disconnection, a society fragmented by competing narratives, where individuals are isolated and alienated from themselves, from others, and from God. When moral truth is no longer considered knowledge, the foundation of human life begins to erode. He writes:

> Moral character is not a matter of the physical body or its 'natural' relations to world and society. As long as the physical realm is regarded as the only subject of knowledge, there will be no moral knowledge and no cognitive foundation of the moral life.[2]

Willard's analysis begins with the Enlightenment, which sought to elevate reason and scientific inquiry as the ultimate arbiters of truth. While this shift brought undeniable advances in understanding and technology, it also led to the marginalization of spiritual and moral realities. Willard argued that this intellectual shift created a false dichotomy between the "factual" and the "spiritual," relegating morality to the realm of subjective opinion rather than objective truth. This relegation of morality to subjectivity left modern individuals without a coherent foundation for answering life's most important questions: What is good? What is true? What is beautiful? For Willard, this void contributed directly to the crisis of meaning in the modern world. He taught that without the foundation of moral knowledge, the human soul cannot find rest or direction.

Willard also identified the fragmentation of modern life as a direct consequence of the disappearance of moral knowledge. In a world where individuals are bombarded by competing ideologies and incessant distractions, it becomes increasingly difficult to live a life of integrity. A life where one's beliefs, actions, and desires are aligned or congruent. Willard described this fragmentation as a profound spiritual malaise. The modern self is divided, pulled in multiple directions, and unable to rest in a coherent understanding of its purpose. This fragmentation is evident in the way many approach their lives, compartmentalizing their work, relationships, and spirituality into separate spheres. Willard argued that this disintegration leads to a profound sense of emptiness, as individuals are unable to see their lives as part of a larger, meaningful whole. When

---

2. Willard, *Disappearance of Moral Knowledge*, 371.

life is lived in fragments, it loses its depth and significance. We are left with activity but no direction, busyness but no peace.

In response to this crisis, Willard called for a renovation of the human heart, a transformation that begins with the recovery of moral knowledge and extends to every aspect of life. He believed that moral knowledge is not merely about adhering to rules but about understanding the nature of goodness as rooted in the character of God. Moral truth is not an abstract set of principles but a reflection of the divine reality that calls us into a relationship with our Creator.

This renovation requires a re-centering of life around the kingdom of God. For Willard, the kingdom is not a distant, future reality but a present invitation to live under God's rule, where love, truth, and justice are the defining realities. He wrote, "Living in the kingdom of God is a matter of living with God's action in our lives."[3]

This integration of "God's action in our lives" begins with the recognition that moral truth is not an optional add-on to life but its very foundation. It continues with the intentional pursuit of spiritual formation, where the heart, mind, body, and will are brought into harmony under the lordship of Christ. As Willard explained in *The Great Ommission*:

> Christian spiritual formation, in contrast, is the redemptive process of forming the inner human world so that it takes on the character of the inner being of Christ himself. In the degree to which it is successful, the outer life of the individual becomes a natural expression or outflow of the character and teachings of Jesus.[4]

This process, he believed, is the only way to address the disconnection and fragmentation of modern life, offering a pathway to the wholeness and meaning that so many desperately seek.

The Call to Spiritual Formation

Dallas Willard's response to the fragmentation and disconnection of modern life was rooted in his vision of spiritual formation, a process by which individuals are transformed into the image of Christ through intentional practices, relationships, and surrender to God. For Willard, spiritual formation was not merely about personal improvement or moral

---

3. Willard, *Living in Christ's Presence*, 76.
4. Willard, *Great Omission*, 105.

behavior; it was about aligning the entire person—heart, mind, body, and will—with the kingdom of God. This process, he believed, was the antidote to the dehumanizing forces of modernity, offering a path toward integration, purpose, and authentic living. Willard's approach to spiritual formation is most fully articulated in *Renovation of the Heart*, where he emphasized that transformation begins with the inner life—the heart or the "spirit" of a person. He believed that outward behaviors naturally flow from the condition of the heart, and any attempt to change behavior without addressing the underlying motivations ultimately falls short. He writes, "The shaping and reshaping of the inner life is, accordingly, a problem that has been around as long as humanity itself; and the earliest records of human thought bear eloquent witness to the human struggle to solve it, but with very limited success, one would have to say."[5]

This perspective stands in contrast to the reductionist approaches of modern psychology, which often focus solely on modifying external behaviors or managing symptoms. Thinkers such as B. F. Skinner, who emphasized behaviorism, and Sigmund Freud, who delved into the subconscious, offered frameworks that regularly failed to address the spiritual dimension of human existence. Willard contended that these approaches, while useful for understanding certain aspects of the human psyche, were ultimately insufficient because they overlooked the soul's need for redemption and transformation.

Spiritual formation, as Willard saw it, was not limited to religious practice; it encompassed every aspect of life. He believed that the mind must be renewed through engagement with truth, the body disciplined through intentional habits, and relationships cultivated in a way that reflects God's love. This holistic approach set him apart from many of his contemporaries, offering a vision of transformation that integrated the intellectual, emotional, and physical dimensions of human life.

Central to Willard's concept of spiritual formation was the role of the will. While many modern thinkers emphasized the power of external forces—social, economic, or psychological—Willard insisted that individuals have the capacity and responsibility to choose their response to these influences. Drawing from thinkers like Frankl, who highlighted the human ability to find meaning even in suffering, Willard argued that the will must be trained to desire what is good and true.

---

5. Willard, *Renovation of the Heart*, 20.

This training requires intentionality. Willard often spoke of the importance of "spiritual disciplines" as tools for shaping the will and aligning it with God's purposes. Practices such as prayer, fasting, solitude, and study were not ends in themselves but means of creating space for God to work in the heart. These disciplines, Willard explained, open us to the power of the Spirit, enabling us to live in a way that we could not achieve through sheer effort.

One of Willard's sharpest critiques was directed at the modern church's failure to emphasize discipleship and spiritual formation. In *The Great Omission*, he lamented that many churches had reduced the Christian life to a set of beliefs rather than a way of being. He writes, "We have lost discipleship largely because, in the evangelical tradition, we have lost Christ as Teacher."[6] Willard argued that the church must move beyond a focus on attendance and programs to become a place where people are taught to live in the reality of the kingdom of God.

Willard also emphasized the importance of community in the process of spiritual formation. He believed that transformation does not happen in isolation but within the context of relationships. The church, as a community of believers, serves as a training ground for living out the values of the kingdom. In this, Willard's ideas align with those of Martin Buber, who saw human relationships as the arena in which individuals encounter the divine. This emphasis on community also speaks to the critiques of modernity offered by Jacques Ellul and others, who warned of the isolating effects of technological and bureaucratic systems. Willard's vision of spiritual formation offered a counternarrative to this isolation, calling individuals to reconnect with one another in love, humility, and shared purpose.

For Willard, spiritual formation was not only about personal transformation but also about resisting the dehumanizing forces of the modern world. He saw the pursuit of spiritual disciplines as an act of rebellion against a culture that prioritizes productivity, consumption, and self-gratification. Willard's call to embrace simplicity, silence, and Sabbath stands in stark contrast to the frenetic pace of modern life. This resistance to cultural norms aligns with the critiques of consumerism and distraction offered by Wendell Berry and other contemporary thinkers. Like Berry, Willard believed that meaning is found not in the accumulation

---

6. Willard, *Great Omission*, 167.

of possessions or achievements but in the cultivation of a life that reflects God's love and creativity.

Ultimately, Willard's vision of spiritual formation is about becoming like Christ, not merely imitating his actions but embodying his character. This process requires a reorientation of the heart, a renewal of the mind, and a willingness to surrender to God's work in every area of life. Willard wrote, "Discipleship is a life of learning from Jesus Christ how to live in the Kingdom of God now, as he himself did."[7] This vision of transformation offers a powerful response to the crisis of meaning in the modern age. It calls for individuals to move beyond the surface-level distractions of modernity and into a life of depth, purpose, and joy.

Life in the Kingdom

The Divine Conspiracy is the cornerstone of Willard's response to the meaning crisis, offering a vision of life rooted in God's presence and authority. Willard's teaching on the kingdom calls individuals to reimagine their existence as participants in God's redemptive work, a perspective that challenges the nihilism, consumerism, and despair of the modern age. In *The Divine Conspiracy*, Willard reinterprets Jesus' teachings on the kingdom, emphasizing that the kingdom is not merely a future hope but a present invitation. He explained that the kingdom is wherever God's will is done, both in the world and within the hearts of individuals. This reality, according to Willard, transforms how people understand their lives and their place in the world. The kingdom of God is not about earning or achieving but about living in the reality of God's rule, where love, justice, and peace prevail.

Willard's perspective contrasts sharply with both the secular narratives of progress and the spiritual escapism found in some religious traditions. Where modernity often places ultimate hope in technological or political solutions, and some religious frameworks emphasize disengagement from the world, Willard's kingdom theology bridges the present and the eternal. It calls individuals to live with intention and purpose, fully engaged in the world while anchored in the eternal reality of God's reign.

This idea finds resonance in the work of N. T. Wright, who similarly emphasizes the "now and not yet" nature of the kingdom. Like Willard,

---

7. Willard, *Great Omission*, 62.

Wright critiques modern Christians' tendency to reduce the gospel to either a set of doctrines or a future salvation while neglecting its transformative implications for the present. Both thinkers call for a holistic understanding of faith that encompasses all aspects of life, offering a compelling counternarrative to modern disillusionment.

Willard often described discipleship as "apprenticeship" to Jesus, a process of learning how to live as he lived.[8] This apprenticeship is not a passive belief but an active participation in the life and mission of the kingdom. Willard believed that the Sermon on the Mount, often dismissed as an unattainable ideal, is actually a blueprint for life in the kingdom, a way of living that reflects God's character and priorities. This vision of discipleship challenges the modern tendency to compartmentalize faith, reducing it to a set of private rituals or propositional beliefs. Instead, Willard argued that discipleship must touch every aspect of life, from relationships and work to habits and desires. This integrated approach echoes the teachings of Abraham Kuyper, who emphasized that every "square inch of creation" belongs to the Lord.[9] Like Kuyper, Willard called believers to live with a holistic sense of purpose, recognizing that the kingdom of God encompasses all areas of life.

Willard also explored the ethical implications of living in the kingdom, particularly in how it shapes attitudes toward power, justice, and forgiveness. He believed that life in the kingdom requires a radical reorientation of values, where love becomes the defining ethic. This love is not sentimental or self-serving but sacrificial and transformative, reflecting the nature of God. Willard explained that the kingdom calls individuals to love not only their neighbors but also their enemies, embodying the radical forgiveness and grace that Jesus demonstrated.

This ethic of love stands in stark contrast to the political ideologies of the modern world, which often prioritize power, control, and retribution. Willard's call to live with humility and grace similarly echoes the ideas of Reinhold Niebuhr, who emphasized the tension between idealism and realism in Christian ethics. Like Niebuhr, Willard recognized the world's brokenness but insisted that Christians are called to live as agents of reconciliation, embodying the values of the kingdom even in the midst of conflict and imperfection. One can see this balance in Willard's discussion on divorce in *The Divine Conspiracy*. He writes:

---

8. Willard, *Great Omission*, xi.
9. Kuyper, *Abraham Kuyper*, 488.

> Hard hearts may make divorce necessary to avoid greater harm, and hence make it permissible. But kingdom hearts are not hard, and they together can find ways to bear with each other, to speak truth in love, to change—often through times of great pain and distress—until the tender intimacy of mutual, covenant-framed love finds a way for the two lives to remain one, beautifully and increasingly.[10]

At its core, Willard's vision of the kingdom is a message of hope. He believed that the despair of modernity could be overcome by living in the reality of God's presence and purposes. This hope is not a passive optimism but an active engagement with the world, rooted in the conviction that God is at work to redeem and restore. This hopeful vision offers a powerful response to the nihilism that permeates much of modern thought. By calling individuals to live as participants in the kingdom, Willard provides a framework for finding meaning, not in the fleeting achievements of the world but in the eternal reality of God's love and grace.

The Spirit of the Disciplines

Willard was careful to emphasize that spiritual disciplines are not ends in themselves but means of grace—tools that enable individuals to align their lives with God's will. He explained, "The disciplines are activities of mind and body purposefully undertaken, to bring our personality and total being into effective cooperation with the divine order."[11] By engaging in these practices, individuals create space for the Holy Spirit to shape their inner lives, cultivating virtues such as patience, humility, and love. This understanding of spiritual disciplines contrasts with the asceticism of earlier Christian traditions that sometimes viewed discipline as a form of punishment or self-denial for its own sake. Willard instead saw the disciplines as liberating, freeing individuals from the compulsions and distractions that prevent them from living fully in God's presence.

Willard divided the spiritual disciplines into two categories: disciplines of engagement and disciplines of abstinence. The former, such as prayer, worship, and study, are practices that actively engage the individual with God and community. The latter, including fasting, solitude,

---

10. Willard, *Divine Conspiracy*, 172.
11. Willard, *Spiritual Disciplines*, 68.

and silence, involve withdrawing from distractions and attachments to create space for reflection and renewal.

Through the disciplines of engagement, Willard argued, individuals come to know God more intimately and experience the joy of his presence. Practices like worship and study nourish the mind and heart, providing the intellectual and spiritual foundation for a life rooted in truth. Willard frequently stressed the importance of study, encouraging Christians to engage deeply with Scripture and theological works to develop a well-formed understanding of their faith.

On the other hand, the disciplines of abstinence serve to counteract the excesses and distractions of modern life. Fasting, for example, teaches individuals to rely on God rather than on material comforts, while solitude creates space for self-examination and communion with God. In a culture driven by constant connectivity and consumption, these practices serve as a form of resistance, reminding individuals of their dependence on God and their need for simplicity.

One of Willard's most counterintuitive insights was his claim that discipline leads to freedom. He argued that the habits and routines individuals cultivate shape their character and capacity for freedom. Just as an athlete trains their body through disciplined practice to perform at a high level, so too must Christians train their hearts and minds to live as disciples of Jesus. Willard explained:

> One must train as well as try. An athlete may have all the enthusiasm in the world; he may "talk a good game." But talk will not win the race. Zeal without knowledge or without appropriate practice is never enough. Plus, one must train wisely as well as intensely for spiritual attainment.[12]

This concept resonates with the broader philosophical tradition of virtue ethics, particularly as articulated by Aristotle. For Aristotle, the development of virtuous habits enables individuals to achieve human flourishing (*eudaimonia*). Willard's adaptation of this principle within a Christian framework underscores the idea that freedom is not the absence of restraint but the ability to live in alignment with one's highest purpose. By cultivating spiritual disciplines, individuals become the kind of people who naturally embody the values of the kingdom of God.

The spiritual disciplines also serve as a counternarrative to the values of modernity, which often prioritize productivity, efficiency, and

---

12. Willard, *Spiritual Disciplines*, 98.

self-gratification. Willard critiqued the cultural obsession with "doing" over "being," arguing that the relentless pursuit of success and achievement leaves little room for reflection, rest, or relationship. This critique aligns with the warnings of Jacques Ellul, whose analysis of technology and its dehumanizing effects complements Willard's insights. They recognized that the tools and systems of modern life, while offering convenience and progress, often come at the cost of spiritual depth and relational connection. Willard's call to embrace simplicity and solitude can be seen as a practical response to Ellul's diagnosis, offering a way to reclaim the sacred in an increasingly mechanized world.

The ultimate purpose of the spiritual disciplines, Willard maintained, is to cultivate a life of love, joy, and peace—the fruit of the Spirit (Gal 5:22–23). These virtues are not achieved through sheer effort but emerge naturally as individuals align their lives with the reality of God's kingdom. This emphasis on character formation distinguishes Willard's approach from legalistic or transactional models of spirituality.

The disciplines are not about earning God's favor but about positioning oneself to receive his grace and participate in his work. By fostering intimacy with God, cultivating virtue, and resisting the distractions of modern life, these practices enable individuals to live with intention and purpose. They restore the integrity of the self, aligning the heart, mind, body, and will under the lordship of Christ.

A Culminating Vision

Dallas Willard's life and work offer a profound response to the crisis of meaning that has plagued modernity. In a world marked by fragmentation, distraction, and disillusionment, Willard's teachings illuminate a path toward wholeness, purpose, and eternal significance. His vision of life in the kingdom of God, cultivated through spiritual formation and the disciplines of grace, provides not only an intellectual critique of modernity's failures but also a practical roadmap for living as whole persons under God's reign.

At the core of Willard's response is his insistence that the human heart was made for integration—for alignment with God's truth, goodness, and beauty. The modern world, with its competing narratives and relentless pace, pulls individuals in countless directions, leaving them fragmented and exhausted. Willard's call to discipleship is, at its heart, a call to wholeness. By aligning every aspect of life with the reality of God's kingdom, individuals can find the peace and purpose that modernity so often fails to deliver.

In this, Willard's vision resonates with the teachings of other thinkers who sought to address the spiritual and existential void of modernity. Like Frankl, who saw meaning as essential to human flourishing even in the darkest circumstances, Willard believed that life's ultimate meaning is found not in self-fulfillment but in self-giving love and participation in God's redemptive work. Where Jacques Ellul critiqued the dehumanizing effects of technology and consumerism, Willard offered practices of simplicity, silence, and Sabbath as pathways to rediscovering humanity's sacred calling. His work stands as both critique and cure, addressing the root causes of disconnection while offering a practical means of transformation.

Willard's emphasis on spiritual disciplines challenges the passive, convenience-driven ethos of modern life. He insisted that transformation into Christlikeness requires intentionality, commitment, and perseverance. This call to intentional living is not about striving in human effort but about partnering with God in the process of sanctification. In this partnership, Willard saw the disciplines as tools for cultivating the virtues that reflect God's character: love, joy, peace, patience, and kindness.

Central to Willard's teaching is the idea that the kingdom of God is the ultimate source of meaning. This kingdom, he explained, is not a distant utopia or an abstract ideal but a present reality that infuses every aspect of life with significance. For Willard, living in the kingdom means seeing all of life—work, relationships, suffering, and joy—as opportunities to participate in God's redemptive purposes.

This vision challenges the nihilism of modernity, which often reduces life to a series of random events or material pursuits. Willard's kingdom theology affirms that every moment is charged with eternal significance, offering a counternarrative to the despair and cynicism of the age. In the kingdom, even the smallest acts of love and faithfulness become part of God's great story of redemption. Willard's writings invite us to embrace this story, to see our lives not as isolated fragments but as threads in the tapestry of God's eternal plan.

Willard's legacy extends far beyond his writings. His influence can be seen in the lives of countless individuals who have been transformed by his teachings, as well as in the broader renewal movements that have embraced his vision of spiritual formation and kingdom living. Through works like *The Spirit of the Disciplines* and *The Renovation of the Heart*, Willard has inspired a new generation of Christian disciples and thinkers like John Mark Comer, who focus on calling believers to be committed to living with intentionality, humility, and love.

But perhaps Willard's greatest legacy is his unwavering belief in the transformative power of the gospel. Willard's teachings remind us that meaning is not found in fleeting pleasures or worldly achievements but in the daily act of living in harmony with God's will. His work calls us to cultivate the inner life, to embrace the practices that lead to transformation, and to see every moment as an opportunity to reflect the love and grace of Christ.

As we conclude this journey through the voices of meaning, Dallas Willard stands as a culminating figure, offering a vision of life that is whole, integrated, and eternally significant. His invitation to live as apprentices of Jesus is a call to rediscover the joy and purpose for which we were created, to become participants in the great story of God's kingdom, and to find, at last, the meaning we long for.

Conclusion to Part III

This journey through the voices of restoration has by no means been exhaustive. The modern crisis of meaning has prompted many profound thinkers, writers, and artists to call the world back to its foundations in purpose, truth, beauty, and goodness. Figures like Søren Kierkegaard, who explored the leap of faith and the tension of existence; Flannery O'Connor, whose stories illuminated the grotesque to reveal grace; or Dietrich Bonhoeffer, who offered a vision of costly discipleship in the face of tyranny, could each have been fitting additions to this section. Others, like Hannah Arendt, Simone Weil, and Franz Kafka, also stood against the tide of fragmentation and disenchantment, offering unique paths toward re-enchantment and restoration.

The voices included here—Chesterton, Marcel, Niebuhr, Frankl, Lewis, Tolkien, Ellul, Schaeffer, and Willard—were chosen not because they exhaust the well of wisdom available but because they represent a tapestry of perspectives that together weave a coherent response to the modern malaise. In their unique way, each of these figures stokes in us a longing for the transcendent, providing breadcrumbs that guide us back to the source of meaning. They address different aspects of the crisis, from the fragmentation of knowledge to the erosion of moral and spiritual frameworks, offering a vision of life that integrates reason, imagination, and faith.

Chesterton invites us to rediscover wonder and the sacredness of the ordinary, grounding us in the joy of creation. Marcel calls us into the mystery of relational being, challenging the isolation of modernity. Niebuhr wrestles with history's tensions and human frailty, offering a realistic yet hopeful framework for engagement with the world. Frankl reminds us of the resilience of the human spirit and the necessity of finding meaning even in suffering. Lewis and Tolkien, through apologetics and myth, reawaken our imaginations and call us to a vision of eternal beauty and truth. Ellul critiques the dehumanizing forces of technology and propaganda, urging us to resist and reclaim our humanity.

Schaeffer steps into this conversation as a crucial bridge between cultural critique and theological restoration. While Ellul exposed the dangers of a technological society that strips life of its sacredness, Schaeffer called believers not only to resist these forces but to rebuild on a foundation of biblical truth. His vision of Christianity as a total worldview—one that integrates faith, philosophy, art, and culture—challenged modernity's false dichotomies between sacred and secular, reason and revelation. Schaeffer's legacy lies in his insistence that Christianity is not only intellectually defensible but also existentially satisfying. It is a faith that provides both truth and meaning. His work prepared the ground for what Dallas Willard would later cultivate: the formation of a deeply rooted, spiritually disciplined life that resists both the shallowness of contemporary Christianity and the nihilism of secularism.

Finally, Willard provides the practical means of living a transformed life, offering the tools and vision for participating in the kingdom of God. If the other voices diagnose the crisis and illuminate the path to meaning, Willard calls us to walk that path, to cultivate the kind of spiritual life that is capable of sustaining a rich and enduring faith. Together, these voices form a symphony of restoration. They do not merely critique modernity; they offer a path forward. Their works do not point us to themselves but to something greater, to a transcendent reality that satisfies the deepest longings of the human heart. They remind us that the search for meaning is not a futile endeavor but an essential one, and they provide the courage to confront the emptiness of modern life with the hope of rediscovery.

As we turn to the fourth and final part of this book, we transition from diagnosis and exploration to application and vision. Part IV: Toward Wholeness serves as the culmination of our journey, offering a roadmap for reclaiming meaning in a world marked by fragmentation and despair. If the voices of restoration in Part III pointed us toward the transcendent (illuminating paths of hope, imagination, and purpose), this final section is about the courageous act of walking those paths. It is about the practical and profound challenge of integrating the eternal truths of the Christian worldview into the very fabric of our lives and communities.

CONCLUSION TO PART III

This is not merely an intellectual exercise or a theoretical reflection. It is an invitation to live differently and to embrace a way of being that sees beyond the disjointed narratives of modernity. It is a call to view the world anew, to perceive it as God intended: as a canvas of divine beauty, a stage for profound relationships, and a place where every act of faithfulness participates in the restoration of all things. The vision ahead requires us to step into the tension of our age, not as passive observers but as active restorers, gathering the broken pieces of our lives and our culture and allowing God's truth, beauty, and goodness to form them into something whole.

The journey to wholeness is not an escape from the world's brokenness; it is a transformative engagement with it. It begins with the fragmented self, often torn apart by the demands of modernity, and moves outward to rediscover the sacred in a disenchanted world, to restore relationships, to reimagine work as sacred calling, and to rekindle a sense of wonder through beauty and the arts. At its heart lies the Christian metanarrative, the story that makes sense of every longing, every fracture, and every hope. This is the story that has carried countless souls through history's darkest nights and continues to illuminate the way forward.

Ultimately, this final section is about more than personal restoration; it is about becoming restorers. As individuals find meaning and integration through Christ, they are called to bring that meaning into their homes, their communities, and the broader culture. This is a vision not just of personal transformation but of cultural renewal, where the light of the gospel permeates every sphere of life, offering hope to a world still searching for its foundation. Let us now embark on this final movement of the journey, one that challenges us to embrace integration and redemption with open hearts. Together, we will explore what it means to live as people who are not only restored but also as those entrusted with the sacred task of restoration.

PART IV

Toward Wholeness
Reclaiming Meaning with a Restored Vision

16

The Fragmented Self
Moving Toward Integration

LET'S THINK ABOUT THE shattered mirror analogy we spoke of in chapter five. Each fragment reflects a piece of the world, yet none can offer the whole image. Light bounces off the jagged edges, distorting what once was clear, cohesive, and beautiful. This is the condition of the modern soul: a collection of fragments, each fighting for dominance yet incapable of wholeness. In a world defined by division and distraction, we carry this fractured self into every relationship, every decision, every moment, feeling the sharp edges of disconnection with ourselves, with others, and with the transcendent God who made us.

This is not how it was meant to be. We were created for unity—body, mind, heart, and spirit—woven together in the seamless image of God. But the pressures of modernity and postmodernity have pulled us apart. Modernity's unyielding faith in reason disconnected us from the sacred, reducing us to economic units or biological machines. Postmodernity promised liberation from oppressive narratives but left us drowning in a sea of relativity, disoriented and untethered. Together, they have left us estranged from ourselves, unable to find coherence in a world without anchors.

This fragmentation is more than a cultural or philosophical crisis; it is a deeply personal one. It manifests in our daily lives: the gnawing anxiety that keeps us awake at night, the sense of purposelessness that dulls our days, and the inability to reconcile the pieces of who we are. We feel it when our minds know one thing yet our hearts desire another; when our bodies ache for rest yet our wills press forward in relentless productivity. We feel it when we long for connection but settle for distraction, endlessly scrolling through digital feeds that promise intimacy but deliver only isolation.

But there is hope. The gospel speaks directly to our fractured condition, not only diagnosing our brokenness but also offering a way forward. In Christ, the fragments of our lives can be gathered, restored, and made whole. The Christian faith does not force us to choose between the intellectual and the mystical, the sacred and the practical, the spiritual and the physical. Instead, it integrates them all into a cohesive vision of what it means to be fully human.

This chapter is a call to reject the fragmentation that the world imposes and to embrace the life of integration that God offers. It is not an easy path, nor is it a quick fix. But it is the only way to reclaim meaning in a world that desperately longs for it. Together, let us explore what it means to move from fracture to wholeness, to be people whose lives reflect the light of God's truth, beauty, and goodness in a way that is clear, cohesive, and profoundly transformative.

Diagnosing the Fracture

The self, as conceived in Scripture, was never meant to be fragmented. Humanity was created as an integrated whole—mind, heart, body, and spirit—united in perfect harmony, reflecting the image of God (Gen 1:27). This unity enabled us to live in right relationship with God, with one another, and with creation. The fall disrupted this order, introducing dissonance into every aspect of life. The soul that once walked confidently in the presence of God now hides in shame and fear, alienated not only from the Creator but also from itself (Gen 3:8–10).

Modern life, in many ways, exacerbates this fragmentation. Modernity's embrace of hyper-rationalism and the industrialization of society reduced the human person to mere intellect and productivity. The Enlightenment's insistence on reason above all else severed the mind from the heart, relegating spiritual truths to the realm of subjective feeling. The rise of consumerism further divided the self by commodifying identity. We are told to define ourselves by what we consume, what we achieve, and how we present ourselves to the world. The result is a disjointed existence, where individuals are alienated from their true selves, their neighbors, and their Creator.

Postmodernity, rather than healing this wound, deepened it. The rejection of metanarratives left individuals adrift, unsure of their place in the world. In this landscape, the self is no longer a unified whole but a collection of competing identities, each vying for dominance. This "self" is perpetually reinvented, shaped by cultural trends and personal whims, yet it lacks any solid foundation. The postmodern individual inhabits a fractured frame closed off from transcendence and vulnerable to the chaos of relativism.

In stark contrast to modern and postmodern conceptions, the Bible presents the self as an integrated being, designed for wholeness in relationship with God. The *Shema* of Deut 6:4–5, "Love the Lord your God with all your heart, all your soul, and all your strength," calls for a holistic devotion that engages every part of our being. Jesus reaffirms this in Matt 22:37, adding "with all your mind," emphasizing the necessity of intellectual engagement alongside emotional, physical, and spiritual devotion.

Fragmentation, therefore, is not merely a sociological problem but a theological one. Paul's lament in Rom 7 captures the internal dissonance of a fractured self: "For I do not do what I want, but I do the very thing I hate" (Rom 7:15). This is the plight of humanity apart from God, torn between the desires of the flesh and the calling of the Spirit. The fragmentation we experience is the echo of Eden's curse, where sin corrupted the harmony between the components of our being.

The good news is that Scripture offers hope for restoration. In Christ, the disjointed self finds its integration. Paul's vision in 1 Thess 5:23 is not of partial redemption but of complete sanctification: "May the God of peace himself sanctify you entirely; and may your whole spirit and soul and body be kept sound and blameless at the coming of our Lord Jesus Christ." This wholeness is not achieved through human effort but through divine grace, as the Spirit works to reconcile every part of our being to the will of God.

The effects of this fragmentation are evident in the malaise of contemporary culture. Anxiety and depression have reached epidemic levels, fueled by a relentless pace of life and the unattainable demands of consumerism. Identity crises abound as individuals struggle to reconcile their online personas with their real selves. Relationships are increasingly transactional, reflecting the commodification of the self.

Even within the church, fragmentation has taken root. The overemphasis on theological propositionalism by some has reduced faith to a mere intellectual exercise, while others have veered toward emotionalism, neglecting the mind in their pursuit of spiritual experience. This divide reflects the broader cultural disintegration and underscores the need for a holistic theology that embraces both head and heart, intellect and mystery.

The diagnosis is clear: humanity is deeply fragmented, a reflection of the fall and a result of the cultural forces of modernity and postmodernity. Yet, this diagnosis is not without hope. The biblical vision of the self offers a way forward, grounded in the integrative work of Christ and the sanctifying power of the Spirit.

The Path Toward Integration

If fragmentation is the condition of the fallen self, then integration is the promise of redemption. The gospel offers a way forward, not through a piecemeal effort to cobble together our shattered identities but through the comprehensive work of Christ, who makes all things new. Integration, in the Christian vision, is not simply a return to a premodern ideal but a movement toward wholeness rooted in God's transformative grace. It is a journey of restoration, where the broken pieces of our lives are brought into alignment with the divine image in which we were created.

At its core, integration begins with reconciliation to God. Without this anchoring relationship, any attempt at self-unity is bound to falter. The gospel declares that Christ not only restores our relationship with the Creator but also mends the internal fractures of the self. The apostle Paul speaks to this in Eph 2:14, proclaiming that Christ "is our peace, who has made us both one and has broken down in his flesh the dividing wall of hostility." While Paul is addressing the division between Jew and gentile, the principle of reconciliation extends inward as well. Christ destroys the walls that separate our mind from our heart, our body from our soul, and our will from God's purposes.

This integration is not a theoretical concept but a lived reality, one that encompasses every dimension of our being. The call to love God with heart, soul, mind, and strength is not merely an ancient creed but a roadmap for holistic living. To engage the mind is to seek truth, to reason faithfully, and to love God with all intellectual vigor. Yet this intellectual pursuit must not stand apart from the deep affections of the heart, which stir us to love, worship, and delight in God's presence. The strength of the body is also drawn into this harmony, as physical existence is neither incidental nor inferior but integral to the human experience. And through it all, the spirit—the innermost core of our being—must be continually renewed by the Holy Spirit, who unites and sanctifies the whole person.

This journey toward integration requires us to embrace the richness of the Christian faith, which refuses to divide intellect from mystery, theology from experience, or the spiritual from the practical. The Bible itself models this integration. Its pages are filled with doctrine that challenges the mind, poetry that stirs the heart, laws that govern physical action, and prayers that draw the spirit toward God. Consider the Psalms, where David wrestles with profound theological questions even as he pours out his soul in raw, unfiltered emotion. Or look to Paul, whose letters combine rigorous logic with soaring doxology, reminding us that the pursuit of God encompasses both reason and wonder.

Integration is not achieved through human effort alone. It is the work of the Spirit, who transforms us into the likeness of Christ, "from one degree of glory to another" (2 Cor 3:18). This process, known as sanctification, is the gradual alignment of every aspect of our being with the will of God. It is not instantaneous, nor is it without struggle. Like Paul, we may find ourselves crying out, "Who will deliver me from this body of death?" (Rom 7:24). Yet the answer is always the same: "Thanks be to God through Jesus Christ our Lord!" (Rom 7:25).

The Spirit's work of integration does not erase our individuality but redeems it. Modernity's reductionist tendencies have often treated the self as a machine to be optimized, while postmodernity's relativism has encouraged a formless fluidity. The gospel rejects both extremes, affirming that each person is uniquely created and uniquely redeemed. In Christ, we discover not only our purpose but also our identity. An identity that is unified and self-rooted in God's eternal design.

Integration is also inherently relational. Just as no part of the self can function in isolation, so no person can achieve wholeness apart from community. The fractured self cannot be healed by retreating inward; it must reach outward, engaging with others in relationships marked by love, forgiveness, and mutual encouragement. This mirrors the relational nature of God himself, who exists eternally as Father, Son, and Spirit. The church, as the body of Christ, becomes the primary context for this relational integration, offering a space where individuals are nurtured, challenged, and transformed in the context of community.

Finally, integration is eschatological. It looks forward to the day when Christ will make all things new, when every fracture will be healed and every tear wiped away. In this life, our journey toward wholeness is marked by imperfection, yet it is guided by the hope of ultimate restoration. As Paul writes in Phil 1:6, "He who began a good work in you will bring it to completion at the day of Jesus Christ." This hope sustains us as we seek to live integrated lives in a world that remains deeply fragmented.

The path toward integration is both demanding and freeing. It calls us to surrender every aspect of ourselves to the transforming work of Christ. It invites us into a life of wholeness, where the fragments of modernity and postmodernity are not discarded but redeemed, made into something more beautiful than we could have imagined. And it assures us that, though the journey may be long, we do not walk it alone. The Spirit goes before us, and the body of Christ walks beside us, leading us ever closer to the fullness of life that God intends.

Practices of Integration

Having diagnosed the fracture of the self and traced the path toward integration, we now turn to the practical outworking of this vision. Integration is not merely a concept to be understood; it is a way of life to be embraced. If the Spirit's sanctifying work is the source of our integration, then our role is one of faithful participation. Just as a vine grows by the nourishing work of the gardener, so the fractured self begins to flourish as we cooperate with the Spirit through intentional practices that align our lives with God's design. These practices, rooted in the wisdom of Scripture and the lived tradition of the church, guide us toward a holistic faith that engages the mind, stirs the heart, nurtures the spirit, and honors the body.

The mind, often the casualty of both modernity's cold rationalism and postmodernity's skepticism, is central to this journey. To love God with our minds is not simply to assent to theological propositions but to actively cultivate intellectual discipleship. Paul exhorts believers to be "transformed by the renewal of your mind" (Rom 12:2), a process that requires both discipline and delight. This renewal involves immersing ourselves in the truths of Scripture, which not only inform but also transform. It also means engaging with the great thinkers of the Christian tradition, whose insights illuminate the contours of God's reality.

Yet intellectual cultivation is not an end in itself. The mind, renewed by truth, must work in harmony with the heart. The heart, in biblical thought, is not merely the seat of emotion but the center of the will, the core of our being that directs all we do. Practices of worship, prayer, and gratitude recalibrate the heart's affections, aligning them with God's purposes. In Ps 51:10, David cries, "Create in me a clean heart, O God, and renew a right spirit within me." This is the cry of a soul seeking integration, a plea for God to reorder the disordered loves that fragment the self.

Prayer, in particular, becomes a means of knitting the mind and heart together in communion with God. In prayer, we speak and listen, reason and feel, offering the entirety of ourselves to the One who knows us fully. Prayer is not simply a task but a posture, a constant awareness of God's presence that integrates the ordinary and the sacred. This immensely important dimension of faith does not bypass the intellect but elevates it, drawing it into the fullness of worship.

Integration also requires attention to the spirit, the innermost part of our being that connects us to God. The spirit, though often neglected in the noise of modern life, is the wellspring of our relationship with the divine. Practices of silence and solitude, long treasured in Christian tradition, allow the spirit to breathe in the presence of God. Jesus himself modeled this rhythm, withdrawing to solitary places to pray (Mark 1:35). These practices, far from being escapist, ground us in the reality of God's love and equip us to engage the world with renewed purpose.

The body, too, must not be forgotten. Modern culture often treats the body as either a tool to be optimized or a canvas for self-expression, ignoring its sacred role in the integrated life. Paul's declaration that our bodies are temples of the Holy Spirit (1 Cor 6:19–20) calls us to honor God through physical stewardship. This includes rest, exercise, and mindful living, but it also encompasses practices like fasting and Sabbath-keeping, which remind us that the body is not an obstacle to spirituality but an essential part of it. Fasting trains the body to align with the spirit, while Sabbath restores its rhythms, anchoring us in God's provision and presence.

Community, while often seen as external to the self, is vital to integration. We are relational beings, created in the image of a relational God, and our wholeness is incomplete without connection to others. The church, as the body of Christ, becomes the primary context for this relational integration. Within its fellowship, we find accountability, encouragement, and the shared practices of worship and service that draw us closer to God and one another. The "one another" commands of Scripture (i.e. love one another, bear one another's burdens, forgive one another) are not just ethical imperatives but pathways to healing and wholeness.

These practices are not checkboxes in a spiritual to-do list but means of grace, ways in which we open ourselves to the Spirit's transformative work. They are practices of alignment, drawing the fragmented parts of our lives into harmony with God's will. They are also profoundly countercultural, resisting the fragmentation and distraction that the world imposes. In embracing these practices, we declare that our lives are not our own, that we belong wholly to the One who created, redeemed, and sustains us.

Living as an Integrated Person

Integration is not merely a personal triumph; it is a testimony. The world, fractured and restless, looks for evidence that wholeness is possible. An integrated person becomes such evidence, not through perfection but through a life that reflects coherence, purpose, and peace. To live as an integrated person is to embody the unity of mind, heart, body, and spirit in daily rhythms, relationships, and callings. It is to live a life centered on God, whose truth, beauty, and goodness restore the harmony that sin has broken.

This integrated life is not withdrawn from the world's fragmentation but fully engaged with it, bearing witness to the transformative power of the gospel. It begins with the self, yet it does not end there. Wholeness in Christ compels us outward: toward God, toward others, and toward the broader creation. As we experience healing and restoration, we are drawn into the mission of God, now as his hands and feet to bring that same healing to the world.

An integrated person approaches life with clarity, not because every question has been answered but because every question is grounded in the ultimate answer: the person of Jesus Christ. This clarity does not eliminate mystery; rather, it embraces it, holding the tension between knowing and trusting. Such a life demonstrates a faith that is as intellectual as it is experiential, a faith that both reasons and worships.

In practical terms, living as an integrated person means embracing life's complexities with courage and hope. It means thinking deeply about the world while also being moved by its beauty and brokenness. It means using one's body not only as a tool for productivity but as a vessel for service and worship. It means orienting the heart toward what is true and good, refusing to be captive to fleeting desires or trivial distractions. And it means living with a spirit attuned to God, responsive to his leading and open to his transforming power.

This integration manifests in relationships, where the fragmented self once sought to use others for affirmation or validation. The integrated person, secure in Christ, becomes a source of love, forgiveness, and encouragement. Relationships cease to be transactional and instead reflect the divine relationality of the Trinity. In families, workplaces, and communities, the integrated life brings stability, compassion, and hope.

Integration transforms our engagement with the world. The person who is whole in Christ no longer sees work as mere drudgery or as the ultimate source of identity but as a sacred calling to participate in God's creative and redemptive purposes. The integrated person approaches the natural world with wonder and care, seeing it not as a resource to exploit but as a gift to steward. This holistic vision draws every aspect of life into alignment with God's kingdom.

The integrated life is not static. It is a continual process of growth, refinement, and dependence on God's grace. Each day offers opportunities to deepen this wholeness, whether through small acts of obedience, moments of reflection, or significant choices that require trust. Even setbacks and struggles become part of this journey, as the Spirit uses them to shape us more fully into the image of Christ.

Living as an integrated person is not only possible but deeply needed in a world desperate for coherence and hope. The fractured culture around us will not be healed by words alone; it must see lives that reflect the peace and purpose of God's restoration. As we live this way, we become living parables of the gospel, inviting others into the wholeness that only Christ can bring.

This brings us to the next step in our journey: the rediscovery of the sacred. If integration begins with the self, it finds its ultimate fulfillment in reconnecting with the transcendent. The longing for wholeness is inseparable from the longing for something beyond ourselves.

17

The Resurgence of the Sacred
Longing for Transcendence

TO BE HUMAN IS to long for something beyond ourselves, to seek a reality greater than what we can see, touch, or fully comprehend. The fractured self, once it begins to find integration, instinctively reaches outward, yearning for transcendence. This longing is no accident: it is the imprint of the Creator, a whisper of eternity placed within every human heart (Eccl 3:11). It is the cry of a soul that knows it was made for more than the fleeting and finite; it is a thirst for the sacred.

In the previous chapter, we explored the path from fragmentation to integration, rediscovering how Christ heals the internal fractures of the self. Yet integration, while necessary, is not sufficient on its own. The self, no matter how whole, was never meant to be an isolated entity. True wholeness is not found in self-sufficiency but in a connection to the transcendent—a reality that grounds, fulfills, and transforms us. This chapter builds on that foundation by moving outward from the integrated self to the universal longing for the sacred.

The modern world, however, has tried to silence this longing. The forces of secularization, as we have seen, have confined humanity to what Charles Taylor calls "the buffered self," a way of seeing the world that excludes the transcendent.[1] In this frame, everything is flattened: beauty reduced to aesthetics, morality to social constructs, and love to mere biology. Yet the human soul resists this reduction. Even in a secular

---

1. Taylor, *Secular Age*, 27.

age, the sacred refuses to be erased. It breaks through in art, in ritual, and in those moments of wonder that leave us breathless, hinting at a reality beyond the material.

This longing is evident all around us, from the mythic storytelling that captivates audiences to the rise of secular spiritual practices like mindfulness and meditation. But these reflections of the sacred, though compelling, are incomplete. They point toward something greater but cannot satisfy the soul's deepest thirst. Like the woman at the well in John 4, humanity drinks from broken cisterns, only to find itself thirsty again. The sacred, we discover, cannot be manufactured or contained; it must be received as a gift from the One who is holy.

We must rediscover the sacred not as an abstract idea or a fleeting experience but as the very heartbeat of reality. It is an invitation to recognize the ways in which the sacred calls to us, to embrace its transformative power, and to reclaim its central place in our lives. As we do, we move closer to the wholeness for which we were created, becoming not only integrated individuals but also participants in a story far greater than ourselves. We have to pause and look upward, allowing the sacred to lift our gaze beyond the confines of the immanent and into the eternal. It is only by reconnecting with the sacred that we can fully live as the people God intended us to be: whole, worshipful, and deeply connected to him.

The Longing for the Sacred in a Secular World

To understand the resurgence of the sacred, we must first confront its absence, or rather, the attempt to suppress it. The modern world is often described as secular, yet it is anything but devoid of spiritual yearning. Beneath the surface of rationalism and materialism lies a profound and persistent hunger, a longing for meaning, connection, and transcendence. This longing, though often unacknowledged, pulses through the heart of human culture, breaking through even in a world that has tried to confine itself to the purely immanent.

The modern age, shaped by centuries of secularization, narrows reality to what can be seen, measured, and controlled. In this worldview, the transcendent—the idea of something beyond the material—is either optional or irrelevant. Yet, this frame of reference consistently proves insufficient. Even those who profess no belief in God are haunted by a sense of transcendence, an inexplicable yearning that no amount of progress or productivity can quench.

This longing is increasingly being articulated by contemporary voices, both secular and religious. Psychologist Jordan Peterson, in his lectures and works like *We Who Wrestle With God*, regularly focuses his analyses on biblical archetypes, highlighting the enduring power of the Bible to address fundamental human questions. He defines God as "what we encounter when we are moved to the depths."[2] Peterson argues that stories such as Cain and Abel or the Exodus resonate because they reflect universal patterns of human experience, pointing toward higher truths about suffering, morality, and redemption. His lectures on the Bible have drawn millions, many of whom identify as secular but are captivated by the profound psychological and spiritual insights of these ancient texts.

Similarly, John Vervaeke, a cognitive scientist, has explored the concept of "relevance realization" and its connection to humanity's pursuit of meaning. Vervaeke's work emphasizes the importance of practices like meditation and mindfulness in fostering states of consciousness that transcend the mundane. Though his framework is not explicitly religious, his recognition of humanity's need for meaning aligns with the sacred longing described in religious traditions.

Rod Dreher's *The Benedict Option* has added another layer to this conversation, offering a vision for how faith communities can reclaim sacred practices in a secular age. Dreher emphasizes the necessity of intentional living, where believers create spaces of transcendent meaning in contrast to the desacralized culture around them. For Dreher, reclaiming the sacred is not merely about personal spirituality but about preserving and embodying the truths of the Christian faith within a fragmented society. Other commentators like Justin Brierley have noted the cracks in secular modernity's facade. Brierley, in his work on faith and reason (*The Surprising Rebirth of Belief in God*), highlights the growing acknowledgment among intellectuals that secular frameworks fail to answer humanity's deepest existential questions.

Popular culture also reflects this longing. The rise of mythic storytelling in film and literature, whether in Tolkien-inspired epics or the moral complexities of superhero narratives, reveals an ever-increasing hunger for stories that speak to eternal truths. These tales of sacrifice, redemption, and the battle between good and evil resonate because they echo the

---

2. Peterson, *We Who Wrestle with God*, 5.

archetypes embedded in the human psyche. As Peterson and others have observed, these stories are compelling precisely because they point beyond themselves to universal truths about human nature and the divine.

Yet these echoes of the sacred, however powerful, remain incomplete. Mindfulness practices and archetypal storytelling may momentarily satisfy, but they cannot address the deepest questions of human existence: Why are we here? What is the purpose of life? What happens after death? The sacred cannot be manufactured or contained within the immanent frame; it must be received as a gift from the Creator.

The persistence of these questions, even in a secular age, reveals a profound truth: the sacred is not gone, only hidden. The immanent frame may attempt to suppress transcendence, but it cannot eliminate the deep-seated awareness of God that resides in every human soul. This longing, far from being a relic of the past, is the heartbeat of humanity, calling us to rediscover the sacred source of all meaning.

Rediscovering the Sacred in Christianity

The echoes of transcendence that ripple through modern culture and intellectual discourse are compelling but incomplete. They hint at a sacred reality beyond the confines of materialism and secularism, but only in Christianity is this longing fully satisfied. Christianity does not merely describe the sacred; it immerses us in it. It reveals the sacred as personal, transformative, and redemptive, calling us into a relationship with the Creator whose presence imbues all things with meaning.

Charles Taylor's concept of "fullness" in *A Secular Age* aligns closely with the Christian understanding of the sacred.[3] Taylor speaks of fullness as the experience of living in connection with something larger than oneself, a sense of purpose that transcends the material. Christianity not only affirms this yearning but reveals its source: the Creator who made humanity for communion with him. This relationship, disrupted by sin, is restored through Jesus Christ. In him, the sacred is no longer distant or abstract but incarnate, near, and accessible.

Christianity uniquely integrates the sacred with the ordinary. Bread and wine, water and oil—elements of the earth—become means of grace in the sacraments. This connection contrasts sharply with secular spirituality, which often isolates the sacred from daily life. In Christianity, the

---

3. Taylor, *Secular Age*, 6.

ordinary becomes enchanted; the mundane is charged with divine meaning. As Gerard Manley Hopkins wrote, "The world is charged with the grandeur of God."[4]

This integration extends to Christian practices. Prayer, for instance, is not self-help or mindfulness but a dialogue with the living God. Contemplative traditions, such as those of the desert fathers, teach believers to dwell in silence and awe, experiencing the sacred presence of God. Worship, too, is transformative. When believers gather as the church, they join a transcendent community (past, present, and future), lifting their voices in eternal praise (Heb 12:22–24). The sacred realities of worship reorient hearts and minds toward God's glory, offering not just a fleeting escape but an enduring transformation.

The communal nature of the sacred is central to Christianity. The church, as the body of Christ, is a living temple where God's presence dwells. Here, believers find not only connection with God but also with one another. This sacred community becomes a foretaste of the kingdom to come, where relationships are restored and love reigns.

Unlike the ephemeral experiences offered by secular spirituality, the Christian encounter with the sacred is enduring. It does not fade with time but deepens, reorienting all of life around God's presence. Jesus offers living water that becomes "a spring of water welling up to eternal life" (John 4:14). The sacred, as revealed in Christianity, is not an abstraction or a fleeting sense of awe; it is a relationship with the living God who transforms and redeems.

The Call to Reclaim the Sacred

Rediscovering the sacred is only the beginning; reclaiming it requires action. The longing for transcendence, deeply embedded in every human soul, is not meant to end in acknowledgment but in participation. The sacred is an invitation to live differently, to embrace a re-enchanted vision of the world where worship becomes a way of life and the ordinary is imbued with divine purpose.

The church is central to this reclamation. As the body of Christ, it serves as both a sacred community and a witness to the world. Through worship, teaching, and communal life, the church becomes a bridge between the immanent and the transcendent. Worship is not merely

---

4. Hopkins, "God's Grandeur."

ceremonial; it is formative. In liturgy, prayer, music, and sacrament, believers are drawn into God's presence. These rhythms shape hearts and minds, re-centering them in God's reality.

Sacred art and beauty also play a vital role in reclaiming the sacred. Cathedrals, hymns, and stained glass communicate truths that words cannot fully capture. Beauty reflects the divine and awakens the longing for transcendence. In a culture that often trivializes or commodifies beauty, the church's commitment to sacred art becomes a countercultural witness, inviting all to glimpse the glory of God.

Reclaiming the sacred extends beyond the church walls into every aspect of life. Practices like Sabbath-keeping, silence, and attentiveness to creation allow believers to cultivate a sacred awareness. The Sabbath is not merely a day of rest but a declaration of God's sovereignty and provision. Silence creates space for God's voice in a noisy world, and creation, seen through the eyes of faith, becomes a canvas of divine artistry.

Reclaiming the sacred is not simply an internal realization or private spiritual practice; it is a focus that reshapes every aspect of life. To live with a renewed sense of the sacred is to live with an entirely transformed orientation toward the world, where everything is reconnected to its ultimate purpose and meaning in God. The consequences of this reorientation ripple outward, transforming how we understand ourselves, how we engage with the created world, and how we relate to one another.

Reclaiming the sacred begins by reshaping our self-understanding. In a culture that often reduces identity to fragmented roles or fleeting preferences, the sacred self stands anchored in God's truth. To see oneself as sacred is to recognize that we are not accidents of biology, nor are we simply products of cultural constructs. We are *imago Dei*—image-bearers of the Creator—designed for communion with him and charged with reflecting his character in the world.

This identity is both humbling and exalting. It reminds us of our utter dependence on God and of the profound dignity he has bestowed upon us. As David declared long ago, "What is man that you are mindful of him. . .? Yet you have made him a little lower than the heavenly beings and crowned him with glory and honor" (Ps. 8:4–5). To live as a sacred self is to reject the modern compulsion to craft our own identities and instead to receive our identity as a gift, rooted in the One who made us.

A renewed sense of the sacred also transforms the way we see the world. Creation is no longer a backdrop for human activity, nor is it a resource to be exploited or consumed. Instead, it becomes a living testimony to God's glory. The psalmist's declaration "the earth is the Lord's and the fullness thereof" (Ps 24:1) reminds us that the world is not ours to own but God's to reveal. Every mountain peak and flowing river, every grain of sand and breath of wind, is charged with divine meaning. This sacred perspective calls us to stewardship. To care for creation is not merely an ethical responsibility but an act of worship. It is to treat the natural world as a sacred trust, reflecting the Creator's care and creativity. This vision also awakens wonder, inviting us to rediscover the world as a theater of God's majesty.

Perhaps most profoundly, reclaiming the sacred reshapes our relationships. To view others as sacred is to see them as bearers of God's image, deserving of dignity, love, and respect. This sacred lens challenges the transactional and often dehumanizing nature of modern relationships. It calls us to live with generosity, forgiveness, and humility, knowing that every person we encounter is infinitely valuable to God.

The sacred life also draws us into deeper community, for the sacred cannot thrive in isolation. Just as God exists eternally in relational love as Father, Son, and Spirit, so we are called to reflect that relationality in our lives. Relationships become a space where the sacred is experienced and expressed, where love is not merely a feeling but an act of worship. Sacred community becomes a foretaste of the relational harmony we were created to enjoy.

Reclaiming the sacred also provides a renewed sense of hope in a fractured and disenchanted world. The sacred reminds us that life is not random or meaningless but part of a divine story that is moving toward ultimate redemption. This hope does not erase the struggles and sorrows of life but places them within a larger context. Even suffering can be imbued with purpose when viewed through the sacred lens, for it becomes a means by which God refines and redeems.

Living with a sense of the sacred reorients us toward God's kingdom, where he is actively working to restore all things. This hope gives meaning to our daily lives, calling us to participate in his redemptive work. It assures us that, even in the midst of chaos, God's purposes will prevail.

Reorienting Around the Holy

To reorient our lives around the holy is to realign our entire being with the truth of God's presence. No longer living as if the world is a cold and indifferent place but as if it is saturated with divine purpose. The recognition of the sacred does not merely lead to a more contemplative life; it transforms how we move, how we think, and how we relate to everything around us. Once we recover the sense of God's presence, we begin to see with new eyes. And what we see is not just an individual path of enlightenment but an interconnected web of relationships, each marked with divine significance.

The longing for transcendence, once fulfilled, does not leave us isolated in personal piety; rather, it spills over into a longing for restored community. True holiness is never self-contained; it always reaches outward. The same God who calls us into intimacy with himself calls us into communion with one another. The sacred, when properly understood, does not remove us from the world but reorients us within it. It reconciles not only our fragmented souls but also our fractured relationships, pulling us out of self-absorption and into the sacred bonds of love, friendship, and fellowship.

This restoration of community is not an abstract ideal but a lived reality that echoes the very nature of God. The Triune God is, in his essence, a relationship of love. To be drawn into the life of God is to be drawn into a relational existence, where love of God and love of neighbor are not separate commands but two sides of the same truth (Matt 22:37–39). To seek God is to seek reconciliation, to desire wholeness not only for ourselves but for those around us. Sin isolates, fractures, and divides; the sacred gathers, restores, and unites.

But this reclamation of the sacred is not an endpoint; it is a gateway. The more we reorient around the holy, the more it begins to shape every aspect of life. Our self-understanding is transformed. We no longer see ourselves through the lens of our failures or successes but through the reality of being beloved in Christ. Our vision of creation shifts, and we no longer view the world as mere material but as the theater of God's glory. Lastly, our relationships are renewed. We no longer see people as instruments of our own fulfillment but as sacred reflections of God's image.

The sacred, once reclaimed, does not remain static. It grows, deepens, and expands, reaching into every corner of our existence. It is not a passive realization but an active force that reshapes how we love, how we work, and how we live together. From here, the journey moves outward, calling us to embody the sacred not just in personal devotion but in the formation of communities marked by truth, goodness, and beauty. It is in these sacred communities that the brokenness of human connection is healed and the love of God becomes tangible.

The task before us is not simply to see the sacred but to live it. To allow its reality to permeate our relationships, our vocations, and our vision for the world. The restoration of the sacred is not just for us; it is for the renewal of all things. It is a call to walk as people who are not only transformed but who participate in the transformation of others. This is the truest form of community, and to the establishment of that, we now turn.

18

Restoring Relationships

The Sacredness of Community

We live in a world more connected than ever before yet profoundly disconnected where it matters most. In the age of instant communication, social media, and virtual interactions, billions of people can reach across continents with a single click. Yet, beneath this façade of connectedness lies a deeper loneliness, a crisis of intimacy and belonging that technology cannot solve. The irony is striking: we have the tools to communicate with almost anyone at any time, but we are losing the art of truly relating to one another. The result is a society plagued by isolation, anxiety, and fractured relationships.

This crisis is not just cultural or psychological; at its core it is spiritual. This crisis reflects humanity's estrangement from the God who made us for relationship. Humanity's story begins and will end with relationships: humanity walking in communion with God in the garden and the redeemed gathered in perfect fellowship around his throne. In between lies a history of relational brokenness healed only through the reconciling work of Jesus Christ. The cross is not merely a symbol of individual salvation; it is the ultimate act of relational restoration, mending the rift between humanity and God and between one another.

Yet, even among Christians, the sacredness of relationships is often neglected. Some retreat into the solitude of hyper-individualism, prioritizing personal spirituality over communal life. Others, weary of relational wounds, are tempted to withdraw from meaningful engagement, building walls instead of bridges. Still others view relationships through a transactional lens, measuring their worth by what they can gain rather than what they can give. All the while, the biblical vision of community—rooted in the love of the Triune God and modeled by Christ himself—offers a radically different way of living.

Jesus was a master of relationships. His life was marked by profound relational intimacy and radical hospitality. He wept with friends, dined with outcasts, and forgave those who betrayed him. At the table, he broke bread not only with his disciples but also with sinners, inviting them into the fellowship of God's kingdom. His ministry was not a lecture but a life shared. A model of sacred community that continues to invite us to the table of grace.

If the meaning we long for is to be discovered, we must reclaim the sacredness of relationships in an age of profound relational disconnection. We need to see relationships not as incidental but as central to our purpose and identity, rooted in the very nature of God. We need to reject both the hyper-individualism of our culture and the ascetic withdrawal of some religious mindsets, embracing instead a vision of community that reflects the relational love of Christ.

To live as sacred people in sacred community is not to retreat from the world but to engage it with intentional love and hospitality. The gospel compels us to invite others into fellowship, to extend grace at the table, and to live in such a way that our relationships become a witness to the reconciling power of Christ. In this fractured age, the church has the opportunity to be what it was always meant to be: a sacred community that draws people not to itself but to the God who restores all things.

The Challenge of Community in a Disconnected Age

The age of hyper-connectivity has given rise to an unsettling paradox: while technology allows us to communicate with anyone, anywhere, at any time, we are lonelier than ever before. Social media platforms promise to connect us, yet studies show that excessive use often leads to feelings of isolation and inadequacy. Relationships, once built on shared physical presence and deep conversations, are increasingly reduced to likes, retweets, and shallow interactions. The resulting loneliness epidemic is not just a societal inconvenience; it is a profound existential crisis, leaving people adrift in a sea of relational fragmentation.

This crisis is well-documented. Scholars like Sherry Turkle, in her book *Alone Together*, have explored how digital communication has replaced genuine connection, creating an illusion of intimacy while eroding the relational depth humanity needs. Turkle argues that while technology offers convenience, it also distances us from the vulnerability and presence required for authentic relationships. This erosion is part of a larger cultural movement that prioritizes autonomy and self-expression over communal bonds, further isolating individuals. From her studies, Turkle made the following assessment:

> We have seen young people try to reclaim personal privacy and each other's attention. They crave things as simple as telephone calls made, as one eighteen-year-old puts it, "sitting down and giving each other full attention." Today's young people have a special vulnerability: although always connected, they feel deprived of attention.[1]

As people drifted away from faith and its communal structures, they lost the relational anchors that give life coherence. This decline of shared belief systems has not only fractured relationships but also left individuals without the framework to form deep, lasting bonds. In the absence of a sacred center, people are left to navigate relationships based on utility rather than love, reducing others to means to an end. At the heart of this crisis lies modernity's disposition towards hyper-individualism, a worldview that exalts personal freedom and self-fulfillment above all else. This emphasis on the autonomous self has weakened the communal ties that once bound societies together. Relationships, once seen as sacred and integral to human flourishing, are now often viewed as optional, even burdensome.

Rapid advancements in technology have exacerbated this crisis by rewiring our relational habits. The rise of virtual interactions has diminished our capacity for embodied presence, a critical component of genuine relationships. Relationships require vulnerability and shared space, yet technology often circumvents these, offering instead curated images and performative interactions that leave people feeling both overexposed and unseen. The existential and relational disconnectedness of our age is both a root and a fruit of the meaning crisis. Disconnection isolates individuals, cutting them off from the relational richness that gives life purpose, while the loss of purpose further entrenches relational breakdown.

---

1. Turkle, *Alone Together*, 294.

The Christian vision offers a compelling antidote: a community rooted in the love of God, where relationships are not transactional but sacred.

The Relational God and the Sacred Call to Community

Humanity's longing for connection is not a cultural artifact or a product of evolution—it is woven into the fabric of existence. The impulse to bond, to know and be known, reflects a deeper reality: we are created in the image of a relational God. This truth is not abstract theology but a profound declaration of what it means to be human. At the heart of reality is not isolation or competition but love and communion. To grasp this is to uncover the sacredness of relationships and the divine invitation to live in community.

God exists coequally and coeternally as a Trinity: Father, Son, and Holy Spirit united as one being in three distinct persons maintaining a perfect relationship of mutual love, honor, and delight. This reality is not incidental to God's nature; it is his essence. The Triune God is the ultimate model of relationship, and every human bond echoes this divine pattern. Augustine, in his writings on the Trinity, marveled at the mystery of a God who is both unity and community, drawing humanity into the relational life of the divine.

This relationality is not a passive ideal but an active force. In creation, God speaks into being not just a solitary man but a humanity designed for partnership and communion. "It is not good that the man should be alone" (Gen 2:18). This declaration is more than a comment on Adam's solitude; it is a revelation of God's intention for human flourishing through relationships. From the beginning, relationships were sacred, a reflection of the love shared within the Trinity.

Yet, as the book of Genesis reveals, this sacred design was shattered. The fall introduced suspicion, shame, and blame, fracturing the harmonious relationships between humanity and God, humanity and one another, and humanity and creation itself. Adam and Eve, once naked and unashamed, now hide from God and each other, their intimacy replaced by fear and division.

This fragmentation reverberates through history, manifesting in the relational crises of our own time. Theologian Miroslav Volf identifies exclusion as one of humanity's deepest wounds, rooted in our alienation from God. Volf argues that sin disintegrates relationships by turning people inward, fostering isolation and hostility. This turning inward and away from others is the antithesis of the divine relationality we were created to reflect. Borrowing from Alvin Plantinga, Volf writes, "If the process of creation takes place through the activity of 'separating-and-binding,' should not then sin be described as some 'devastating twister' that both explodes and implodes creation, pushing it back toward the 'formless void' from which it came."[2] Where God brought creation, harmony, and relationship out of the formless void, sin and the brokenness produced by permeated the world after the fall seeking to undo what God declared "very good" (Gen 1:31).

Into this brokenness steps Christ, the ultimate reconciler. His life, death, and resurrection are not merely acts of individual salvation but profound works of relational restoration. The apostle Paul makes this clear when he writes, "All this is from God, who through Christ reconciled us to Himself and gave us the ministry of reconciliation" (2 Cor 5:18–19). Christ's atonement repairs the fractured relationship between humanity and God, and through this restored connection, he empowers us to heal our relationships with one another.

Jesus' ministry was saturated with relational intentionality. He invited fishermen to follow him, befriended tax collectors and sinners, wept with grieving sisters, and washed the feet of his disciples. He broke societal norms by engaging with Samaritans, women, and the marginalized, embodying the sacred truth that no relationship is insignificant. His table fellowship, in particular, became a profound act of inclusion and restoration. In sharing meals with outcasts, Jesus declared that the hingdom of God is a place of radical welcome, where all who will follow him are invited to the table. The church, as the body of Christ, is the continuation of this relational mission. It is not merely a gathering of individuals but a sacred community where the broken are mended, the alienated find belonging, and the fractured bonds of humanity are restored.

This sacred community stands in stark contrast to the transactional relationships of modern culture. Within the church, relationships are not defined by utility but by mutual love and sacrifice. Paul's vision of the church in Eph 2:19–22 captures this beautifully: "You are no longer strangers and aliens, but you are fellow citizens with the saints and members of the household of God... Christ Jesus Himself being the cornerstone." The

---

2. Volf, *Exclusion and Embrace*, 66.

church is not merely an institution; it is a household, a family where the sacredness of relationships is rediscovered and celebrated.

To live relationally is to live in alignment with the God who made us for communion. This call is not optional; it is central to the Christian life. As Jesus prayed in John 17:21, "That they may all be one, just as You, Father, are in Me, and I in You, that they also may be in Us." This unity is not a vague ideal but a lived reality made possible through Christ's reconciling work.

In answering this sacred call, we embody the relational nature of God, becoming conduits of his love in a world desperate for connection. This is not a retreat from the world's fragmentation but an engagement with it, offering a countercultural vision of relationships rooted in grace, humility, and hospitality. As we turn to explore what this looks like in practice, we begin to see how the sacredness of community transforms not only individuals but entire societies. Relationships, when restored in the light of God's love, become a powerful witness to the kingdom of God breaking into the world.

The Vision for Community

Community, in the biblical sense, is not a peripheral aspect of faith but its living heart. It is in the context of relationships, restored and centered in God, that the gospel is most fully lived out. Yet this vision of community is not abstract or unattainable; it is a deeply practical call to action that challenges us to reimagine our lives as intertwined with others in ways that reflect the love of Christ.

At Jesus's table, boundaries of social status, morality, and ethnicity dissolved. The sinner sat alongside the righteous, the outcast alongside the insider, and all were welcomed not because of their worthiness but because of his grace. The table became a sacred space where relationships were healed, hearts were opened, and the kingdom of God was made manifest. This vision of the table challenges us to rethink the spaces where we build community. In a world of closed doors and exclusive circles, we are called to open our homes, hearts, and churches as places of hospitality. Hospitality is not about impressing others but about creating spaces where strangers can become friends and the broken can feel whole. It is the act of making room for others at the table of our lives.

Modern relationships are often transactional, based on mutual benefit or convenience. The Christian vision calls us to something far deeper: transformational relationships rooted in sacrificial love. This is the kind of love Jesus demonstrated when he washed the feet of his disciples, a task reserved for the lowest servant. It is a love that humbles itself, seeks the good of the other, and expects nothing in return.

To restore relationships, we must move beyond self-interest and embrace vulnerability. This requires risk—risking rejection, risking discomfort, risking misunderstanding. Yet it is only in vulnerability that true connection is formed. As Brené Brown, a leading researcher on vulnerability, has observed, "Vulnerability is the birthplace of connection and the path to the feeling of being truly loved." For Christians, this path is not walked alone but in the strength of the Holy Spirit, who empowers us to love as Christ loves.

Building and restoring relationships requires intentionality. It is not enough to desire community; we must cultivate it through concrete practices. Here are steps toward restoring relationships and creating sacred community:

1. *Practice Presence*: In a world of distractions, one of the most countercultural acts is to be fully present. Whether in conversations with a friend, a shared meal with family, or prayer with a fellow believer, being present communicates value and love. Put away the phone, make eye contact, and listen deeply.

2. *Prioritize the Gathering of the Church*: The church is not simply a place to consume spiritual content but a family to belong to. Regular participation in worship, small groups, and communal activities strengthens the bonds that hold the body of Christ together. The early church in Acts 2:42–47 thrived because of its commitment to "fellowship, the breaking of bread, and prayers."

3. *Extend Forgiveness and Seek Reconciliation*: Broken relationships cannot be mended without the hard work of forgiveness. True forgiveness is not forgetting or excusing wrongdoing but releasing the hold of bitterness and seeking peace. Jesus calls us to this radical forgiveness, instructing us to reconcile even before offering our gifts at the altar (Matt 5:23–24).

4. *Engage in Acts of Service*: Serving others shifts the focus from ourselves to the needs of those around us. It breaks down barriers of

pride and self-sufficiency, fostering relationships built on humility and compassion.

5. *Intentionally Create Community*: Whether it's inviting neighbors to a meal, hosting a Bible study, or simply making time to visit someone in need, creating spaces of welcome reflects the hospitality of Christ. These spaces need not be perfect; they need only be open.

When relationships are restored and community is cultivated, lives are transformed. And not just the lives of those within the community but also those on the outside looking in. A church that lives as a sacred community becomes a beacon of hope in a fractured world. It demonstrates the reconciling power of the gospel, inviting others to experience the love of Christ not through words alone but through the tangible witness of lives lived together in harmony and grace.

The church must recover its role as a sign of contradiction to the world's disintegration. This does not mean retreating into isolation but standing as a visible alternative. Being a community where love triumphs over division, forgiveness over bitterness, and selflessness over self-interest. Such a community becomes irresistible, drawing people not to itself but to the God who alone makes it possible.

This vision of community is not a utopian dream but a lived reality, rooted in the love of the Triune God and modeled by Christ. It calls us to open our lives to others, to embrace vulnerability, and to create spaces where relationships can flourish. It is an invitation to live as sacred people in a sacred community, offering the world not just a solution to its relational crisis but a glimpse of the kingdom of God. As we take steps toward this vision, we do more than restore relationships, we participate in God's work of restoration, becoming agents of reconciliation in a world desperate for wholeness. In doing so, we fulfill the sacred call to love God and love our neighbor, living out the greatest commandment in ways that transform both our lives and the lives of those around us.

A Sacred Fellowship in a Fragmented World

The Christian vision of restored relationships and sacred community is a hope that pulses with life, a healing balm in a world shattered by loneliness and hyper-individualism. In an age where technological connection often masks deep relational alienation, where people live side-by-side yet remain strangers, and where community is increasingly shaped by consumer preference rather than covenantal commitment, the church stands as a countercultural witness to something far greater: a family not bound by bloodlines, status, or choice but by the unbreakable grace of the gospel.

Before creation, before time itself, relationship was at the center of reality. God did not create out of a need for love but out of an overflow of an eternal love. He made humanity in his image, not as isolated beings but as creatures meant for communion with him and with one another. Sin fractured this design, turning love into self-interest, community into competition, and fellowship into fear, but Jesus Christ, through his life, death, and resurrection, not only reconciles us to God but also to each other. The walls that divide us—ethnic, economic, social, ideological—are torn down by and in him, and in their place, a new humanity is formed, one bound not by convenience but by covenant, not by fleeting emotions but by eternal love.

This sacred fellowship is not a retreat from the world but a mission to it. It is not an escape from the brokenness of life but an embodiment of Christ's radical love within it. The church is not called to be an enclave of the comfortable but a home for the weary, the wandering, and the wounded. In a world that builds walls, sacred community builds bridges. It rejects both the transactional relationships of a consumer-driven culture, where people are valued only as long as they are useful, and the ascetic withdrawal of those who abandon the world in the name of holiness. Instead, it follows Christ's example. The One who sat at the table with sinners, who touched the untouchable, who called the forsaken his friends, and who, even on the cross, spoke words of welcome: "Today you will be with me in paradise" (Luke 23:43).

The table of Christ is not a place of exclusion but of invitation. It is where enemies become brothers, where strangers find belonging, and where the broken are restored. And the church, as the body of Christ, is called to embody this invitation, to be the living extension of his welcome. In a society where loneliness has become an epidemic, where trust is eroded, and where fear of the other is cultivated, the church must be the place where love is tangible, where hospitality is not a performance but a way of life, and where people are seen, known, and cherished.

But sacred community is not built in theory; it is forged in practice, in the daily, often difficult work of love. It is easy to speak of community; it is far harder to live in it. True fellowship requires vulnerability, a willingness to be known not just in strength but in weakness. It demands forgiveness, even when wounds still ache. It calls for patience, for bearing with one another in grace rather than in judgment. Sacred community is not formed by perfect people but by people willing to extend the same mercy they have received.

To live in sacred community is to participate in God's mission of restoration. It is to embody, in our relationships, a glimpse of the coming kingdom, where every tribe and tongue will one day gather around the great table of fellowship, no longer divided by sin or strife but united in worship of the Lamb. This is not a distant dream but a present calling. The church is not just waiting for the kingdom; it is called to be a foretaste of it. Every meal shared, every burden carried together, every act of sacrificial love is a reflection of what is to come.

As this chapter draws to a close, the call to sacred community becomes clear: we are not meant to walk this journey alone. The Christian life is not an isolated ascent but a shared pilgrimage. We were created for relationships that reflect the relational nature of God, and we are transformed by the love of Christ so that we might, in turn, pour that love into others. To belong to the family of God is to become part of his ongoing work of reconciliation, to invite the world into the joy of restored relationship, and to embody the love that speaks louder than words.

But sacred community is not an end in itself; it is the foundation for living out the gospel in every sphere of life. Love of neighbor does not stop at the church door; it shapes our vocation, our work, and our engagement with the world. As we move forward, we will explore how restored relationships do more than transform how we love one another; they redefine how we live. The next chapter turns to the sacredness of work and vocation, examining how the love of God and neighbor shapes our participation in his creative and redemptive purposes. Relationships are the root, but the fruit is a life fully engaged in the mission of God, where every act, whether in community, at the table, or in the workplace, becomes a reflection of his kingdom come.

19

Work, Calling, and the Kingdom of God

WORK OCCUPIES A CENTRAL place in human life. From the humblest tasks to the most complex endeavors, work shapes our days, our identities, and often our sense of purpose. Yet, in a world increasingly defined by hyper-automation, careerism, and disillusionment, work has become a source of frustration and alienation for many. Some see it as a necessary evil, a relentless grind to pay bills and survive. Others idolize it, chasing success and productivity in a futile attempt to fill a deeper void. In both cases, work is stripped of its sacredness, reduced to either a burden or a badge of worth.

But what if work is more than a means to an end? What if it is not only a reflection of who we are but also of who God is? From the opening pages of Genesis, the Bible reveals that work is not an accident of human existence but an integral part of God's design. Humanity's first commission was to fill, subdue, and cultivate the earth, mirroring the creative work of the Creator. Far from being a curse, work was embedded in the fabric of creation, a sacred vocation that dignifies and enriches human life.

Yet, as with so much of God's good creation, work was marred by the fall. The ground became cursed, and labor turned from a joy to a toil. In our time, this brokenness manifests in many ways: in the dehumanizing effects of hyper-automation, where efficiency is valued over creativity and relationships; in the rise of burnout culture, where people's worth is tied to their productivity; and in the erosion of vocation, where the question of why we work is overshadowed by the relentless demand to work.

This loss of meaning in work is as much a spiritual problem as it is an economic one. The meaning crisis that pervades our culture is deeply connected to the way we view and approach work. When work becomes disconnected from its sacred purpose, it loses its ability to fulfill the deep human longing for purpose, dignity, and contribution. But the gospel offers a different vision. In Christ, work is redeemed, restored to its rightful place as a sacred calling and a means of glorifying God.

This chapter seeks to reclaim a biblical understanding of work: not as a drudgery or an idol but as an act of worship and a vital part of our identity as image-bearers. It will explore how Scripture frames work as central to what it means to be human, how our role as stewards and sub-creators reflects God's own creative nature, and how work, done faithfully, contributes to the advancement of his kingdom. It will also address the challenges of hyper-automation and the growing disconnect between work and meaning, offering practical steps for embracing work as a sacred vocation.

To recover a biblical vision of work is to take a significant step in addressing the meaning crisis of our age. Wherever we are called—whether in boardrooms, classrooms, kitchens, or construction sites—we are called to work as unto the Lord, offering our labor for his glory and the good of his kingdom. In doing so, we reclaim work not just as a necessity of survival but as a sacred act of creation, stewardship, and worship. This is not just about how we work; it is about why we work and who we work for. It is about finding meaning in the ordinary and seeing the extraordinary purposes of God in the labor of our hands.

Designed for Work

When God created the world, he worked—fashioning the heavens and the earth, separating light from darkness, and declaring each aspect of creation "good." And when he created humanity, he gave them a task that reflected his own creative work: to fill, subdue, and cultivate the earth. This commission, often called the *creation or dominion mandate*, establishes work as sacred, woven into the fabric of human identity and purpose.

In Gen 1:26–28, God declares his intention for humanity to "have dominion" over the earth, to care for it and cultivate its potential. This is reiterated in Gen 2:15, where Adam is placed in the garden "to work it and keep it." These passages make it clear that work is not a result of sin or a punishment for the fall but an essential part of God's design for humanity.

Work, in this sense, is not limited to agriculture or manual labor; it encompasses any activity that develops, sustains, and beautifies creation. Whether through art, science, teaching, or business, humans are called to bring order out of chaos, to steward resources wisely, and to contribute to the flourishing of the world. This is what N.T. Wright describes as "signposting" God's kingdom, revealing his glory through faithful and creative labor.[1]

Human work is sacred because it reflects the nature of the God who created us. In Gen 1:27, humanity is described as being made in the image of God, or *imago Dei*. This means that our capacity to create, steward, and innovate mirrors God's own creative work. J. R. R. Tolkien captures this beautifully in his concept of "sub-creation," articulated in his essay *On Fairy-Stories*. Tolkien argues that as creatures made by a Creator, humans are designed to imitate his creativity, fashioning beauty and meaning in the world around them.[2]

But this reflection of God's image is not merely about producing or achieving; it is also about relationality and purpose. God's work in creation was not done in isolation but as an outpouring of his relational nature as Father, Son, and Spirit. Similarly, human work is not meant to be an isolated endeavor but a communal one, connecting us to others and to the created world.

Work also serves as an act of stewardship, a way of honoring the Creator by caring for his creation. In Gen 2:15, the Hebrew word for "keep" carries the connotation of guarding, preserving, and nurturing. Stewardship, then, is not just about maintaining the status quo but about cultivating the earth's potential in ways that glorify God and benefit others. This stewardship extends beyond the physical environment to include relationships, culture, and institutions. Artists steward beauty; teachers steward knowledge; business leaders steward resources; parents steward the next generation. Each act of stewardship is a response to the

---

1. Wright, *Surprised by Hope*, 216.
2. Tolkien, *On Fairy Stories*, 10.

sacred trust God has given humanity, a way of participating in his ongoing work of creation.

It is worth noting that in the pre-fall world, work was not burdensome but joyful. Adam and Eve worked in harmony with creation, experiencing the satisfaction of tending the garden and enjoying the fruits of their labor. This joy reflects the intrinsic value of work as something that fulfills human purpose and glorifies God. It is a glimpse of the eternal reality described in Rev 22:3, where God's people will serve him in the new creation, not out of obligation but out of delight.

This biblical vision of work challenges the narratives of both secularism and escapism. In a culture that often devalues work as a necessary evil or idolizes it as a source of identity, Scripture offers a third way: work as a sacred calling that reflects the nature of God and fulfills his purposes. Work, in this sense, is not about achieving status or accumulating wealth but about participating in God's creative and redemptive purposes. As we labor faithfully in whatever tasks God has given us, we reveal his glory and contribute to the flourishing of the world. This is the foundation for understanding work not as a burden or a means to an end but as a profound and joyful act of worship. From this understanding, we can begin to address the distortions of work in modern culture and recover its sacred purpose in the midst of a meaning-starved world.

The Crisis of Work in Modern Culture

While work was originally designed as a sacred calling, modern culture has distorted its purpose, stripping it of its sacredness and reducing it to either a burden or an idol. This distortion has contributed significantly to the meaning crisis of our time. By dehumanizing labor, idolizing productivity, and embracing hyper-automation, our culture has severed work from its divine purpose, leaving individuals alienated and adrift.

One of the defining features of the modern work crisis is the dehumanization of labor. Industrialization, with its emphasis on efficiency and mechanization, transformed work into a means of production, prioritizing output over the well-being of the worker. This shift reflects the ways in which workers have become disconnected from the fruits of their labor, the creative process, and, ultimately, from themselves. Modern dehumanization compounds this fallenness, creating environments where individuals feel like cogs in a machine rather than image-bearers contributing to God's creation. This mechanistic view of labor robs work of its inherent dignity, reducing workers to their utility and perpetuating the sense of meaninglessness that plagues so many.

Alongside the dehumanization of labor is the cultural idolization of productivity. In a world driven by metrics, deadlines, and endless to-do lists, success is often measured solely by output. This obsession with productivity creates a relentless pressure to perform, leaving little room for reflection, rest, or relational depth. Work becomes not a means of glorifying God but a means of proving one's worth.

This idolization also feeds into the narrative of self-sufficiency, where individuals are expected to derive their identity and value from their achievements. Tim Keller wrote about the danger of idolizing our work in the book *Every Good Endeavor*. He writes:

> If an idol is a good thing turned into an ultimate thing, then a corporate idol is an overemphasis and absolutizing of an admirable cultural trait. We should expect, then, that each culture's emphases have some beneficial influences on work and yet at the same time harmfully distort it.[3]

Work is a good thing, but when we look to our careers for identity, we enter the realm of idolatry and inevitably encounter disillusionment because even the most successful achievements fail to satisfy the deeper longings of the soul.

Perhaps the most pressing challenge of our time is the rise of hyper-automation and artificial intelligence, which are rapidly transforming the nature of work. Tasks once requiring human skill and creativity are increasingly being performed by machines, promising greater efficiency but often at the cost of human engagement. While automation has undeniable benefits, it also poses profound questions about the future of work and its role in human flourishing. As machines take over more tasks, the challenge for humanity is not merely economic but existential: How can we reclaim work as a meaningful and sacred endeavor in an increasingly automated world?

At the opposite end of the spectrum from overwork is disengagement—the perception that work is meaningless or merely a means to survive. For many, this is the result of being in jobs that feel disconnected from their passions or values. The rise of "quiet quitting," where individuals do the bare minimum to keep their jobs, reflects a broader cultural

---

3. Keller, *Every Good Endeavor*, 137.

disillusionment with work. This disengagement is deeply tied to the loss of a transcendent framework for understanding work. Without the biblical vision of work as a sacred calling, people are left to navigate their careers in isolation, searching for fulfillment in roles that often feel arbitrary or unimportant. The result is a growing sense of despair, where work feels like a treadmill rather than a journey toward something meaningful.

Modern culture's fragmentation of work from identity further exacerbates the crisis. In the biblical worldview, work is integrated into a holistic understanding of human purpose, tied to our identity as image-bearers and stewards of creation. In contrast, contemporary narratives often compartmentalize work as a separate sphere, disconnected from spiritual life and relational flourishing.

This compartmentalization creates a profound dissonance, where individuals struggle to reconcile their work with their deeper values and calling. The result is not only personal dissatisfaction but also a diminished capacity for work to contribute to the flourishing of communities and cultures. Work, divorced from its sacred context, becomes an isolated endeavor, stripped of the relational and spiritual dimensions that make it meaningful.

The crisis of work in modern culture is not merely a matter of economic systems or technological advancements; it is a spiritual issue rooted in humanity's estrangement from God's design. To address this crisis, we must recover a vision of work that reconnects it to its sacred purpose, integrates it into the larger narrative of God's kingdom, and restores its role as a source of meaning and human flourishing.

Understanding Calling and Vocation

The distortions of work in modern culture—its dehumanization, idolization, and disconnection—highlight the need to recover a biblical understanding of calling and vocation. While contemporary narratives often reduce work to a career or a means of self-fulfillment, Scripture presents a richer, more integrated vision. Work, when rightly understood, is not merely about what we do but about who we serve.

The word *calling* has its roots in the idea of being summoned, of responding to a voice that draws us into purpose. In the biblical narrative, this calling originates with God, who invites his people to live in relationship with him and to participate in his work. This is seen most clearly in passages like Gen 12:1–3, where God calls Abram to leave his homeland and become a blessing to the nations, or Exod 3:10, where Moses is called to deliver Israel. These callings are not merely about tasks; they are about aligning lives with God's purposes.

The New Testament deepens this understanding, presenting calling as both a universal invitation to follow Christ and a personal vocation within the kingdom of God. Paul reminds believers in 1 Cor 7:17 to "lead the life that the Lord has assigned to him, and to which God has called him." This life encompasses not only spiritual practices but also daily work, relationships, and community engagement. Calling, then, is holistic, encompassing every aspect of life and centering it on God.

One of the great challenges in modern culture is the conflation of job and calling. While jobs can be part of a calling, they are not synonymous with it. A job is a role; a calling is a purpose. The biblical concept of vocation (*vocare*, meaning "to call") goes beyond occupation to encompass the entirety of life lived in service to God and others. This understanding liberates work from the narrow confines of careerism and elevates it to a sacred act, regardless of its societal status.

Dorothy Sayers, in her essay *Why Work?*, captures this idea beautifully: "The only Christian work is good work well done."[4] Whether one is a teacher, artist, farmer, or engineer, work becomes Christian when it is done with excellence, integrity, and a heart oriented toward God's glory. This perspective frees believers from the pressure to find the "perfect job" and invites them to see every task as an opportunity to reflect God's character and contribute to his kingdom.

One of the most radical implications of the biblical view of work is its inclusivity. No task, however mundane or unnoticed, is insignificant in the eyes of God. Paul's exhortation to the Colossians on this topic is particularly powerful. He writes, "Whatever you do, work heartily, as for the Lord and not for men, knowing that from the Lord you will receive the inheritance as your reward" (Col 3:23–24). This means that sweeping floors, preparing meals, writing code, or managing teams can all be sacred acts when done with a heart that seeks to honor God.

This vision transforms how we approach our daily work. It shifts the focus from personal gain to faithful stewardship, from self-fulfillment to service. It also provides a profound sense of purpose, reminding us that even in tasks that feel routine or thankless, we are contributing to God's

---

4. Sayers, *Why Work*, 8.

redemptive mission. Our work, no matter how small, participates in the larger story of his kingdom.

While the universality of calling provides a foundation, discerning one's specific vocation requires prayer, reflection, and wisdom. Frederick Buechner's famous definition offers a helpful framework: "The place God calls you to is the place where your deep gladness and the world's deep hunger meet."[5] This intersection of passion, talent, and need can guide believers in understanding how their unique gifts and circumstances align with God's purposes.

Scripture provides numerous examples of diverse callings. Joseph served as an administrator in Egypt, using his wisdom to save countless lives during famine (Gen 41:46–57). Lydia, a merchant, supported Paul's ministry through her resources and hospitality (Acts 16:14–15, 40). Paul, though a missionary, continued his trade as a tentmaker, demonstrating the dignity of manual labor alongside spiritual leadership (Acts 18:3–4). These examples remind us that God calls his people to various vocations, from leadership and business to ministry and the arts. What unites these callings is not the nature of the work but the heart behind it—a desire to serve God and advance his kingdom.

A critical but often overlooked aspect of vocation is its relational dimension. Calling is not discerned or lived out in isolation; it is shaped and affirmed within the context of community. The church, as the body of Christ, plays a vital role in helping believers discover and fulfill their callings. Through mentorship, encouragement, and shared discernment, the church becomes a space where gifts are recognized and nurtured for the common good.

This communal aspect reminds us that calling is not solely individual but corporate. As members of the body of Christ, we are called to work together, each contributing our unique gifts to build up the church and bear witness to God's kingdom in the world. This interdependence reflects the relational nature of God and provides a countercultural vision of work that values collaboration over competition.

---

5. Buechner, *Wishful Thinking*, 119.

For the Glory of God and the Advancement of His Kingdom

When work is reclaimed as a sacred calling, no longer confined to the narrow metrics of personal fulfillment or societal productivity, it is reoriented around its ultimate purpose: glorifying God and advancing his kingdom. This kingdom perspective transforms not only how we view our labor but also how we engage with the world through it.

As previously noted, work, when done faithfully, is not separate from worship; it *is* worship. The Reformers emphasized this truth in the doctrine of the "priesthood of all believers," which affirmed that all work, not just ecclesiastical roles, can glorify God when undertaken with a heart of service. Martin Luther famously declared that

> when a prince sees his neighbor oppressed, he should think: That concerns me! I must protect and shield my neighbor. . . . The same is true for shoemaker, tailor, scribe, or reader. If he is a Christian tailor, he will say: I make these clothes because God has bidden me do so, so that I can earn a living, so that I can help and serve my neighbor.[6]

This vision shifts the focus from the nature of the work to the heart behind it. As Paul exhorts in 1 Cor 10:31, "Whatever you do, do all to the glory of God." The farmer plowing his fields, the teacher nurturing young minds, the artist creating beauty—all participate in worship when their work is offered to God with reverence and joy. This sacred perspective breathes life into even the most mundane tasks, infusing them with eternal significance.

Work, done unto the Lord, also becomes a powerful tool for advancing his kingdom. This impact manifests in several ways:

1. *Building Culture:* Christians who approach their work with creativity and integrity contribute to the flourishing of culture. J. R. R. Tolkien and C. S. Lewis exemplify this through their literary works, which not only entertained but also illuminated profound spiritual truths. Similarly, Christian scientists, entrepreneurs, and public servants can shape their fields in ways that reflect God's justice, beauty, and love.

2. *Serving Others:* At its core, kingdom work is others-focused. Jesus himself modeled this in his ministry, which often involved meeting

---

6. Luther, "Sermon in the Castle Church at Weimar."

physical and social needs: feeding the hungry, healing the sick, and welcoming the outcast. In the same way, our labor, whether directly or indirectly, should serve the well-being of others. A nurse caring for patients, an engineer designing safer infrastructure, or a chef preparing nourishing meals all embody the love of Christ through their work.

3. *Promoting Justice and Mercy:* Work can also be a means of addressing systemic brokenness in the world. From advocating for ethical practices in business to creating opportunities for marginalized communities, Christians can use their vocations to enact justice and extend mercy. "To act justly, love mercy, and walk humbly with your God" (Mic 6:8) becomes a guiding principle for how we engage with the systems and structures of our workplaces.

4. *Witnessing Through Excellence:* Daniel, in the courts of Babylon, serves as a powerful biblical example of how excellence in work can bear witness to God's sovereignty. By performing his duties with skill and integrity, Daniel earned the respect of kings and pointed others to the God he served. Today, Christians who strive for excellence in their professions provide a compelling testimony to the world, showing that their ultimate accountability is to a higher standard.

While work is sacred, it must also be balanced with rest. The biblical rhythm of work and Sabbath reminds us that we are not defined solely by our labor. Rest is not just a cessation of activity; it is an act of trust, a declaration that God is the ultimate provider. The Sabbath was instituted to reorient humanity's focus from productivity to dependence on God, teaching us to delight in him and his creation.

In an age of burnout and perpetual busyness, Sabbath rest becomes a countercultural act of worship. It not only renews our strength but also recalibrates our priorities, reminding us that our worth is not tied to what we produce but to who we are in Christ. This balance of work and rest ensures that labor remains a joy rather than a burden, a reflection of God's rhythm in creation.

To view work as worship and kingdom service is to reclaim it as a meaningful and transformative act. This reclamation directly confronts the meaning crisis, offering a vision of labor that restores dignity and purpose. This vision challenges us to approach our vocations with intentionality, seeking not just personal success but eternal impact. It calls us to align our work with the values of God's kingdom, to serve others selflessly, and to strive for excellence that glorifies him. In doing so, we become co-laborers with Christ, advancing his purposes in a world desperately in need of hope.

A Sacred Offering

Work, when seen through the lens of the biblical narrative, is far more than a means of survival or a path to personal success; it is a sacred offering and an integral part of what it means to be human and to participate in God's redemptive purposes. From the first commission in the garden to the promise of the new creation, work is woven into the story of God's relationship with humanity. It reflects his creativity, extends his care for creation, and serves as a tangible act of worship and service.

Reclaiming this vision of work challenges us to reorient our perspective. No matter the task, whether building skyscrapers, raising children, or filing documents, we are called to work as unto the Lord, offering our labor for his glory and the advancement of his kingdom. This sacred perspective imbues even the most mundane tasks with eternal significance, transforming the ordinary into the extraordinary.

In an age marked by the dehumanization of labor, the idolization of productivity, and the rise of hyper-automation, the biblical understanding of work provides a powerful antidote to the meaning crisis. It restores dignity to workers, purpose to their tasks, and hope to their futures. By grounding work in the character and mission of God, we reclaim its sacredness and rediscover its role in shaping both individual lives and the broader culture.

Yet, this vision does not promise ease. The post-fall reality of toil remains, and challenges will persist. But the gospel assures us that our labor is not in vain. As Paul reminds us in 1 Cor 15:58, "Therefore, my beloved brothers, be steadfast, immovable, always abounding in the work of the Lord, knowing that in the Lord your labor is not in vain." This promise gives us strength to persevere, knowing that our efforts, however small, contribute to God's eternal plan.

The call to sacred work is not an isolated one; it is deeply connected to the larger story of God's kingdom. Just as work reflects God's creativity and care, so too does beauty. In the next chapter, we will explore how the arts and the pursuit of beauty serve as powerful witnesses to God's glory, offering glimpses of transcendence and inspiring wonder in a disenchanted world. Together, work and beauty form a tapestry that reveals the grandeur of God and invites us to participate in his redemptive mission.

20

The Sacred Balance

Embracing the Objective and the Subjective

IMAGINE WALKING INTO A church building or cathedral. Sunlight streams through stained glass, casting vibrant colors on the stone floor. A symphony of voices swells in worship, filling the air with transcendent beauty. In that moment, awe takes hold, not merely of your emotions but of your whole being, lifting you toward the divine.

Now imagine a different scene. A scholar sits at a desk, surrounded by books, poring over Scripture and theological texts. With careful precision, they trace the unshakable truths of the Christian faith: the historical resurrection of Christ, the reliability of God's word, the coherence of the gospel. Their mind is engaged, their understanding deepened, and their faith fortified.

Which of these is the truer expression of Christianity? The answer is both.

The Christian faith is neither empty-headed nor cold-hearted. It does not pit the intellect against the emotions but calls for a sacred balance between them. To follow Christ is to engage both the mind and the heart, to think deeply about the truths of God while also feeling deeply the awe, wonder, and love that those truths inspire. Christianity is a faith that grounds itself in the objective reality of God's word while drawing believers into a subjective, personal, and transformative encounter with him.

This balance, however, is not always easy to maintain. Our culture often pressures us to choose between head and heart, intellect and emotion. On one side, the intellectualism of modernity reduces faith to mere doctrine or rational argument, stripping it of its experiential power. On the other side, the emotionalism of postmodernity exalts subjective feelings while dismissing the importance of objective truth. Both approaches fall short of the rich, holistic faith that Christianity offers.

Scripture itself models this sacred balance. The psalmists, for instance, wrestle intellectually with profound questions about God and existence, yet they do so with raw, unfiltered emotions—lamenting, rejoicing, and praising. Jesus, in his ministry, engaged both the mind and the heart of his listeners. He reasoned with the Pharisees and taught profound theological truths, but he also wept with the grieving, celebrated with the joyful, and embraced the outcast. The early church, too, was marked by both rigorous teaching and vibrant worship, uniting objective doctrine with the subjective wonder of encountering the Holy Spirit.

This chapter is a call to recover and embrace this sacred balance. It challenges the false dichotomy that divides intellect from emotion, reason from experience, truth from beauty. Instead, it invites believers to see these dimensions as complementary, each enriching the other in the pursuit of God.

As we explore this theme, we will examine how Christianity is a faith firmly rooted in objective truth and also profoundly experiential. We will look at how the intellectual pursuit of God strengthens faith, while the subjective awe of God deepens it. Together, these elements form a holistic vision of what it means to walk with Christ, equipping believers to navigate a world that desperately needs both clarity of thought and depth of feeling.

To follow Christ is to engage the whole self—mind, heart, and soul. It is to know the unshakable truths of the gospel and to feel their transformative power. It is to reason with conviction and to worship with abandon. This sacred balance is not just a theological ideal; it is the essence of a vibrant and meaningful faith. It is to rediscover what it means to think deeply, feel deeply, and live fully in the light of God's truth and love.

The Objective Foundation— Christianity as a Faith of Truth

At the heart of Christianity lies a foundation that is both firm and unshakable: its objective truths. Unlike philosophies or religions that center on abstract ideas or subjective experiences alone, the Christian faith is deeply rooted in historical realities and coherent reason. This grounding provides a clarity and stability that transcends emotional fluctuations and cultural shifts. To embrace Christianity fully is to recognize it as a faith not only of the heart but also of the mind.

The gospel is not a myth, a mere moral tale, or a set of philosophical musings. It is anchored in historical events that took place in real time and space. The incarnation of Jesus Christ, his crucifixion under Pontius Pilate, and his resurrection on the third day are not allegories; they are facts attested to by eyewitnesses and preserved in Scripture. Paul, writing to the Corinthians, emphasized the historical nature of the resurrection: "For I delivered to you as of first importance what I also received: that Christ died for our sins in accordance with the Scriptures, that He was buried, that He was raised on the third day" (1 Cor. 15:3–4). Christianity invites believers not to a blind leap of faith but to a reasoned trust grounded in evidence.

Throughout history, the intellectual robustness of Christianity has been a powerful testimony to its truth. Apologists such as Augustine, Thomas Aquinas, C. S. Lewis, and countless others have demonstrated how faith and reason complement each other. Lewis, in *Mere Christianity*, argued that Christianity is not only logical but also uniquely capable of making sense of the human condition: our moral awareness, our longing for meaning, and our capacity for love. This intellectual tradition invites believers to engage their minds, exploring the depths of Scripture and the riches of theology as acts of worship.

At the core of Christianity's objective foundation is the word of God. Scripture, inspired by the Holy Spirit, provides a reliable and authoritative guide for faith and practice. Jesus himself affirmed the enduring truth of Scripture, declaring, "Heaven and earth will pass away, but my words will not pass away" (Matt 24:35). The Bible's coherence, fulfilled prophecies, and transformative power testify to its divine origin and reliability.

Scripture does not shy away from intellectual rigor. Its pages are filled with profound theological truths, complex narratives, and moral instructions that invite careful study and reflection. From the creation account in Genesis to the vision of the new creation in Revelation, the Bible challenges readers to engage their minds, not just their emotions. This intellectual engagement is not a detour from faith but an essential part of it. As believers wrestle with the word, they encounter the God who reveals himself through it.

Faith in Christianity is often misunderstood as irrational belief or wishful thinking. Yet the biblical definition of faith is far more robust. In the letter to the Hebrews, faith is described as "the assurance of things hoped for, the conviction of things not seen" (Heb 11:1). This is not blind trust but confident reliance on the character and promises of God, rooted in his proven faithfulness. Consider the example of Abraham, who is commended in Scripture for his faith. Abraham did not trust God arbitrarily; he trusted him because he knew God's character and had witnessed his faithfulness. This reasoned trust is the essence of Christian faith. It is a reliance on the objective truths of who God is and what he has done, leading to a life of obedience and hope.

The objective truths of Christianity provide a necessary foundation for the believer's journey. They ground us when emotions waver, guide us when cultural trends shift, and sustain us in times of doubt. Yet this foundation, as essential as it is, does not stand alone. Christianity is not merely a set of propositions to be affirmed but a dynamic relationship with the living God, one that also engages the heart and soul.

The Subjective Experience— Christianity as a Faith of Wonder

If the objective truths of Christianity form the foundation, its subjective experiences provide the breath of life that animates faith. The gospel is not merely a series of historical facts or theological doctrines; it is an invitation to encounter the living God. This encounter is deeply personal, engaging the heart, emotions, and imagination in transformative ways. Christianity is a faith not only to be understood but also to be felt and lived.

Subjective experiences, whether moments of awe in nature, the inexplicable peace of prayer, or the stirring of the heart in worship, invite us to marvel at the depth of the gospel in ways that purely intellectual engagement cannot. They remind us that faith is not simply about knowing; it is about being known. As Paul writes, "Now I know in part; then I shall know fully, even as I have been fully known" (1 Cor 13:12). This is the essence of faith: an encounter with the sacred that engages both the mind and the heart.

The subjective experience of Christianity often begins with a sense of awe. Beauty, in its various forms, has a unique power to awaken the soul and point it toward the divine. The psalmist declares, "The heavens declare the glory of God, and the sky above proclaims his handiwork" (Ps 19:1). Creation itself becomes a canvas of divine artistry, inviting humanity to marvel at the Creator's handiwork.

Beyond nature, art and music have long been vehicles through which believers encounter God. Handel's *Messiah*, with its soaring choruses, moves hearts to worship. The intricate storytelling of Tolkien's *The Lord of the Rings* reveals echoes of redemption and hope. These works, inspired by the Christian imagination, do more than entertain; they draw people into the mystery of God's beauty. In these moments, faith is not a detached intellectual exercise but an embodied experience of awe and wonder.

Emotions, often dismissed as unreliable or secondary, play a vital role in the Christian life. Throughout Scripture, we see God engaging with his people in profoundly emotional ways. David's psalms are a masterclass in the full range of human emotions—joy, sorrow, anger, gratitude, and hope—all laid bare before God. "My soul thirsts for God, for the living God" (Ps 42:2), David writes, expressing a yearning that is both deeply personal and profoundly theological.

The emotional life of faith is not an escape from reality but an encounter with it. The joy of salvation, the sorrow of repentance, the hope of resurrection—all are experiences that deepen our connection with God. Mary's song of praise in Luke 1:46–55 exemplifies this, as her heart overflows with gratitude and wonder at God's redemptive work. These emotions do not stand apart from objective truth but flow directly from it, as the reality of God's actions evokes a response of love, awe, and worship.

Worship is where the subjective experience of faith often reaches its most profound expression. In worship, believers encounter God not as an abstract concept but as a present and personal reality. Whether through the soaring hymns of a choir, the quiet reflection of prayer, or the participatory beauty of liturgical rituals, worship draws the believer into communion with God.

The act of worship engages all of the senses. The spoken word stirs the mind, the music moves the heart, and the sacraments—bread, wine, water—connect the spiritual with the tangible. This holistic engagement reflects the incarnation itself, where God became flesh and dwelt among us (John 1:14). Just as Christ's physical presence bridged the divide between the heavenly and the earthly, worship bridges the divide between the objective and subjective dimensions of faith.

In worship, believers are reminded of the truths they hold dear, but they are also invited to experience these truths in a transformative way.

The doctrine of God's sovereignty becomes a reason for praise; the reality of Christ's sacrifice evokes gratitude; the promise of the Spirit's presence fills hearts with peace. Worship is a divine encounter, a sacred space where the intellectual and emotional aspects of faith converge.

While the objective truths of Christianity provide the framework, subjective experience fills it with depth and vibrancy. It is one thing to know intellectually that God is love; it is another to feel his love in prayer, worship, or the beauty of creation. These experiences do not replace objective truth but affirm and illuminate it, making the reality of God's presence tangible in the life of the believer. This interplay of head and heart, reason and emotion, is essential for a faith that is both robust and alive.

The Necessity of Integration—Faith Rooted in Both

Faith that relies solely on intellectual rigor risks becoming cold and detached, while faith driven entirely by emotion can veer into instability and superficiality. Christianity, however, calls believers to a holistic approach. One that unites the objective truths of the gospel with the subjective experiences of encountering God. This integration is not a balancing act but a weaving together, where both dimensions enrich and strengthen each other, forming a faith that is both deeply grounded and profoundly alive.

The history of Christianity offers cautionary tales of what happens when the head and the heart are severed. Intellectualism can lead to a faith that is purely cerebral, reducing belief to an abstract set of principles while neglecting the relational and transformative aspects of the gospel. This was the danger faced by the Pharisees, whom Jesus criticized for their meticulous knowledge of the law but lack of love and mercy (Matt 23:23). Their faith, while intellectually rigorous, became a burden rather than a source of life.

On the other hand, emotionalism risks divorcing faith from its doctrinal foundation, making it subject to the whims of personal feeling. The heart is deceitful (Jer 17:9) and therefore must be guarded under the authority of the word. In times of emotional high, a strictly subjective faith may seem vibrant, but when feelings wane or trials arise, it can falter. Without the grounding of objective truth, subjective experiences lose their anchor, leaving believers vulnerable to doubt and confusion.

Jesus himself exemplifies the perfect integration of head and heart. His teachings reveal profound intellectual depth, engaging the minds of his listeners with parables, debates, and theological insight. He reasoned with the Pharisees about the nature of the law (Matt 22:41–46), used logic to dismantle false arguments (Mark 12:18–27), and articulated the truths of the kingdom in ways that challenged and inspired.

Yet, Jesus also engaged deeply with the emotions of those around him. He wept at the tomb of Lazarus (John 11:35), showing compassion for those who grieved. He expressed anger at the money-changers in the temple (John 2:15), displaying righteous indignation at injustice. His interactions with individuals, from the woman at the well to the tax collector Zacchaeus, revealed not only his knowledge of their hearts but his willingness to meet them in their deepest emotional and spiritual needs. Jesus' life and ministry demonstrate that truth and love, intellect and emotion, are not opposing forces but complementary aspects of a holistic faith.

The church serves as a vital community where this integration is nurtured. Through teaching, worship, and fellowship, believers are invited to grow both in their understanding of God's truth and in their experience of his presence. Sermons and Bible studies engage the mind, while worship and prayer stir the heart. Sacraments such as baptism and communion connect theological truths with tangible experiences, reminding believers of the reality of God's grace in ways that resonate deeply.

The church also provides accountability and encouragement, helping believers avoid the extremes of intellectualism and emotionalism. In community, faith is sharpened and deepened, as the head and the heart are shaped in tandem. The church becomes a place where the richness of Christian doctrine and the beauty of Christian experience coexist, each pointing to the fullness of life in Christ.

The integration of head and heart is not simply a matter of balance; it is a recognition of their interdependence. The objective truths of Christianity provide the foundation upon which subjective experiences are built. Without these truths, experiences lack direction and meaning. Conversely, the subjective aspects of faith—wonder, worship, and love—breathe life into the objective, transforming doctrine into devotion and knowledge into relationship.

This integration is beautifully described in Eph 3:17–19, where Paul prays that believers "may have strength to comprehend with all the saints what is the breadth and length and height and depth, and to know the love of Christ that surpasses knowledge." Here, the intellectual comprehension of God's love is intertwined with an experiential knowing that goes beyond mere understanding. The two are not in competition but in harmony, drawing believers into a fuller relationship with God.

To integrate head and heart is to embrace the fullness of what it means to follow Christ. It is to engage with the unshakable truths of Scripture while allowing those truths to transform the soul through worship, beauty, and relationship. This holistic vision equips believers not only to navigate their own faith journeys but also to bear witness to a world in need of both clarity and wonder. By embracing both the intellectual and the experiential dimensions of Christianity, believers discover a faith that is deeply rooted and vibrantly alive, capable of withstanding the storms of life and radiating the beauty of God's truth and love to others.

An Invitation to Wonder

A few years ago, I found myself immersed in the writings of Gregory of Nyssa, one of the Cappadocian Fathers whose works often tread the line between theological precision and poetic wonder. In one passage, Gregory described humanity's relationship with God as an eternal ascent—a journey of ever-deepening intimacy with the infinite, where each revelation of his glory only leaves us yearning for more. He likened this to Moses on Mount Sinai, where the presence of God is veiled in darkness, inviting not rejection but awe. A mystery to step into rather than away from.[1]

Reading those words, I was struck by how his articulation of the gospel truth captured something profoundly paradoxical. Here was a faith not merely a system of doctrines to be cataloged but a sacred mystery, infinitely knowable yet never fully comprehended. Gregory's vision of faith was simultaneously grounded in the objective truths of the gospel and aflame with the subjective wonder of a soul communing with its Creator. For a moment, I felt as though I was standing on Sinai with Moses, enveloped in the incomprehensible yet deeply personal love of God.

That moment didn't just move me emotionally; it unsettled me intellectually. It made me question how often modern Christianity, shaped by the demands of hyper-objectivity, has lost its capacity to articulate the mystery of the gospel. Have we become so consumed with dissecting and explaining the truth that we've forgotten how to marvel at it? And more than that, have we forgotten how to invite others into that marvel?

---

1. Gregory, *Life of Moses*, II, 242.

Modernity has given us an unparalleled capacity to understand the mechanics of the world, but in its pursuit of precision, it has often relegated the subjective—those moments of wonder, awe, and mystery—to the periphery of human experience. Faith, love, and beauty, once considered signposts of divine reality, are now often dismissed as emotional residue, things to be managed or minimized but certainly not explored.

Yet the subjective is indispensable, especially when it comes to our faith. This is not to suggest that truth is relative or that we abandon the objective realities of God's word. Far from it. Rather, the subjective complements the objective, providing a window through which we glimpse the divine, not in its fullness, but in its splendor. The truths of the gospel are not dry propositions to be categorized; they are mysteries that ignite both our minds and our hearts.

One of the greatest gifts of faith is the freedom to embrace both the objective and the subjective. The certainty of truth and the mystery of wonder. This freedom allows us to approach God with both our intellect and our emotions, to know him as he has revealed himself and to stand in awe of the infinite depths that remain beyond our comprehension. Every moment of understanding, every glimpse of his beauty, every stirring of the soul is an invitation to go deeper. Faith is not the absence of questions but the courage to ask them, knowing that even in our searching, we are held by the One who is truth itself.

And this is the heart of the gospel: not a cold, calculated system of facts but a living, breathing relationship with the Creator of the universe. It is a story of love so profound that it shatters our attempts to reduce it to mere logic yet so grounded in reality that it anchors us when feelings waver. It is the story of a God who stepped into the subjective messiness of human life to redeem us, not just as thinkers but as lovers, dreamers, and seekers.

As I reflect on my own journey, I realize that some of the most transformative moments of my faith have come not from solving mysteries but from surrendering to them. The times when I stopped striving to understand everything and simply marveled at the God who understands me. The moments when I allowed myself to rest in the tension of knowing in part and trusting fully. And the times when I let the truth of the gospel take root not just in my mind but in the deepest corners of my soul.

So, I invite you to do the same. Step into the mystery. Allow the objective truth of Scripture to ground you, but don't stop there. Let them awaken your heart to the wonder of God's love, the beauty of his creation, and the depth of his grace. Resist the urge to tame the sacred or reduce it to something manageable. Instead, let it captivate you, challenge you, and draw you closer to the One who is both knowable and infinitely beyond knowing.

You don't have to choose between reason and wonder, between truth and mystery. In Christ, the two come together in perfect harmony. He is the Word made flesh, the truth that loves, the light that shines in the darkness. And he invites you to see, to taste, to marvel, and to live a life that is not confined by the limits of what you can explain but expanded by the endless possibilities of what you can experience in him.

Come, then, and stand at the edge of the infinite. Gaze into the mystery. Take a step of faith. And know that in this sacred balance of the objective and the subjective, you will find not contradiction but the fullness of life and the God who makes all things new.

21

Towards a Christian Metanarrative
The Story That Won't Die

IMAGINE A TINY MUSTARD seed, so small it seems inconsequential. It falls to the ground, buried in the soil, and is forgotten. Days pass, then weeks, with no sign of life. It seems as though the seed has vanished, swallowed by the earth. But then, almost imperceptibly, a shoot emerges, tender yet unrelenting. Over time, it grows into a towering tree, its branches providing shelter, its roots digging deep, unshaken by wind or storm.

This is the image Jesus uses to describe the kingdom of God: "It is like a grain of mustard seed that a man took and sowed in his garden, and it grew and became a tree, and the birds of the air made nests in its branches" (Luke 13:19). What begins as small and seemingly fragile becomes a force of transformation, shelter, and flourishing. This is the story of Christianity. A seed buried, dismissed, and often opposed yet growing triumphantly throughout history.

In every age, attempts have been made to bury the Christian story. Enlightenment thinkers sought to reduce it to superstition, insisting reason had replaced faith. Totalitarian regimes sought to silence it, claiming their ideologies would create a better world. Postmodern philosophers deconstructed it, asserting that no single story could hold ultimate truth. Yet, like the mustard seed, the gospel has continued to grow, rooted in the soil of history and flourishing in the hearts of those who believe.

Why does the Christian story endure when so many other narratives fade? The answer lies in its unparalleled power to address the deepest questions of human existence: Why are we here? What is our purpose? How do we make sense of suffering? Where do we find hope? The Christian metanarrative—creation, fall, redemption, and restoration—offers not only a coherent framework for understanding these questions but also a transformative hope that speaks to the heart and mind alike.

This chapter is the culmination of our journey through this book. Here, we will explore how the Christian story uniquely answers the crisis of meaning in our age, providing a foundation that is both intellectually satisfying and personally transformative. We will see how it harmonizes reason and wonder, truth and beauty, offering a vision of life that no other worldview can match. And we will celebrate the reality that, like the mustard seed, this story continues to grow, triumphant and unstoppable, because it is true.

As we embark on this final chapter, let the image of the mustard seed remind us of the resilience and power of the gospel. The Christian story cannot be buried because it is the story of the One who conquered death, the One whose kingdom will have no end. It is the story that will not die, for it is the story of life itself.

The Framework of the Christian Metanarrative

The Christian story unfolds as a grand narrative, a unified and sweeping account of reality that begins with the very foundations of existence and culminates in the eternal restoration of all things. It is not a series of isolated events or abstract truths; it is a cohesive framework that speaks to the deepest longings of the human heart and addresses the profound questions of life. This story—creation, fall, redemption, and restoration—offers the most compelling and comprehensive vision of meaning, purpose, and hope the world has ever known.

The Christian story begins in a garden, not a battlefield. Unlike many ancient myths that depict creation as the result of cosmic violence or chaos, the Bible presents the world as the intentional work of a good and loving Creator. "In the beginning, God created the heavens and the earth" (Gen. 1:1). These opening words set the stage for a reality imbued with purpose, beauty, and order.

God's creation is marked by goodness. Repeatedly, the narrative of Genesis declares, "And God saw that it was good" (Gen 1:10, 12, 18, 21, 25). Humanity, uniquely made in the image of God (*imago Dei*), is the crowning achievement of this creation. "So God created man in his own image, in the image of God he created him; male and female he created them" (Gen 1:27). This declaration affirms the intrinsic dignity and worth of every human being, setting Christianity apart from worldviews that reduce humanity to mere products of chance or biology. Humanity's restlessness, the desire for meaning and fulfillment, is rooted in the truth that it was created for communion with God.

The Christian story begins with harmony—between humanity and God, humanity and creation, and humanity with one another, but the garden is not the end of the story. Humanity's rebellion against its Creator mars the goodness of creation. In Gen 3, Adam and Eve's choice to disobey God introduces sin, suffering, and death into the world. The fall is not merely an ancient tale; it is a theological explanation for the brokenness we see and feel in our lives and our world.

The effects of the fall are comprehensive. Alienation replaces communion: humanity is separated from God, from one another, and from creation itself. Paul describes this reality in his Letter to the Romans when he writes, "For the creation was subjected to futility, not willingly, but because of him who subjected it, in hope that the creation itself will be set free from its bondage to corruption" (Rom 8:20–22). The beauty of creation now bears the scars of human rebellion, and the harmony of relationships is shattered.

John Calvin wrote, "The surest source of destruction to men is to obey themselves."[1] This insight captures the essence of the fall: humanity's rejection of God's authority in favor of self-rule. The fall explains why even the most well-intentioned human efforts cannot ultimately resolve the problems of sin and suffering. It diagnoses the root of the meaning crisis, pointing to humanity's estrangement from God as the source of despair.

However, the darkness of the fall is not the final word. The Christian story turns on the axis of redemption, the climactic act of God entering into human history to restore what was lost. This redemption is accomplished through the life, death, and resurrection of Jesus Christ, who takes upon himself the weight of human sin and offers reconciliation with God.

In John 1:14, the Gospel proclaims, "The Word became flesh and dwelt among us, and we have seen his glory, glory as of the only Son from the Father, full of grace and truth." The incarnation of Christ is the

---

1. Calvin, *On the Christian Life*, 9.

ultimate expression of God's love, as the infinite Creator takes on the limitations of humanity to rescue his creation. Through the cross, Jesus bears the penalty of sin, satisfying the demands of justice while extending mercy to all who believe. As Paul writes, "For our sake he made him to be sin who knew no sin, so that in him we might become the righteousness of God" (2 Cor 5:21).

The resurrection is the triumphant vindication of Christ's work. It is the event that declares death defeated, sin overcome, and hope restored. The resurrection is the decisive moment in which God's new creation broke into history. It is not only the basis for Christian hope but also the turning point of the entire story, demonstrating that God's grace is greater than humanity's rebellion.

The Christian metanarrative concludes with a vision of ultimate restoration, where God's redemptive work is brought to its fulfillment. In the book of Revelation, the risen Christ declares, "Behold, I am making all things new" (Rev 21:5). This promise is not a return to Eden but the creation of something even greater, a renewed heaven and earth where sin, death, and despair have no place.

This hope is not escapism; it is transformative. The promise of restoration empowers believers to live with purpose and resilience in the present, knowing that their labor is not in vain (1 Cor 15:58). The vision of the New Jerusalem, where God dwells with his people, provides the ultimate answer to the meaning crisis: a world fully reconciled to its Creator, filled with joy, peace, and eternal communion. The early church father Irenaeus famously said:

> For the glory of God is the living man, and the life of man is the vision of God. If the revelation of God by the creation already gives life to all the beings living on earth, how much more does the manifestation of the Father by the Word give life to those who see God![2]

This fullness of life is realized in the final chapter of the Christian story, where the fullness of God's glory is revealed and his people are restored to the life for which they were created.

The framework of the Christian metanarrative is both profound and personal. It explains the beauty and brokenness of the world, offers redemption through Christ, and promises a future filled with hope. It is

---

2. Irenaeus, *Against Heresies*, 4.20.7.

a story that resonates because it is true. It is a story that answers not only the mind's questions but also the heart's deepest longings.

The Christian Story and the Crisis of Meaning

In an age of disillusionment and despair, the Christian story offers a compelling and transformative response to the crisis of meaning. Unlike fragmented worldviews or temporary philosophies, it addresses the deepest questions of life with coherence and power. The Christian metanarrative not only satisfies the intellect but also resonates with the heart, offering clarity where there is confusion, hope where there is despair, and justice where there is brokenness. It speaks to the universal longings of humanity, showing that these desires are fulfilled in the God who made us, loves us, and will ultimately restore all things.

Christianity affirms that humanity is not the result of blind chance or random processes but the intentional creation of a loving and purposeful God. Humanity, uniquely made in God's image, possesses intrinsic dignity and worth. This foundational truth stands in sharp contrast to materialistic views, which reduce humanity to mere biology, and postmodern perspectives, which deny any ultimate purpose. As C. S. Lewis observed, "You have never talked to a mere mortal."[3] Every person reflects God's eternal image, imbuing life with immeasurable value.

This narrative also addresses the question of purpose. The Christian story declares that humanity's highest calling is to glorify God and enjoy him forever. This is not an abstract or burdensome purpose but one that infuses every aspect of life with meaning. Jonathan Edwards beautifully described this truth, writing, "The enjoyment of God is the only happiness with which our souls can be satisfied."[4] Unlike secular narratives, which often struggle to define purpose or leave it to individual construction, the Christian worldview provides a transcendent purpose rooted in the unchanging character of God. This purpose shapes how believers approach work, relationships, and their stewardship of the world.

Perhaps most poignantly, Christianity speaks to the question of destiny. At the heart of the crisis of meaning is the fear of death and the anxiety that life ultimately leads to nothingness. The gospel proclaims the hope of resurrection, a future where death is defeated and life is restored. Paul's

---

3. Lewis, *Weight of Glory*, 46.
4. Edwards, "Christian Pilgrim," *Works* II: 244.

words in Rom 6:5 capture this assurance: "If we have been united with him in a death like his, we shall certainly be united with him in a resurrection like his." This hope does not merely comfort; it transforms, providing a foundation for courage, endurance, and joy in the face of mortality.

Integral to the Christian story is its ability to harmonize justice and mercy, offering what no other worldview can: the assurance that every wrong will be made right and that God's justice will prevail. The Bible consistently declares that God is a just judge who will hold every person accountable for their actions. "For we must all appear before the judgment seat of Christ, so that each one may receive what is due for what he has done in the body, whether good or evil" (2 Cor 5:10). Unlike human systems of justice, which are often flawed or incomplete, God's judgment is perfect, rooted in his omniscience and righteousness. This reality offers profound hope in a world where evil frequently seems unchecked and injustices go unanswered.

Christianity assures believers that evil will not have the final word. However, the Christian story does not stop at justice. It also offers mercy, beautifully harmonized in the person of Jesus Christ. On the cross, justice and mercy meet, as Christ bears the penalty for sin, satisfying the demands of divine justice while extending mercy to all who believe. As Paul writes, God is both "just and the justifier of the one who has faith in Jesus" (Rom 3:26). This reconciliation of justice and mercy is unparalleled, providing both accountability and grace.

At the heart of the Christian story is the gospel, the good news that Jesus Christ has overcome sin, death, and despair. This message addresses the crisis of meaning with unmatched power. It speaks hope into suffering, declaring that pain and hardship are not meaningless but are part of God's redemptive work. Paul's words in Rom 8:18 resonate deeply: "For I consider that the sufferings of this present time are not worth comparing with the glory that is to be revealed to us." This perspective transforms suffering from a source of despair into an opportunity for growth, perseverance, and trust in God's ultimate plan.

The gospel also redeems failure. Christianity does not shy away from humanity's brokenness but confronts it with the promise of grace. When we were wrong, God came to right us, and that is the whole meaning of the story of the world. Through Christ, failure is not the end of the story. Sins are forgiven, lives are restored, and identities are renewed as believers are adopted into God's family. This assurance offers profound comfort to those burdened by guilt or shame, pointing them to the transformative power of the cross.

The Christian story offers a joy that endures beyond circumstances. It does not merely provide answers; it transforms lives. It reconciles reason with imagination, justice with mercy, and suffering with hope. Unlike fleeting happiness, the joy of the gospel is rooted in God's unchanging character. Jesus himself promised this to his followers: "These things I have spoken to you, that my joy may be in you, and that your joy may be full" (John 15:11). This joy sustains believers through trials, enabling them to face life's challenges with confidence and hope.

The Enduring Power of the Gospel

The Christian story is not merely a private narrative of personal faith; it is a world-shaping, history-altering force. For over two millennia, the gospel of Jesus Christ has demonstrated unparalleled resilience and transformative power. Against persecution, skepticism, and cultural shifts, the gospel continues to rise, revealing its enduring relevance and truth. As historian Tom Holland observed in his work *Dominion*, the West owes its morals and most cherished values not to ancient Greece or Rome but to the transformative impact of Christianity. Sociologist Rodney Stark echoes this, noting the profound societal impact of Christianity, from the elevation of human dignity to the shaping of modern justice systems. The power of the gospel is seen not only in its ability to endure but also in its capacity to transform individuals, societies, and entire civilizations. It is a story that has triumphed not because it imposes itself but because it speaks to humanity's deepest needs, offering a compelling, liberating, and redemptive vision of life.

Throughout history, many have attempted to suppress or dismiss the Christian story. The early church faced brutal persecution under the Roman Empire, yet it grew at an astonishing rate. In a world dominated by power and cruelty, Christianity's radical ethic of love and forgiveness stood out. As Stark notes in *The Rise of Christianity*:

> Christianity taught that mercy is one of the primary virtues—that a merciful God requires humans to be merciful. Moreover, the corollary that because God loves humanity, Christians may not please God unless they love one another was something entirely new. Perhaps even more revolutionary was the principle that Christian love and charity must extend beyond the

boundaries of family and tribe, that it must extend to "all those who in every place call on the name of our Lord Jesus Christ" (1 Cor. 1:2). Indeed, love and charity must even extend beyond the Christian community.[5]

This countercultural compassion drew people to the gospel not through coercion but through witness.

The resilience of Christianity continued through the Enlightenment, a period when reason and science were seen as incompatible with faith. Yet, as Holland and Stark demonstrated, the very values championed by the Enlightenment—human rights, equality, and dignity—are deeply rooted in the Christian worldview. The secular world, often unknowingly, continues to draw upon the moral capital of Christianity, even as it seeks to distance itself from its origins.

Persecution has also been unable to extinguish the gospel's flame. From the Soviet Union to modern-day regimes hostile to Christianity, attempts to silence the church have often had the opposite effect. In many cases, faith has flourished under pressure, as believers have demonstrated courage and hope rooted in the resurrection. The blood of martyrs, as Tertullian famously observed, has truly been the seed of the church.

The gospel's power is most vividly seen in the lives it transforms. From the apostle Paul, who turned from persecutor to preacher, to Augustine, whose restless heart found peace in God, history is filled with stories of individuals radically changed by the message of Christ. This transformation is not confined to the past. Today, testimonies of lives redeemed from addiction, despair, and purposelessness bear witness to the ongoing work of the gospel.

On a societal level, Christianity has profoundly shaped the moral and cultural foundations of the modern world. The Christian emphasis on the inherent worth of every individual revolutionized ancient conceptions of power and hierarchy. In Rome, where infanticide and slavery were accepted practices, Christianity introduced a radical ethic of human dignity, proclaiming that all are equal before God. The Christian story, Holland writes, "is the principal reason why, by and large, most of us who live in post-Christian societies still take for granted that it is nobler to suffer than to inflict suffering."[6]

---

5. Stark, *Rise of Christianity*, 212.
6. Holland, "Why I was wrong about Christianity," September 14, 2016.

Rodney Stark also emphasizes Christianity's role in advancing justice and compassion. Hospitals, orphanages, and charities owe their origins to the Christian commitment to care for the vulnerable. The abolition of slavery in the Western world was driven by Christian convictions, with figures like William Wilberforce tirelessly advocating for freedom based on the belief that all people are made in the image of God. These societal transformations are not incidental but are deeply rooted in the gospel's vision of redemption and restoration.

Even in the arts and sciences, the Christian story has left an indelible mark. From the architectural beauty of cathedrals to the music of Bach and Handel, from the literary genius of Dante and Milton to the scientific endeavors of Kepler and Newton, Christianity has inspired creativity that reflects the glory of God. These contributions are not merely cultural artifacts; they are expressions of a worldview that sees all of life as a stage for God's redemptive work.

The enduring power of the gospel is further demonstrated by its global and cross-cultural appeal. Unlike ideologies bound by geography or ethnicity, the Christian story transcends cultural barriers, speaking to the hearts of people from every nation and language. The church is now more global than ever, with its center of gravity shifting to the Global South. Africa, Asia, and Latin America are experiencing explosive growth in Christianity, as millions embrace the gospel's message of hope and salvation.

This universality is rooted in the gospel's ability to address universal human needs. Whether in a bustling metropolis or a remote village, the Christian story answers the same questions: Where did I come from? Why am I here? What happens when I die? Its promise of forgiveness, reconciliation, and eternal life resonates with people across cultures and contexts. This global reach underscores the truth of the gospel as not merely one story among many but the story of humanity's ultimate purpose and destiny.

The enduring power of the gospel ultimately reflects the truth of its central event: the resurrection of Jesus Christ. Just as Christ rose from the grave, defeating sin and death, so the gospel rises again and again, undiminished by opposition or neglect. It is a story that cannot be buried because it is the story of life itself. As Paul declares, "For the message of the cross is foolishness to those who are perishing, but to us who are being saved it is the power of God" (1 Cor 1:18).

This story endures not because it is imposed but because it is true. It satisfies the mind's longing for coherence, the heart's yearning for meaning, and the soul's need for redemption. Its impact on history and society testifies to its transformative power, and its ongoing relevance in the modern world demonstrates that it speaks to the deepest needs of humanity.

A Living Invitation

The Christian metanarrative is not merely a story to be admired or analyzed; it is a living invitation. It calls each person to step into the story of redemption, to find their place in the grand narrative of creation, fall, redemption, and restoration. This invitation is not passive. It is active, transformative, and deeply personal. It calls not only for intellectual assent but also for a life reoriented around the gospel's truth and beauty. Through Christ, individuals are invited into a relationship with the living God and into the sacred community of his people, the church.

At the heart of the Christian story is the call to come to Christ. Jesus' invitation is as compelling today as it was two thousand years ago: "Come to me, all who labor and are heavy laden, and I will give you rest" (Matt 11:28). This is a call to lay down the burdens of sin, shame, and striving and to embrace the grace and freedom that only he can offer. The gospel does not demand perfection; it offers forgiveness. It does not require strength; it gives rest.

To be in Christ is to be transformed. Paul captures this beautifully, "Therefore, if anyone is in Christ, he is a new creation. The old has passed away; behold, the new has come" (2 Cor 5:17). This transformation is not superficial; it is a re-creation, a renewal of the very essence of who we are. Through Christ, we are reconciled to God, adopted into his family, and given a new identity as his beloved children. This is not a distant or abstract relationship but an intimate, personal communion with the creator who knows us fully and loves us completely.

The invitation to follow Christ is also an invitation to join his body, the church. Christianity is not a solitary journey but a communal one. From its earliest days, the church has been a sacred community where believers are united not by culture, status, or background but by their shared faith in Christ. As Paul writes to the church at Corinth, "For in one Spirit we were all baptized into one body—Jews or Greeks, slaves or free—and all were made to drink of one Spirit (1 Cor 12:13).

The church is more than a gathering of individuals; it is the living temple of God, the place where his Spirit dwells. Within this community, believers find encouragement, accountability, and belonging. The church becomes a tangible expression of the gospel, a family where the love of Christ is made visible through acts of service, worship, and fellowship.

Reflecting on the sacredness of Christian community, Bonhoeffer writes in *Life Together*, "Christianity means community through Jesus Christ and in Jesus Christ. No Christian community is more or less than this."[7] To be part of the church is to be drawn into a sacred fellowship that transcends time and space, uniting believers across generations and around the world.

This sacred community also plays a vital role in the Christian's growth and mission. Through worship, teaching, and the sacraments, the church nurtures faith and equips believers to live out the gospel. And as the body of Christ, the church is sent into the world as his hands and feet, embodying his love and proclaiming his truth. The invitation into Christ is inseparable from the invitation into his church. It is the community that reflects the glory of God and extends his invitation to others.

To accept the invitation of the Christian story is to step into a life of purpose, hope, and mission. It is to live in the light of God's grace and to reflect his love to a world in need. The gospel calls believers not only to be recipients of its truth but also participants in its unfolding story. As Paul writes, "For we are His workmanship, created in Christ Jesus for good works, which God prepared beforehand, that we should walk in them" (Eph 2:10). This call is both individual and communal. Each believer is uniquely gifted and called to contribute to God's kingdom, whether through acts of service, creative expression, or faithful witness in daily life. Yet, this work is never done in isolation. It is carried out in partnership with the church, the sacred community through which God's mission advances.

Living the story also means living with hope. The Christian narrative is not static; it is moving toward a glorious conclusion. The promise of restoration, of a new heaven and new earth where God dwells with his people, is not a distant dream but a future reality that shapes the present. As the apostle John describes in Revelation, "Behold, the dwelling place of God is with man. He will dwell with them, and they will be His people, and God Himself will be with them as their God. He will wipe away every

---

7. Bonhoeffer, *Life Together*, 21.

tear from their eyes, and death shall be no more" (Rev 21:3–4). This hope empowers believers to face life's challenges with courage and resilience, knowing that their labor is not in vain and that the story does not end in despair but in eternal joy.

The gospel is not exclusive in its invitation; it calls out to all who are weary, broken, and searching for meaning. It is a story that welcomes the doubter, the skeptic, the outcast, and the sinner. It proclaims that there is no life too far gone, no sin too great, and no heart too hardened for the grace of God. It calls out to every soul: come to Christ, join his body, and live as a participant in the greatest story ever told. It is a summon to be transformed, to find meaning, and to share in the hope of restoration. It is the invitation of a lifetime, one that echoes through history and resounds in eternity.

As the book draws to a close, the challenge remains open: Will you accept this invitation? Will you step into the story that has changed the world and continues to change lives? The Christian story endures because it is true, and it calls you to find your place within it. The seed has been planted, and the tree has grown. The invitation is before you. Will you come?

Conclusion
Living as Restorers

THE WORLD IS ACHING, an unrelenting hum of longing reverberating across generations, cultures, and societies. Beneath the surface of technological advancement and modern comforts lies a profound and persistent hunger: for meaning, for connection, for wholeness. This longing, unspoken yet undeniable, is the thread that has woven together every page of this book.

We began by tracing the unraveling of meaning in the rise of modernity, as the sacred was pushed to the margins and the mechanistic worldview left humanity with facts but no purpose. The situation worsened in the era of postmodernity, where truth was deconstructed, leaving only fragmented stories and fractured souls. New Atheism, in turn, sought to fill the void with the cold logic of materialism, offering answers devoid of transcendence and hope.

Yet, even in the darkest wilderness of this crisis, voices have risen, calling us back to wonder, truth, and the sacred. These messengers of meaning—Chesterton, Lewis, Schaeffer, and others—have pointed toward the only story that can truly satisfy the restless heart: the Christian story. It is a story that does not shy away from humanity's brokenness but speaks directly to it, offering redemption, restoration, and hope.

Now, as we come to the conclusion of this journey, the question remains: What do we do with this story? If the Christian narrative truly provides the answer to the crisis of meaning, how then should we live? The answer is both profound and simple: we are called to live as restorers.

To live as a restorer is to embrace the story of Christ as not just a truth to believe but a life to embody. It is to carry the light of hope into a world still drenched in despair and "longing for more." It is to participate in the work of restoration, mending what has been broken, healing what has been wounded, and pointing others toward the wholeness found in Christ. In this conclusion of the book, we will weave together the threads of the journey that we have taken, pointing to the ultimate answer for meaning and wholeness in the story of Christ. It will also call us to live out that story, not merely as recipients of its truth but as ambassadors of its transforming power.

The Unraveling of Meaning

The modern world was born out of the Enlightenment's ambition to cast off the shadows of superstition and tradition, replacing them with the steady light of reason, progress, and human ingenuity. For a time, it seemed that this promise of modernity might deliver. The rise of science and technology brought remarkable advancements, transforming the ways we understand and navigate the world. Yet, beneath these surface achievements, cracks began to form. The sacred order that had underpinned centuries of human life was eroded and with it, the sense of meaning that had given purpose and direction to individual and communal existence.

The unraveling of meaning began with modernity's shift away from the transcendent. The mechanistic worldview that emerged in the Enlightenment reimagined the universe as a machine—complex, intricate, and ultimately self-sustaining. God, once the center of the cosmos, was pushed to the periphery or dismissed entirely. In his place stood humanity, exalted as the master of its own destiny. While this shift brought freedom from certain oppressive structures, it also severed the connection to a larger story that gave life coherence and depth. The result was a world of facts without values, knowledge without wisdom, and progress without purpose.

This fracture deepened with the rise of postmodernity. Where modernity had sought to construct meaning through reason and science, postmodernity declared the entire project futile. It rejected the grand narratives that had once framed human life, replacing them with skepticism, relativism, and fragmentation. Truth was no longer seen as something objective or universal but as a construct, subjective and fleeting. While postmodernity's critique of modernity exposed its limitations, it left humanity further adrift, without a shared story to anchor meaning.

The final blow came with the rise of New Atheism, which sought to fill the void left by postmodernism's deconstruction. Figures like Richard Dawkins and Christopher Hitchens championed a worldview rooted in materialism, insisting that the universe is the product of blind chance and that life's only purpose is survival. In this narrative, humanity is reduced to atoms and instinct, with no ultimate significance or destiny. New Atheism dismissed the sacred as a delusion and the transcendent as a relic of the past. But in doing so, it offered little to address the existential despair that inevitably arises when meaning is stripped away.

The consequences of these shifts are profound. The unraveling of meaning has left individuals and societies fragmented, anxious, and alienated. The result is what sociologist Zygmunt Bauman called "liquid modernity"—a state of constant flux where stability, certainty, and coherence are elusive.[1] This unraveling has also distorted the way we see ourselves and others. Without a transcendent framework, human beings are often valued not for their inherent worth but for their utility, productivity, or conformity to societal norms. Relationships become transactional, communities dissolve into isolated individuals, and the sense of belonging that once anchored human life fades away. The modern world, for all its advancements, has left many feeling untethered, yearning for something more.

Yet, even in the midst of this unraveling, the longing for meaning persists. The human heart continues to ache for connection, transcendence, and purpose. This ache is not a flaw but a signpost, pointing toward the story we were created to inhabit. We are reminded again of Lewis's quote, "If I find in myself desires which nothing in this world can satisfy, the only logical explanation is that I was made for another world."[2]

The unraveling of meaning is not the end of the story. It is the backdrop against which the Christian narrative shines most brightly. As the threads of modernity's promises fray and postmodernity's critiques falter, the gospel offers a vision of life that is coherent, compelling, and redemptive. It invites us to step out of the immanent frame and into the transcendent story of creation, fall, redemption, and restoration—a story that not only explains our longing but fulfills it.

---

1. Bauman, *Liquid Modernity*, 12.
2. Lewis, *Mere Christianity*, 75.

Voices in the Wilderness

Amid the unraveling of meaning brought about by modernity's exaltation of reason, postmodernity's deconstruction of truth, and New Atheism's reductionist materialism, there have been voices calling out from the wilderness, refusing to let humanity's search for meaning be extinguished. These messengers of meaning did not merely critique the cultural forces of their time but offered profound insights that pointed the way back to wonder, purpose, and transcendence. Each of them, in their own way, sought to rekindle the light of meaning in a world shrouded by despair.

G. K. Chesterton stood as a luminous figure against the rising tide of disenchantment. At a time when the industrial age and materialistic philosophies sought to reduce life to mere mechanics, Chesterton reminded his readers of the enchantment inherent in existence. He saw the world as "a divine drama," where even the mundane was imbued with sacred significance. His writings, particularly in *Orthodoxy*, celebrated the paradoxes of life that pointed beyond human comprehension to the divine mystery. His invitation was clear: to recover a childlike sense of awe and see the sacred in the ordinary, a task essential to reclaiming meaning.

C. S. Lewis followed this path of wonder but went further by exploring the deep longings of the human heart. In his own journey from atheism to faith, Lewis wrestled with the reality of a profound yearning—what he called *sehnsucht*—an insatiable desire for something beyond this world. In *Mere Christianity* and *The Weight of Glory*, Lewis argued that these longings were not illusions but signposts, pointing to the ultimate fulfillment found in God. For Lewis, meaning was not an abstract concept to be deduced but an experience rooted in the ultimate reality of God's presence. His works rekindled the imagination of countless readers, showing that reason and desire, intellect and wonder, could converge in the Christian story.

While Lewis spoke of longing, Viktor Frankl illuminated the redemptive potential of suffering. Writing in the aftermath of the Holocaust, Frankl's *Man's Search for Meaning* offered a stark contrast to the nihilism that often accompanies suffering. Having endured unimaginable horrors, Frankl argued that meaning is not contingent on circumstances but is discovered in the response to them. His philosophy of logotherapy emphasized the necessity of a purpose that transcends the self. Though not explicitly Christian, Frankl's insights resonate deeply with the gospel, which transforms suffering into a pathway to redemption. His work demonstrated that even in the darkest moments, the quest for meaning endures and can triumph.

J. R. R. Tolkien offered yet another perspective on meaning through his mythic storytelling. In works like *The Lord of the Rings*, Tolkien wove narratives of heroism, sacrifice, and hope, which resonated with universal human longings. His concept of *eucatastrophe*—the sudden, unexpected turn toward joy—paralleled the gospel's message of redemption. Tolkien believed that myths were not mere fabrications but reflections of the ultimate story found in Christ. His friendship with Lewis helped to bridge the divide between reason and imagination, showing that the truth of Christianity could be both rationally compelling and profoundly beautiful.

The historical and societal impact of the Christian story was further illuminated by scholars like Tom Holland and Rodney Stark. In *Dominion*, Holland traced how the Christian narrative reshaped Western civilization, embedding values of human dignity, compassion, and justice into its moral fabric. He argued that even secular ethics owe their foundation to the revolutionary ethic of Christianity, which elevated the marginalized and proclaimed the inherent worth of every individual. Similarly, Stark's *The Rise of Christianity* demonstrated how the early church's commitment to mercy, community, and care for the vulnerable set it apart in a world dominated by power and exploitation. These thinkers provided historical evidence that the Christian story is not merely a private faith but a public force for good, offering a vision of meaning that transforms both individuals and societies.

These messengers of meaning, along with many others we have journeyed with together in this book, though diverse in their approaches and contexts, shared a common conviction: the quest for meaning cannot be severed from the transcendent. Together, they form a chorus calling humanity back to the sacred, urging a return to the framework that alone can satisfy the restless heart. Their work stands as a bridge, spanning the chasm created by modernity's disenchanted rationalism and postmodernity's fragmented skepticism. Each voice contributes to the understanding that meaning is not something humanity constructs but something it discovers—ultimately in the person of Christ and the narrative of redemption he embodies. As these voices echo across history and culture, they point us toward the story that fulfills every longing and restores every fragment of meaning lost in the wilderness of modernity's despair.

The Answer in the Christian Story

The Christian story is the ultimate answer to humanity's relentless search for meaning. It is not merely a competing narrative among many; it is the story that makes sense of all stories. This grand metanarrative encompasses the deepest questions of existence, providing coherence to the fragmented and hope to the despairing. It answers the cries of the human heart with a truth that is both profound and personal.

This story begins with the foundational truth that meaning is not something humanity invents but something it receives. The opening chapters of Genesis declare that the universe is not the product of random chaos but of intentional design. Humanity, created in the image of God, has intrinsic worth and a divine purpose: to reflect God's character and steward his creation. This vision of origin sets the Christian story apart from worldviews that reduce humanity to mere biological mechanisms or meaningless cosmic accidents. It affirms that life is inherently sacred and purposeful.

Yet, the Christian story does not gloss over the brokenness of the world. The fall acknowledges the reality of sin and its devastating consequences: alienation from God, from one another, and from creation. This diagnosis of human brokenness explains the profound discontent and fragmentation that have plagued humanity throughout history. Unlike secular narratives that dismiss this brokenness as an unfortunate byproduct of evolution or economic systems, Christianity names it for what it is: rebellion against a holy and loving creator. But this naming is not an act of condemnation; it is the starting point for redemption.

Redemption lies at the heart of the Christian story. In the life, death, and resurrection of Jesus Christ, we see God's answer to the crisis of meaning. Jesus is not merely a teacher of truth or a moral example; he is the truth (John 14:6). His death on the cross satisfies the demands of divine justice, reconciling sinners to God, while his resurrection guarantees the ultimate victory over sin and death. In Christ, the despair of the fall is transformed into the hope of redemption. The gospel is not just good advice; it is good news. News that changed and continues to change everything.

The story does not end with redemption but moves toward restoration. The promise of a new heaven and a new earth, where God will dwell with his people. Unlike worldviews that see history as cyclical or aimless, the Christian story moves toward a glorious conclusion, where every wrong is righted and every longing fulfilled. This hope is not escapism; it empowers believers to live with purpose and resilience in the present, knowing that their lives are part of a larger, redemptive story.

What sets the Christian story apart is its ability to satisfy both the mind and the heart. It offers intellectual coherence, answering the great philosophical questions of origin, purpose, morality, and destiny. At the same time, it speaks to the deepest desires of the human soul: the longing for love, belonging, and transcendence. Christianity is not merely an intellectual framework; it is a lived reality, one that transforms hearts and minds.

Moreover, it alone can uniquely reconcile justice and mercy. In the cross, we see the perfect harmony of these two attributes of God. Justice is not ignored but fulfilled, as Christ bears the penalty for sin. Mercy is not compromised but magnified, as forgiveness is extended to all who believe. This resolution is unparalleled in any other worldview, offering a hope that is both just and compassionate. The promise of final judgment ensures that evil will not go unpunished, while the invitation to grace ensures that no one is beyond redemption.

The Christian story is not merely to be understood; it is to be entered. It calls each person to find their place within its grand arc, to be reconciled to God and transformed by his grace. This is not an abstract call but a deeply personal one. Hear the Lord's words to you:

> Come, everyone who thirsts,
> come to the waters;
> Seek the Lord while he may be found;
> call upon him while he is near;
> let the wicked forsake his way,
> and the unrighteous man his thoughts;
> let him return to the Lord,
> that he may have compassion on him,
> and to our God, for he will abundantly pardon.
> (Isa 55:1, 6–7)

Yet, this invitation is not just a call to God; it is a call into family, into a sacred community, the church, where we are joined with others who share in the mission of restoration. Together, we become part of God's redemptive work in the world, bearing witness to the gospel through acts of love, justice, and compassion. The church is not a refuge from the world but a light within it, pointing others to the hope found in Christ.

The Christian story does more than offer meaning: it reconciles the fragmented self, restores broken relationships, and provides a vision of a future filled with hope. It is the story that answers the crisis of meaning because it is the true story of the One who gives meaning to all things. As we move toward the conclusion of this book, the challenge remains: to not only believe this story but to live it, embodying its truth and sharing its hope with a world still longing for more.

Living as Restorers

The Christian story does not end with us. It is not merely a truth to believe or a hope to cling to but a life to embody. To embrace the gospel is to step into a calling—a calling to live as restorers in a world fractured by despair, alienation, and meaninglessness. In Christ, we are not only recipients of redemption but also agents of restoration, sent out to reflect his light in the darkness and to invite others into the sacred story of hope. This calling is deeply personal, profoundly communal, and undeniably practical. It begins in the heart of every believer, extends to the relationships we cultivate, and radiates outward into the broader culture.

The work of living as restorers begins with allowing the gospel to continually transform us. To be a restorer, we must first experience restoration. In Christ, the fragmented self is made whole, as our identity is no longer defined by the chaos of sin or the shifting sands of culture but by the unshakable truth that we are beloved children of God. Paul reminds us, "You were bought with a price. So glorify God in your body" (1 Cor 6:20). To glorify God is to live as those who have been made new, letting the reality of redemption shape every aspect of our lives.

This means embracing spiritual practices that anchor us in the truth of the gospel. Prayer, Scripture reading, worship, and confession are not mere disciplines; they are means of encountering the living God. They realign our hearts with his, renewing our minds and equipping us to see the world through his eyes. As restorers, we must first be connected to the source of restoration, allowing God's grace to flow into us so that it may flow through us.

Living as restorers also means building sacred relationships. In a world that is profoundly connected technologically yet deeply lonely relationally, we are called to embody the love of Christ in our interactions with others. This begins with seeing every person as made in the image of

God, worthy of dignity, love, and respect. It means cultivating authentic relationships rooted in vulnerability, generosity, and mutual care.

The church, as the body of Christ, is central to this mission. It is a sacred community where believers are nourished and strengthened, but it is also a place that must invite others in. The table of Christ is wide, and we are called to extend his hospitality to the world. This means breaking down barriers of race, class, and culture, creating spaces where people can encounter the love of God through the love of his people.

Jesus's ministry was marked by his willingness to share meals with sinners, outcasts, and those on the margins. As his followers, we are called to do the same. Hospitality is not just about opening our homes but opening our lives. It is inviting others into our joys and struggles, our victories and failures, so they might see the transformative power of the gospel at work in us.

Restorers are not called to retreat from the world but to engage it with the hope of the gospel. This means living out our faith in the places God has called us, in our workplaces, neighborhoods, schools, and communities. Every vocation, when offered to God, becomes a sacred calling (Col 3:23). Whether we are teachers, artists, engineers, parents, or caregivers, our work is an opportunity to reflect God's creativity, stewardship, and love.

Engaging the world as restorers also means addressing the brokenness we see around us. The gospel compels us to pursue justice, care for the vulnerable, and advocate for the oppressed. It calls us to create beauty in a world marked by cynicism, build bridges in a culture of division, and speak truth in an age of relativism. Living as a restorer is not passive; it is an active participation in God's mission of renewal.

Finally, to live as restorers is to live in the hope of the ultimate restoration to come. This hope sustains us in the face of life's challenges, reminding us that our labor is not in vain. It gives us the courage to persevere, the strength to love, and the joy to celebrate, even in the midst of difficulty. As restorers, we are called to embody this hope in our daily lives. This means choosing forgiveness over bitterness, generosity over greed, and faithfulness over despair. It means being peacemakers in a world of conflict, healers in a world of pain, and witnesses to the truth of the gospel in a world hungry for meaning.

The story of Christ is the story that changed everything. It is the story that has redeemed us, the story that sends us, and the story that will one day bring all things to completion. As those who have been invited into this story, we are now commissioned to invite others, living as restorers in a world still drenched in despair and longing for more.

This commission is not a burden but a privilege. It is an opportunity to participate in God's redemptive work, to bring light to the darkness, and to bear witness to the One who makes all things new. As Paul declared almost two millennia ago, "All this is from God, who through Christ reconciled us to himself and gave us the ministry of reconciliation... We are therefore Christ's ambassadors, as though God were making his appeal through us" (2 Cor 5:18–20).

You are called to be a restorer. To embrace this call is to live a life of purpose, hope, and joy. To cultivate a life that reflects the glory of God and the grace of his gospel. The world is still longing for more, and the Christian story is the answer. Let it be your story, and let your life be its witness.

The Answer to Your Longing

The journey of this book has been a journey through the wilderness of modernity's unraveling, the shadows of postmodernity's skepticism, and the barren plains of New Atheism's despair. It has traced the threads of meaning's disintegration and listened to the voices of those who refused to let the light fade—messengers who pointed us back to the sacred, the transcendent, and the beautiful. And ultimately, it has led us to the story that answers every longing: the story of Christ.

The crisis of meaning that defines our age is not an intellectual puzzle to solve but a spiritual hunger to satisfy. It is the groaning of creation, the ache of every human heart, the unspoken yearning for wholeness and purpose. This longing, though often distorted, is a gift, a signpost that points to the One who made us, who knows us, and who loves us.

The Christian story does not shy away from the world's brokenness or the pain of the human condition. It acknowledges the depth of our fallenness while offering the promise of redemption. It proclaims that in Christ, the fractured can be mended, the lost can be found, and the hopeless can be restored. It is a story that does not demand we climb to heaven but tells us that heaven has come down to us.

This story is not a relic of the past or a private refuge for the devout. It is the story of all stories, the truth that makes sense of our existence and redeems our despair. It is the story that rises again and again, triumphant and unshaken because it is rooted in the One who conquered death itself.

You were made for this story. You were made for communion with God, for the joy of his presence, and for the hope of his promises. You were made to live as a restorer, carrying the light of Christ into a world that still longs for more. This is not merely a calling; it is an invitation to step into the greatest story ever told and to let it transform your life.

The choice is yours. You can continue searching, chasing shadows and echoes of meaning, or you can come to the source. The invitation is open. The door is not locked. The table is set. If you are longing for more, Christ is the answer. And his promise stands firm: "Whoever comes to me I will never cast out" (John 6:37).

Bibliography

Baudrillard, Jean. *Simulacra and Simulation*. Translated by Sheila Faria Glaser. Ann Arbor: University of Michigan Press, 1994.
Bauman, Zygmunt. *Liquid Modernity*. Cambridge, UK: Polity, 2000.
Beckwith, Francis, and Gregory Koukl. *Relativism: Feet Firmly Planted in Mid-Air*. Grand Rapids: Baker, 1998.
Berry, Wendall. *The Art of the Commonplace*. Washington, DC: Counterpoint, 2002.
Bonhoeffer, Dietrich. *Life Together: The Classic Exploration of Faith in Community*. Translated by John W. Doberstein. New York: Harper & Row, 1954.
Borgmann, Albert. *Power Failure: Christianity in the Culture of Technology*. Grand Rapids: Brazos, 2003.
Buechner, Frederick. *Wishful Thinking: A Theological ABC*. New York: HarperOne, 1993.
Calvin, John. *On the Christian Life*. Translated by Henry Beveridge. Grand Rapids: Christian Classics Ethereal Library. https://www.grace-ebooks.com/library/John Calvin/JC_On The Christian Life.pdf.
Carpenter, Humphrey. *J. R. R. Tolkien: A Biography*. Boston: Houghton Mifflin, 1977.
Catholic Quotations. "Chesterton." https://catholicquotations.com/chesterton/.
Chesterton, G. K. *The Everlasting Man*. London: Hodder and Stoughton, 1925.
———. *Heretics*. London: Bodley Head, 1905.
———. *Orthodoxy*. London: John Lane Company, 1908.
———. *A Short History of England*. London: Chatto and Windus, 1924.
———. *Tremendous Trifles*. London: Methuen & Co., 1909.
———. *What's Wrong with the World*. New York: Cassell and Company, 1910.
Dawkins, Richard. *The Blind Watchmaker: Why the Evidence of Evolution Reveals a Universe Without Design*. New York: Norton, 1986.
———. *The God Delusion*. New York: Houghton Mifflin, 2006.
———. "Speech at the Edinburgh International Science Festival." In "Editorial: A Scientist's Case Against God." *Independent*, Apr. 15, 1992.
Debord, Guy. *The Society of the Spectacle*. Translated by Ken Knabb. Berkeley, CA: Bureau of Public Secrets, 2014.
Dennett, Daniel C. *Breaking the Spell: Religion as a Natural Phenomenon*. New York: Viking, 2006.

Derrida, Jacques. *Of Grammatology*. Translated by Gayatri Chakravorty Spivak. Baltimore: Johns Hopkins University Press, 1997.
Dostoevsky, Fyodor. *Crime and Punishment*. Translated by Richard Pevear and Larissa Volokhonsky. New York: Vintage Classics, 1992.
———. *Notes from Underground*. Translated by Michael R. Katz. New York: W. W. Norton, 2001.
———. *The Brothers Karamazov*. Translated by Constance Garnett. New York: Farrar, Straus and Giroux, 2002.
Edwards, Jonathan. "The Christian Pilgrim." In *The Works of Jonathan Edwards*. Vol. 2. https://www.ccel.org/ccel/e/edwards/works2/cache/works2.pdf.
Eliot, T.S. "The Hollow Men." https://drbaplit.files.wordpress.com/2018/12/hollow_men_pdf.pdf.
———. *The Idea of a Christian Society*. New York: Harcourt, Brace, & Company, 1940.
———. *The Rock*. New York: Harcourt, Brace, & Company, 1934.
———. *The Waste Land*. New York: W. W. Norton & Company, 2001.
Ellul, Jacques. *The Presence of the Kingdom*. Translated by Olive Wyon. Colorado Springs: Helmers & Howard, 1989.
———. *Propaganda: The Formation of Men's Attitudes*. Translated by Konrad Kellen and Jean Lerner. New York: Vintage, 1973.
———. *The Technological Society*. Translated by John Wilkinson. New York: Alfred A. Knopf, 1964.
Foucault, Michel. *Discipline and Punish: The Birth of the Prison*. Translated by Alan Sheridan. New York: Vintage, 1995.
———. *The History of Sexuality: An Introduction*. Vol. 1. Translated by Robert Hurley. New York: Vintage, 1990.
———. "Nietzsche, Genealogy, History." In *Language, Counter-Memory, Practice: Selected Essays and Interviews*, edited by D. F. Bouchard, 139–64. Ithaca: Cornell University Press, 1977.
Frankl, Victor E. *The Doctor and the Soul: From Psychotherapy to Logotherapy*. Translated by Richard Winston and Clara Winston. New York: Alfred A. Knopf, 1955.
———. *Man's Search for Meaning: An Introduction to Logotherapy*. Translated by Ilse Lasch. Boston: Beacon, 2006.
Freud, Sigmund. *Civilization and Its Discontents*. Translated by James Strachey. New York: W. W. Norton, 1961.
Gallagher, Kenneth T. *The Philosophy of Gabriel Marcel*. New York: Fordham University Press, 1962.
Gregory of Nyssa. *The Life of Moses*. Translated by Abraham J. Malherbe and Everett Ferguson. New York: Paulist, 1978.
Harris, Sam. *The Moral Landscape: How Science Can Determine Human Values*. New York: Free, 2010.
Havel, Václav. *Living in Truth*. Edited by Jan Vladislav. London: Faber & Faber, 1986.
Heidegger, Martin. *The Question Concerning Technology and Other Essays*. New York: Harper, 1977.
Hitchens, Christopher. *God Is Not Great: How Religion Poisons Everything*. New York: Twelve, 2007.
Holland, Tom. *Dominion: How the Christian Revolution Remade the World*. New York: Basic, 2019.

Holland, Tom. "Why I Was Wrong About Christianity." New Statesman, Sep. 14, 2016. https://www.newstatesman.com/politics/religion/2016/09/tom-holland-why-i-was-wrong-about-christianity.

Hobbes, Thomas. *Leviathan*. London: J. M. Dent & Sons, 1914.

Hooper, Walter, ed. *The Collected Letters of C.S. Lewis*. Vol. 3. New York: HarperCollins, 2007.

Hopkins, Gerard Manley. "God's Grandeur." https://www.cslewisinstitute.org/wp-content/uploads/KD-2018-Summer-POEM-Gods-Grandeur-6448.pdf.

Hume, David. *An Enquiry Concerning Human Understanding*. Chicago: Open Court, 1900.

Huxley, T. H. "Agnosticism." *Collected Essays*. New York: D. Appleton, 1898.

Irenaeus. *Against Heresies*. Translated by Robert M. Grant. Abingdon, UK: Routledge, 2002.

Keller, Timothy. *Every Good Endeavor: Connecting Your Work to God's Plan for the World*. New York: Dutton, 2012.

King, Martin Luther, Jr. "Facing the Challenge of a New Age." Martin Luther King, Jr. Research and Education Institute. https://kinginstitute.stanford.edu/king-papers/documents/facing-challenge-new-age-address-delivered-naacp-emancipation-day-rally.

———. "I Have a Dream." Teach Tennessee History. https://teachtnhistory.org/file/I Have A Dream Speech.pdf.

———. "Letter from Birmingham Jail." California State University, Chico. https://www.csuchico.edu/iege/_assets/documents/susi-letter-from-birmingham-jail.pdf.

Kuyper, Abraham. *Abraham Kuyper: A Centennial Reader*. Edited by James D. Bratt. Grand Rapids: Eerdmans, 1998.

Lewis, C. S. *The Abolition of Man*. New York: HarperOne, 2001.

———. *The Great Divorce*. New York: HarperOne, 2001.

———. *Mere Christianity*. New York: HarperOne, 2001.

———. *The Problem of Pain*. New York: HarperOne, 2001.

———. *Surprised by Joy: The Shape of My Early Life*. New York: HarperOne, 2001.

———. *The Screwtape Letters*. New York: HarperOne, 2001.

———. *The Weight of Glory and Other Essays*. New York: HarperOne, 2001.

Luther, Martin. "Sermon in the Castle Church at Weimar." In *Werke: Kritische Gesamtausgabe*, Vol. 36, 314–19. Weimar: Herman Böhlaus Nachfolger, 1883–1980.

Lyotard, Jean-François. *The Postmodern Condition: A Report on Knowledge*. Translated by Geoff Bennington and Brian Massumi. Minneapolis: University of Minnesota Press, 1984.

Marcel, Gabriel. *Being and Having: An Existential Diary*. Translated by Katharine Farrer. Westminster, UK: Dacre, 1949.

———. *Creative Fidelity*. Translated by Robert Rosthal. New York: Fordham University Press, 2002.

———. *Homo Viator: Introduction to a Metaphysic of Hope*. Translated by Emma Craufurd. Chicago: Henry Regnery Company, 1962.

———. *The Mystery of Being: Volume I, Reflection and Mystery*. Translated by G. S. Fraser. Chicago: Henry Regnery Company, 1950.

Mumford, Lewis. *The Myth of the Machine: Technics and Human Development*. New York: Harcourt Brace Jovanovich, 1967.

Niebuhr, Reinhold. *The Children of Light and the Children of Darkness*. New York: Charles Scribner's Sons, 1944.

———. *Christ and Culture*. New York: Harper Collins, 1951.

———. *The Irony of American History*. Chicago: University of Chicago Press, 1952.

———. *Moral Man and Immoral Society: A Study in Ethics and Politics*. New York: Charles Scribner's Sons, 1932.

———. *The Nature and Destiny of Man: A Christian Interpretation*. Vols I and II. New York: Charles Scribner's Sons, 1941.

Nietzsche, Friedrich. *The Gay Science*. Translated by Walter Kaufmann. New York: Vintage, 1974.

———. *Thus Spoke Zarathustra*. Translated by Thomas Common. New York: Random House, 1968.

Peterson, Jordan B. *We Who Wrestle with God: Perceptions of the Divine*. London: Portfolio Penguin, 2024.

Sartre, Jean-Paul. *Being and Nothingness*. Translated by Hazel E. Barnes. London: Methuen, 1957.

Sayers, Dorothy L. "Why Work?" In *Creed or Chaos?*, 46–62. Manchester, NH: Sophia Institute Press, 1999.

Schaeffer, Francis. *Escape from Reason*. Downers Grove, IL: InterVarsity, 1968.

———. *The God Who Is There*. Downers Grove, IL: InterVarsity, 1968.

———. *He Is There and He Is Not Silent*. Wheaton, IL: Tyndale, 1972.

———. *How Should We Then Live?: The Rise and Decline of Western Thought and Culture*. Old Tappan, NJ: Revell, 1976.

———. *True Spirituality*. Wheaton, IL: Tyndale, 1971.

Schweitzer, Albert. *Reverence for Life: An Autobiography*. Translated by C. T. Campion. Kansas City: Hallmark Editions, 1971.

Schopenhauer, Arthur. *The World as Will and Representation*. Translated by E. F. J. Payne. New York: Dover, 1969.

Stark, Rodney. *The Rise of Christianity: How the Obscure, Marginal Jesus Movement Became the Dominant Religious Force in the Western World in a Few Centuries*. San Francisco: HarperSanFrancisco, 1997.

Taylor, Charles. *A Secular Age*. Cambridge, MA: Belknap Press of Harvard University Press, 2007.

Tolkien, J. R. R. *On Fairy-Stories*. Edited by Verlyn Flieger and Douglas A. Anderson. London: HarperCollins, 2008.

———. *The Fellowship of the Ring*. London: Harper Collins, 2001.

———. *The Letters of J. R. R. Tolkien*. Edited by Humphrey Carpenter. Boston: Houghton Mifflin, 1981.

———. *The Return of the King*. London: Harper Collins, 2001.

Turkle, Sherry. *Alone Together: Why We Expect More from Technology and Less from Each Other*. New York: Basic Books, 2011.

———. *Reclaiming Conversation: The Power of Talk in a Digital Age*. New York: Penguin, 2015.

Volf, Miroslav. *Exclusion and Embrace: A Theological Exploration of Identity, Otherness, and Reconciliation*. Nashville: Abingdon, 1996.

Wells, H. G. *Mind at the End of Its Tether*. London: Will Heinemann, 1945.

———. *A Modern Utopia*. New York: Thomas Nelson & Sons, 1927.

———. *The Island of Dr. Moreau*. New York: Stone & Kimball, 1946.

———. *The Time Machine*. New York: Penguin Classics, 2005.
Willard, Dallas. *The Disappearance of Moral Knowledge*. Edited by Steven L. Porter, Gregg A. Ten Elshof, and Aaron Preston. New York: Routledge, 2018.
———. *The Divine Conspiracy: Rediscovering Our Hidden Life in God*. San Francisco: HarperOne, 1998.
———. *The Great Omission: Reclaiming Jesus's Essential Teachings on Discipleship*. San Francisco: HarperOne, 2006.
———. *Living in Christ's Presence: Final Words on Heaven and the Kingdom of God*. Downers Grove, IL: IVP Formatio, 2013.
———. *The Renovation of the Heart: Putting on the Character of Christ*. Colorado Springs: NavPress, 2002.
———. *The Spirit of the Disciplines: Understanding How God Changes Lives*. San Francisco: Harper & Row, 1988.
Wright, N. T. *Surprised by Hope: Rethinking Heaven, the Resurrection, and the Mission of the Church*. New York: HarperOne, 2008.

www.ingramcontent.com/pod-product-compliance
Lightning Source LLC
Chambersburg PA
CBHW050838230426
43667CB00012B/2056